Economy, Welfare, and Reforms in Pakistan

Essays in Honour of Ishrat Husain

Economy, Welfare, and Reforms in Pakistan

Essays in Honour of Ishrat Husain

Edited by

VAQAR AHMED *and* MAAZ JAVED

Foreword by

TARIQ BANURI

OXFORD

UNIVERSITY PRESS

OXFORD
UNIVERSITY PRESS

Oxford University Press is a department of the University of Oxford.
It furthers the University's objective of excellence in research, scholarship,
and education by publishing worldwide. Oxford is a registered trade mark of
Oxford University Press in the UK and in certain other countries

Published in Pakistan by
Oxford University Press
No. 38, Sector 15, Korangi Industrial Area,
PO Box 8214, Karachi-74900, Pakistan

ISBN 978-0-19-070881-8

Typeset in Minion Pro
Printed on 55gsm Book Paper

Printed by Kodwavi Printing Services, Karachi

Contents

Foreword

Aconcept that best describes Ishrat Husain's approach and
achievements is 'clinical economist'. This concept was
introduced by Jeffrey Sachs[1] to argue that countries were
complex systems, and that economists, like doctors, needed to
recognise these complexities, provide nuanced, context-sensitive
advice, and back it up with robust feedback systems and a sustained
commitment to professional ethics. Sachs' arguments were in direct
opposition to the prevailing orthodoxy at the international financial
institutions (IFIs), namely the now-discredited Washington Consensus
and its partiality for one-size-fits-all neoliberal prescriptions.

As Johannes F. Linn underscores in his essay in this volume,
Ishrat Husain consistently advocated a pragmatic and nuanced
approach to development policy, which he applied with great success
in country after country—Ghana, Nigeria, Azerbaijan, Tajikistan,
and Turkmenistan. While he departed radically from the prevalent
orthodoxy, he did not seek to advocate an alternative theoretical
framework, such as Mahbubul Haq's human development approach
or Amartya Sen's capability approach, even if at some level he agreed
with them.

Rather, what he advocated is far better described as clinical
economics. It is easy to forget what a radical idea it was at its time.
Today, it may have become acceptable, even to the IFIs, which were
forced into soul-searching because of the past failures. But in the
1980s, going against the prevailing orthodoxy meant risking one's
career and professional prospects.

The 1980s and 1990s, the so-called 'lost decades of development',
witnessed a massive retrenchment of societal agendas under the
combined onslaught of global macroeconomic crises and ill-advised

procrustean policies imposed by IFIs on hapless governments. Some challenged the orthodoxy on theoretical grounds, but others, like Husain, bypassed theoretical debates to focus on pragmatic solutions based on an innovative combination of theory and practice.

In fact, as I have argued in one of my papers from this period,[2] the pragmatic approach consistently produced superior results. In the paper, we distinguished between a 'theory view' and a 'policy view' of macroeconomic analysis, and found that theoretical purity, whether of the left or the right, led countries into sub-optimal choices in comparison to those that opted for a nuanced policy approach.

It would be inappropriate and even self-contradictory to try to represent this approach as an alternative orthodoxy. Also, the very diversity of options and solutions make it difficult to confine it within a simple structure. Yet, it is possible to discern some recurring patterns, all of which are visible in Husain's contributions. These include, first, an uncompromising commitment to poverty eradication. Second, to compensate for theoretical certitudes, there is a focus on institutional strengthening and robust feedback mechanisms (to enable policy to keep track of changing realities). Third, the mobilisation of political commitment is recognised as a prerequisite for the sustained pursuit of the policy objectives.

Linn mentions how Ishrat Husain had to argue with his colleagues at the World Bank to be allowed to push his ideas. It is understandable that the large bureaucracies at IFIs found it difficult to accept, let alone champion, the agenda proposed by him. One reason that may have swayed them is the unique combination of his skills and experience. Very few development economists would have had the experience of a Civil Service of Pakistan officer early on in their careers. Very few civil servants would have channelled this into a rigorous academic programme. The combination is ideally suited to a pragmatic and clinical agenda.

In the 1990s and 2000s, one can find others with similar inclinations, e.g., Manmohan Singh in India, Sartaj Aziz in Pakistan, Joseph Stiglitz in the US, Fernando Henrique Cardoso in Brazil, and Angel Gurria in Mexico. While Sachs does not say so explicitly in his book, his concept may have been developed from observing such professionals. In fact, Sachs was part of the brains trust that Husain established at the World Bank's international finance division.

A number of people have remarked upon Husain's success in several different careers: civil servant, World Bank economist, central banker, academic administrator, and governance czar. Yet, if one follows the logic of Sachs' insights, these are not radically different careers but a unified career trajectory for a special breed of economists who, like doctors, seek to combine theoretical knowledge with clinical experience.

Ishrat Husain's tenure at the State Bank of Pakistan was informed by the same commitment to pragmatic solutions, robust feedback systems, institutional strengthening, and promotion of professionalism. Another word for this approach today is governance, which, not coincidentally happens to be the responsibility entrusted to him by the current government.

Tariq Banuri
Chairman Higher Education Commission (HEC),
Government of Pakistan
February 27, 2021

Notes

1. Jeffry Sachs, *The End of Poverty: Economic Possibilities for Our Time* (New York: The Penguin Press, 2005).
2. Tariq Banuri and Edward Amadeo, 'Policy, Governance, and the Management of Conflict,' in *Economic Liberalization: No Panacea*, ed. Tariq Banuri (Oxford: Oxford University Press, 1992).

Introduction

Abid Q. Suleri

Dr Ishrat Husain is a name that needs no introduction in Pakistan. However, I would like to introduce Dr Husain through his work and my reference point is his flagship book, *Pakistan: The Economy of An Elitist State*. He sounds revolutionary and an opponent of the status quo when substantiating the argument that Pakistan's economy is in the clutches of a narrow elite comprising 1 to 2 per cent from the top, he writes:

> [...] only those who possess assets can benefit from market resources. The markets are rigged by the elites since the state is politically controlled by the same elite for promoting their parochial agenda. The elites get bank loans and never repay, grab their choiced urban land at concessional rates, and secure permits and licenses to set up their businesses without paying a single penny. They know how to conceal income to evade taxes, misclassify the value of imports and real estate in connivance with government officials, sell wheat and sugar to public procurement agencies at prices higher than market rates, divert government subsidies granted in the name of small farmers for their own use, regulate higher tariffs to protect their inefficient industries, etc.[1]

He strives for a progressive, humanitarian, and exploitation-free society and does not only confine to diagnosing the problem but also proposes a solution. He outlines financial, educational, and judicial reforms to set Pakistan free from the elite capture. In his view, only these reforms can liberate Pakistan from the stranglehold of a small elite and ensure that the benefits of economic growth are shared by most of the population, particularly those in the lower income and social strata. He highlights reforms as a tool to shake up the institutional edifice so that they could deliver an inclusive and sustainable economic growth.

However, his diagnosis and policy recommendations, which should be implemented to solve the problem, are not something that distinguish him from many other policy analysts. His distinction lies in the fact that, like many others, he does not have the luxury of packing his bag and sleeping peacefully after giving policy recommendations. In fact, he does the opposite by accepting the challenge to implement what he proposes and is consistently leading by example.

Husain believes that financial sector reforms are a must for inclusive growth and got the opportunity to reform the financial sector of Pakistan through his stint as Governor of the State Bank of Pakistan (SBP) (1999–2005). During his tenure, the banking sector was completely transformed and opened to competition for bringing about efficiency, soundness, and profitability from subsidised support. However, privatisation of the banking sector sans a strong regulator with high quality human resources, technology, and simplified business processes would have led to a major failure. To keep the private banks aligned with national objectives and protect the depositors, he had to first bring his own house in order, i.e., introduce reforms in the SBP. This is what he endeavoured to accomplish. When he took over, only one SBP staff member was a PhD holder. Since then, Husain sent Pakistanis, who got admission in the top 20 economic departments, overseas on a full four-year scholarship that also included a stipend. This is why today there are 30 PhD and numerous foreign degree holders at the SBP.

During his tenure as Governor SBP, he came up with a new monetary policy to not only pull the country out of a serious economic crunch in 1999 but also to revive the economy. It was a time when Pakistan was undergoing international sanctions for conducting nuclear detonations. As a result of his efforts, Pakistan succeeded in stimulating the economy, and achieved 8.4 per cent growth rate in 2005.

In the year 2000, Pakistan was on the verge of bankruptcy. With Husain's efforts, the country not only earned credibility from the

World Bank (WB), but also accumulated over \$12 billion in its foreign exchange reserves. After this, the WB declared Pakistan as one of the top 10 reformers. One of his biggest moves as Governor SBP was that he curtailed black economy by refusing incentives to black marketeers.

As an advocate of Islamic banking, he believes that it can contribute heavily to poverty alleviation, affordable housing, microfinance, financial inclusion, and educational reforms. He argues that Islamic banking is more suitable to fund start-ups, which are otherwise avoided by conventional banks.

The second set of reforms that he believes can help in ending the elite capture is educational reform. He got an opportunity to develop a prototype for reforms in higher education as Dean and Director (2008–2016) of Pakistan's oldest graduate business school, the Institute of Business Administration (IBA). His struggle to transform IBA into an institute of higher learning was unmatched where he played the role of a mentor of the mentors. To materialise his dream to include IBA among the top 100 global business schools, he realigned the institute's programmes with the best international practices, keeping in view local educational needs and circumstances.

At IBA, he not only enhanced the quality of education but also brought in new disciplines, thus turning it into a truly interdisciplinary institute of higher learning. For this, he raised the number of PhDs in the IBA faculty from 20 to 72, sent many other faculty members abroad to pursue doctoral degrees, and also transformed the institute's MBA programme by making the criterion to have a two-year compulsory post-graduation work experience before enrolment. With this change, though the MBA enrolment dropped drastically, the qualitative difference was recognised later on.

Ishrat Husain's successful endeavours included the Responsible Citizen Initiative where it was mandatory for Business Administration students to do an eight-week community-based internship, and the Talent Hunt Programme that brought forward students from backward areas to the institute. These initiatives showed his commitment towards ending elite culture. During his tenure at IBA, he proved that people belonging from different backgrounds could study in the same class. He believed that intellectual curiosity and academic openness are the fundamentals of knowledge which

Pakistan's educational institutions need direly. To all the newcomers at IBA, he said, 'the best way of learning is through inquisitiveness and that no question is a stupid question.' Today, IBA has set such high standards in quality education due to Husain's vision and commitment that other institutions aspire to reach that level.

He raised Rs 5 billion from the private sector and philanthropists for the IBA's infrastructure and faculty development. This infrastructural expansion helped the institute increase its enrolment. Rs 1 billion Endowment Fund at the IBA was one of his biggest achievements in order to take the institute towards sustainability and self-reliance.

The essential ingredients of Husain's IBA transformation model were student admissions on pure merit through entry exams and interviews (no shortcuts or connections); faculty appointments made in transparent manner purely on competence, searching, attracting, retaining, and motivating high calibre individuals to join the faculty; creating opportunities for the community at large to benefit from a first-rate institution; holding classes and exams on time with zero tolerance for plagiarism and cheating; inculcating a sense of social responsibility and serving the downtrodden; opening up the space for talented students from unprivileged families and backward areas to study at the institute and thus move up the social ladder; imbibing a sense of values of integrity and truthfulness, and forging academia-industry partnership.

After his stint at the SBP and before his appointment as the Director of IBA, he was appointed as Chairman National Commission for Government Reforms (NCGR) with the status of a federal minister. The NCGR was tasked with producing analysis and recommendations on how the government, its institutions, and infrastructure could become more effective to meet the social, economic, and political challenges that Pakistan faces in the twenty-first century. The commission took two years to produce a comprehensive report which covered the restructuring of government at the federal and provincial levels, strengthening of the district governments, reorganisation of civil services, revamping of human resource management policies and practices, and reengineering of business processes.

The change in government did not allow him to implement these reforms. However, the report of the NCGR came handy when Prime

Minister Imran Khan appointed him as advisor for institutional reforms and austerity (2018–2021) with the status of a federal minister. This provided him the opportunity to finish his unfinished agenda of the NCGR. His vision for institutional reforms mainly emphasises the change in overall governance structure of the country since it is the fundamental problem which has caused deterioration in the institutions. He prepared an institutional reform bill that may be divided into three phases to cater to the governance-related problems:

1. Restructuring and strengthening of key institutions of economic governance
2. Reorganising the federal government
3. Reforms in civil services

These reforms are ongoing and the Prime Minister himself is looking after the restructuring of the Federal Board of Revenue (FBR) and strengthening of the State Bank as being the key institutions of economy. This time Husain moved incrementally—getting each component deliberated and approved by the political leadership. He successfully established a merit-based criterion for appointing heads of public sector institutions; forty such CEOs/MDs have been appointed under a transparent selection process based on pure merit without any interference from the elected politicians. Similarly, he has put a system for high level promotions in place, where such promotions are not made on seniority but on competence and integrity. This incremental process has its drawback, particularly in a country where patience and perseverance are in short supply and people expect results overnight. However, one believes this approach would produce lasting desirable changes.

Other areas of Husain's interest include food security, climate change, food-energy-water nexus, and regional collaboration. Through his writings, he keeps highlighting the importance of tackling climate change which may threaten our food, energy, and water security. He is a staunch advocate of regional cooperation and believes that CPEC and the Belt and Road Initiative have the potential to uplift not only the economy of Pakistan but the economies of this region, especially to boost and to make the basis for a strong regional trade integration.

Husain's introduction would remain incomplete without mentioning his distinguished career spanning over two decades (1979–1999) at the World Bank. Among the key positions he held at the bank were: Resident Representative to Nigeria; Head of the Debt and International Finance Division; Chief Economist for Africa; Chief Economist for East Asia and Pacific Region, including China; Director of the Poverty and Social Department, and in 1997, was named the Country Director for Central Asian Republics.

It would not be wrong to say that he is using his academic expertise and the World Bank experience to have an impartial socioeconomic system in place in Pakistan that may provide equal access to opportunities to all citizens on the basis of their hard work rather than connections and class. Such a system, in his opinion, has a better chance of survival and is in the best interest of the country for long-lasting peace and sustainable economy.

In recognition to his meritorious services, he was conferred the prestigious award of Hilal-e-Imtiaz by the President of Pakistan in 2003. *The Banker* (London) declared him as the Central Bank Governor of the year for Asia in 2005. He received the Asian Banker Lifetime achievement award in 2006. The President of Pakistan conferred upon him the highest civilian award of Nishan-e-Imtiaz in 2016 for his outstanding public service.

Owing to his scholarly interest in development issues, Husain has authored two dozen books and monographs and contributed more than 40 articles in refereed journals, and 34 chapters in books.

* * *

I have a special regard for Ishrat Husain, even if he did not have the above-mentioned professional achievements to his credit. He is a gem of a person, an excellent human being with a caring heart who believes in grooming leaders among his team members rather than increasing the number of his followers. He is not an ungrateful person and believes in paying back, which is evident from the fact that despite many opportunities he never thought of settling abroad.

During my last two decades of association with him, I was present in the meetings that he was chairing. We were co-panellists and I had the honour of moderating the sessions where he was a keynote speaker. To him, what is being said is more important than who is saying it. I have seen him appreciating the youth and endorsing their ideas when they had a point. He knows the art of agreeing to disagree in an amicable manner when he has a difference of opinion with someone. He tries to explain his point of view without losing his patience and temper when someone disagrees with him. I also had the chance of travelling with him and can vouch for the fact that he can discuss fiction, movies, music, literature, and cuisine as eloquently as he would discuss economy and reforms.

I am extremely grateful to him for his special patronage of the organisation that I represent, Sustainable Development Policy Institute (SDPI). I cannot remember any instance where we requested his time for a seminar/lecture and he refused. That simply shows the importance he gives to sustainable development. I wish him all the success for his latest mission, agenda of institutional reforms, and hoping him many more accomplishments in life.

Note

1. Ishrat Husain, 'The revolt against elitism,' *Dawn*, November 14, 2016.

In Honour of Dr Ishrat Husain

20 Years at the World Bank Dedicated to
Economic and Social Reform

JOHANNES F. LINN

Ishrat Husain joined the World Bank in 1979 as an economist in mid-career. He left the World Bank in 1999, as an accomplished senior manager, to become the Governor of the State Bank of Pakistan. I had the great honour and pleasure to count him as my colleague for the 20 years he worked at the World Bank, as I worked closely with him on various occasions.

It was my privilege to have many distinguished Pakistani economists as colleagues during my time at the World Bank—among them Masood Ahmed, Parvez Hasan, Shahid Husain, Tariq Husain, Homi Kharas, and Shahid Yusuf. Ishrat Husain stood out among them for his unique combination of being a man of ideas, hungry for data and analysis, full of empathy for the people in the developing world, fearless in his pursuit of what he thought was the right course of action, a rebel with a cause—the cause being the fight for development and against poverty around the globe—and a loyal friend. And, while many of us international civil servants stayed in the world of global development challenges, he returned to Pakistan and served his country, a choice I highly respected. In the end, the true test of a policy prescription comes not when you act as an adviser and financier but when you try and implement it yourself as the policymaker.

In this brief account of Ishrat Husain's time at the World Bank I have to be selective. I will highlight those areas of his engagement where I directly worked with him, or where I have a first-hand account of his work. The purpose is not to delve into a deep analysis of his achievements but to share what I saw in him as a colleague and a friend.

After Husain's initial appointment as Country Economist for Liberia and Sierra Leone, in 1980, he was asked to lead the World Bank's support for Ghana's structural adjustment reforms and to prepare the first structural adjustment loan by the Bank to any of its clients. This type of loan—with its financing of a country's general budget in support of policy reforms rather than for a traditional investment project—was a major departure for the Bank. It meant a whole new set of challenges in assisting the government in developing a comprehensive national economic reform programme, and in preparing and supervising the loan, with Husain serving as a pioneer in making it all happen. As chance would have it, I then served as country economist for Thailand at the World Bank and we followed suit quickly with a similar structural adjustment loan for that country, having learned a lot from the Ghana case. Structural adjustment loans (SALs) later on were heavily criticised because they were seen to support narrow neoliberal policy prescriptions of fiscal austerity, price liberalisation, and privatisation under what was referred to as 'the Washington Consensus', but our early SALs were much broader in focus, with institutional reform and concern for poverty very much part of the programme design.

Ishrat Husain's outstanding performance in Ghana caught the attention of the World Bank's senior vice president at the time, Ernest Stern, who decided in 1983 to post Husain as the Bank's resident representative in Nigeria, a major country in dire need of reform. President Ibrahim Babangida had pledged reforms but refused to request IMF financing, which then was a requirement for the Bank to proceed with a SAL. After carefully assessing the quality of the planned reforms and the President's commitment, he decided that an exception to this requirement was called for. His entire management chain, including his vice president, nixed the idea, but he would not give up. He asked Stern to personally visit Nigeria to see for himself. This he did, and then accepted Husain's proposal, albeit with the proviso—in jest or otherwise—that he would be fired if the reforms were not implemented and the loan a failure. As it turned out, the reforms were implemented as long as President Babangida remained in power.

After his four-year assignment in Nigeria, Husain returned to Washington in 1987 and took over the World Bank's central debt and international finance division. He turned what was a traditional data crunching outfit into a modern data management unit, just in time for another developing country debt crisis which unfolded in the late 1980s. I recall vividly a demonstration of the first edition of the World Bank's debt data on a compact disk (CD), as I marvelled at what was then a most modern technology, indeed the first CD I ever saw. He also decided that data management was not enough and brought together bright young economists for in-depth analysis of the global and country debt situation. During the summers, he invited the best global economic thinkers to join his team as visiting fellows, including Kenneth Rogoff, Paul Krugman, and Jeffrey Sachs. One of his achievements at that time was to have the World Bank go on record in support of debt relief for developing countries in crisis, which until that time had been an anathema in the Bank. Previously, debt relief, let alone forgiveness, had not been accepted in the Bank.

In 1991, Ishrat Husain assumed the position of Chief Economist of the World Bank's Africa region. At that time, the criticism over the Bank's structural adjustment in Africa lending reached a crescendo and he was asked to lead a study to review the region's experience with structural reform. The result was a two-volume report which reviewed the experience with structural reforms during the second half of the 1980s in 29 Sub-Saharan African countries. It concluded that reforms, when effectively implemented, did lead to higher GDP growth rates and to reductions in poverty. When reforms lagged or were reversed, economic performance faltered. But the report also noted that '[a]chieving long-term, equitable growth also requires more investment in human capital and infrastructure, greater expansion of institutional capacity, and better governance'.[1]

In 1994, Ishrat Husain moved on from Africa to the World Bank's East Asia and Pacific Region as Chief Economist. After a brief year in that position, he was drafted in 1995 to serve as the World Bank's Director for Poverty and Social Policy. This department was created in response to a call by the Bank's new President, James Wolfensohn, for a much more determined focus on poverty reduction as a key strategic goal of the institution. That position gave him a great opportunity to combine his passion for sound analysis with a focus on effective social policy in the battle against poverty. He contributed greatly to the World Bank's pursuit of its renewed anti-poverty vision.

In 1997, the World Bank traversed another one of its frequent reorganisations. At that time, I served as Vice President for the Europe and Central Asia Region. When I had an opportunity to fill a newly created position of Country Director for Central Asia, I had the great fortune that Husain was ready to join my team. He took responsibility for three countries: Azerbaijan, Tajikistan, and Turkmenistan. All three countries had hit rock bottom of the deep recession following dissolution of the Soviet Union. Tajikistan had just emerged from a deadly civil war. All three countries faced daunting challenges of reform. Husain was once again in his element as a practitioner in the front lines of reform. He took on the job with gusto.

In Tajikistan, even under the most difficult of circumstances, reforms progressed, not least because Ishrat Husain had gained the trust of the country's President, Emomali Rahmon. When, a few years later, Rahmon paid an official visit to Pakistan, he sought out Husain, then Governor of the State Bank of Pakistan, during a state dinner and gave him his fulsome praise for having brought the World Bank and other donors together to help Tajikistan at a critical time. In the case of Azerbaijan, Husain advised the government to set up an oil fund to help manage the expected oil revenues for the benefit of the country, a wise choice as subsequent developments proved. In the case of Uzbekistan, his advice fell on deaf ears under long-time President Islam Karimov, not for lack of trying. His efforts were not helped when Joseph Stiglitz, then World Bank's Chief Economist, visited the country and—as an avid opponent of 'shock therapy' reforms—congratulated the President for the country's painfully slow reforms. Only since the arrival of a new President in 2016 has Uzbekistan embarked on a path towards reform which has now begun to bear fruit.

Twenty years of professional life at the World Bank offered Ishrat Husain many great opportunities to contribute with his insight, energy, commitment, power of persuasion, and exquisite human decency. They also offered him opportunities to grow and to learn in his manifold capacities, in the many countries he worked in, and in the wide range of challenges he faced in managing people, serving clients, and pursuing the best possible pathways for reform. Equipped with this knowledge and experience, Husain has been able to devote his next 20 years and beyond to the service of his country in various capacities, again with the goal to achieve the best possible outcome for the people he is committed to work for, and especially the most vulnerable among them.

Note

1. 'Adjustment in Africa: reforms, results, and the road ahead. A World Bank policy research report,' *World Bank* (Washington, DC: World Bank Group, 1994).

Introduction

Vaqar Ahmed

An effort to compile essays focusing on the state of economy, welfare, and reforms in Pakistan proved to be a daunting task amid the initial days of Covid-19. The authors who have contributed to this festschrift faced a world never seen before. As the timeline of pandemic prolonged, so did the uncertainties associated with economic recovery scenarios. Almost everything—economic growth, job creation, implementation of structural reforms, bringing Sustainable Development Goals (SDGs) back on track, and several other socioeconomic priorities were now linked to medical solutions and how fast these could reach the masses.

This celebratory volume carries policy relevance as Dr Ishrat Husain, was an important part of the government at the time of writing this text and continued to play an important role in envisaging the way forward to Pakistan's economy and institutional reforms. He, along with other cabinet members, faced a formidable challenge. The fiscal year 2019–2020 has already seen an estimated annual loss of Rs 2.5 trillion to the national economy due to the pandemic and still the end of the Covid-19 threat is nowhere in sight. The delays in acquiring and administering the vaccine are bound to increase such economic losses.

In January 2021, the Pakistan Bureau of Statistics released its results from a survey conducted to gauge the impact of Covid-19 on livelihoods. The findings revealed that 20.76 million workforce suffered livelihood losses due to coronavirus-related lockdowns. While many were able to go back to work after the partial lifting of lockdowns by the end of 2020, however, even at the time of writing this text, there were several sectors which could not fully open due to the necessary micro and smart lockdowns.

In such a scenario, even if Pakistan witnesses a V-shaped recovery in economic growth and other related macroeconomic indicators, the pre-pandemic momentum towards structural reforms promised under the IMF programme has been lost. Building back better would certainly require a stronger resolve to address recurrent balance of payment difficulties and reducing public expenditures which keep budget deficit and government's borrowing requirements high.

In view of this, our approach to deciding specific themes of chapters for this festschrift was three-pronged. First, we carefully identified areas of immediate concern for Pakistan's economy. Most of these areas, for example, the management of government budget also present several opportunities. Second, we narrowed down this list and focused on themes where Dr Husain was able to contribute during his career and in various capacities inside and outside of the public sector. Third, we spent a significant amount of time searching for authors who were an authority on these themes and were well-versed with the challenges, opportunities, and Dr Husain's contribution.

Most chapters, therefore, go beyond a standard festschrift approach and readers will note how various authors have presented their own evidence-based perspectives as well. For ease of reference, we have grouped the chapters into five main broad categories namely: macroeconomic management, financial markets, sub-national economic reforms, regional integration, and human development, including women's economic empowerment.

Equally important is to note that most chapters are a result of the contributor's own research, an updated literature review, and at places in-depth interviews with the relevant stakeholders. An example of this is Chapter 2 by Ali Salman and Beenish Javed which is a result of several rounds of national debt conference organised by the Policy Research Institute of Market Economy (PRIME). Their contribution explains how Pakistani economists, including Dr Husain, have approached the domestic and external debt challenge.

Chapter 3 by Zafar Hayat, again, banks on his years of research. He has presented the counter-productive performance of monetary policy in the past towards achieving price stability and economic growth. He presents evidence to indicate that the central bank undermined both the objectives while trying to directly stimulate growth rather than trying to achieve it through price stability.

Some such sentiments are also shared by Bushra Yasmin in Chapter 4, analysing reasons which prevent good quality foreign direct investment from coming to Pakistan. Yasmin also presents some possible recommendations for the future. These suggestions compliment those presented in Hamid Mahmood's Chapter 6 on increasing efficiency of public investments across the country. Almost all chapters under the macroeconomic management theme underscore the need for stronger institutions—an area which is the focus of Shakeel Ahmad's work presented. He has emphasised on how Pakistan will need to encourage innovation and risk-taking in public sector—a key value seen in countries with lean and efficient civil service.

Under the state of sub-national economy, we were able to cover all provinces except Khyber Pakhtunkhwa. The contributing author who had confirmed could not meet the timeline due to personal circumstances. This remains a deficit which may have to be addressed in future such endeavours.

Chapter 9 on the economy of Balochistan from Abdul Salam Lodhi paints a grave picture from a land which carries so much potential waiting to be harnessed through a correction in priorities of Pakistani elites and investments in human capital and enabling infrastructure. He draws from his own research as an academic teaching in one of the leading universities of the province. From another acclaimed academic, Saranjam Baig, we are fortunate to have perspectives from Gilgit-Baltistan (Chapter 10)—a region which was (before the pandemic) and will continue to be highlighted in the 'must-go' tourist destinations of the world. Over the past five years, this region has seen an unprecedented footfall owing to pro-tourism policies of the Pakistan Tehreek-e-Insaf (PTI) government in the region and at the federal level.

Chapters 7 and 8 on the economies of Punjab and Sindh were contributed by two experienced economists currently associated with the provincial planning and development departments. Both chapters highlight the contours of provincial growth strategies and investments required to achieve these.

Pakistan's financial markets have gradually continued to integrate with the rest of the world and now perhaps at a faster pace due to the adoption of digital technologies. The evolution of this sector has been captured in Faheem Sardar's work (Chapter 11). The author invites the relevant institutions and regulatory bodies to put in motion a longer-term vision for this sector's growth and making financial inclusion a more immediate goal. A sub-set of this discussion is then undertaken at length in Chapter 12 by Ahmed Ali Siddiqui who explains the factors behind growth of Islamic banking—a sector which, according to him, will continue to see a record growth given people's preferences and introduction of financial products compliant with Islamic values.

The need for stronger financial inclusion reforms is presented in chapters 13 and 14 by Hadia Majid and Muhammad Arif, respectively. While the former focuses on avenues for women's financial inclusion, the latter makes a case for consciously encouraging entrepreneurship and private enterprise through policy and regulatory measures.

In our last section, authors explain what regional trade and investment integration holds for Pakistan. In Chapter 15, Ghulam Samad and Ghulam Nabi have highlighted prospects of Pakistan's trade with Central Asia and ways through which higher exchange of goods and services may be possible. In Chapter 16, Liaqat Ali Shah explains how the China-Pakistan Economic Corridor (CPEC) and priority special economic zones could mean a revival of competitive manufacturing sector in Pakistan. In Chapter 17, Maaz Javed takes a similar view and goes deeper into how gains from CPEC could be offered to Pakistan's neighbours, including Afghanistan, India, and Iran.

In compiling these contributions, and in my capacity of a volume editor, I was reminded continuously by peers about two important goals. One, of course, to honour the untiring efforts of Dr Ishrat Husain and the other to present a narrative which could highlight post-pandemic priorities of Pakistan's fast-evolving economy. The country and its people hold significant promise. Since 2008, the state has seen strengthening of democratic rule. People have voted for change in 2013 and 2018. Institutions, such as the superior judiciary, have played a responsible role in bringing order to both the executive and legislative branches of the government. Civil society institutions, including policy think tanks and non-profit organisations, have exhibited resilience and a stronger practice of social accountability for demanding improved service delivery in health, education, and various other spheres. The deregulation of media has allowed it to transform into a strong pillar of democracy. And, last but not the least, having over 60 per cent of population still comprising of youth which is more educated than past generations and digitally connected is pushing growth in new economic activities never seen in the past decades. Building on all these episodes of success will now require lasting improvements in governance, social justice, and peace.

Vaqar Ahmed
January 24, 2021

Part

1

MACROECONOMIC MANAGEMENT

CHAPTER 1

Macroeconomic Policy and Management amid Covid-19

Vaqar Ahmed

It is a rare privilege to write this chapter in honour of Dr Ishrat Husain—who remains a mentor to me and somebody who has brought great clarity in my thought process as a student of economics and public policy. My interactions with Dr Husain started in the early 2000s. Pakistan was passing through a turbulent economic and security milieu and he was responsible, in his capacity as Governor of the State Bank of Pakistan, to keep the macroeconomic fundamentals secure, negotiate external assistance to bring stability to the external account, as well as induce critical structural reforms. Later, in the same decade, he contributed immensely to formulate a home-grown approach to improving governance at the National Commission for Government Reforms. He remains an advocate for expedient public administration reforms, which he sees as critical for enhancing development effectiveness.

Our regular meetings continued once he took over as the head of the Institute of Business Administration (IBA) in Karachi. He has taken this school of excellence to new heights. This institution, which is alma mater to several luminaries, is perhaps the go-to place for public and private sector trying to understand business, finance, and the economy.

Perhaps I learned the most from him after 2013 once I got a chance to work under his guidance to formulate a regional trade and investment strategy for Pakistan. This comprehensive research work was requested by the then federal minister for commerce, Khurram Dastgir-Khan. Under Dr Husain's leadership, our team was able to advise and guide the ministry to expedite critical reforms needed to better integrate with the region, optimise benefits from China-Pakistan Economic Corridor (CPEC), and bring greater efficiency in Afghanistan-Pakistan transit trade.

In 2018, Dr Husain was appointed as Prime Minister's Advisor on Institutional Reforms and Austerity. In this capacity, he increased his efforts to reform those government windows responsible for regulatory burden on businesses. Under his leadership, the Pakistan Tehreek-e-Insaf (PTI) government initiated the Pakistan Regulatory Modernization Initiative (PRMI) with the aim to: a) map, rationalise, modernise, and digitise compliance with regulatory governance, and b) digitise all Business-to-Government (B2G) payments of related fees through a consolidated Pakistan Business Portal. The team at the Sustainable Development Policy Institute (SDPI) was able to advocate and help create urgency for the PRMI in the days that followed.[1]

Just when several of these important regulatory reforms were being rolled out, the world braced for perhaps the biggest global challenge of our times—Covid-19. This chapter provides an insight into how Pakistan dealt with the immediate impact of this crisis. At the time of writing this chapter, the crisis is still not over. In fact, many believe that Pakistan has not reached its peak and many more could test positive for the virus in the coming days. Amid these difficult times, the following sections provide an insight into the colossal challenge Dr Husain and his colleagues in the Cabinet had to rise up to.

COVID-19'S IMPACT ON MACROECONOMIC PERFORMANCE

The Covid-19 pandemic brought sharp economic contraction in Pakistan. The economic expansion was targeted at 2.4 per cent during fiscal year 2019–20, however, the real GDP growth contracted by -0.4 per cent with a slow recovery expected in fiscal year 2021 and beyond.[2] Perhaps the biggest hit was taken by the manufacturing sector where growth declined by 5.4 per cent. A significant slowdown set in textile, automobiles, chemicals, leather, iron and steel products, petroleum products, metallic and non-metallic metals, and electronics. The agriculture sector's outlook also became uncertain due to supply chain disruptions and the delayed harvesting on account of the lockdown and locust attacks. After Covid-19 struck, there were four main channels now causing economic slowdown.

First, the supply side channel indicated that disruptions in supply chains and constraints imposed by Covid-19 on international and local movement of industrial inputs resulted in lower-than-expected output. A survey conducted by the Small and Medium Enterprise Development Authority (SMEDA) revealed that 92 per cent of firms had reported a disruption in their supply chain and 23 per cent reported up to 100 per cent loss in their export orders.[3] The micro, small, and medium enterprises were particularly termed vulnerable. In the months that followed, we saw instances of localised and selective lockdowns, eventually resulting in several industries laying off their workers.

Second, the demand side channel indicated that lower orders from abroad translated into reduced earnings.[4] The lay-offs and rise in underemployment in FY20 also triggered lower demand for goods and services at home and a preference for savings. There was some shifting of expenditures at the household level in favour of healthcare, hygiene, and essential needs. In the agriculture and livestock sector, weak purchasing power resulted in farmers not investing in the next season's inputs, which ultimately threatened overall food security in the country.

Third, the financial market channel showed that lower confidence and reduced earnings by both private enterprises and individuals adversely impacted markets for financial instruments. Pakistani currency declined sharply in April and later again in June FY20. Lastly, the cross-border channel indicated that supply-side shocks in other countries started impacting Pakistani manufacturers; border closures resulted in reduced mobility of Pakistani goods abroad.[5]

The investment outlook remained uncertain. With the above-mentioned transmission mechanisms at play, fixed investment-to-GDP ratio was only 13.8 per cent in FY20. Traditionally, during the past economic crises, government's own development budgets were used to stimulate the economy. However, there were limits to this response as the timeline for the reversal of Covid-19 spread was unknown. As government increased spending to cover for better healthcare and social safety nets, the public sector's investment-to-GDP ratio declined in FY21. This also pointed towards a very tight fiscal space to sustain current levels of stimulus over the medium term. This also contributed to the overall slowdown in recovery process.[6]

There were immense difficulties in fiscal management at the federal and provincial level. In the short run, Pakistan was not able to comply with the IMF's requirement of 0.8 per cent of primary budget deficit and this was allowed to expand to 2.9 per cent during FY20. It was not clear back then how the government planned to bring primary deficit to 0.4 per cent in FY21 and keep it at low levels going forward. This was difficult as the Federal Board of Revenue (FBR) had missed the July–February revenue collection target by Rs 484 billion. Besides, government's spending needs to finance healthcare and economic recovery were expected to remain high.

To finance its running and expected expenditures, the government relied on external assistance. The State Bank's working indicated that Pakistan's borrowing needs during FY20 would increase by another $1.9 billion. To cater to these needs, the government prepared Pakistan's Pandemic Preparedness and Response Plan (PPPR). The multilateral and bilateral partners promised to provide $4.4 billion over the next 15 months to finance this plan.[7] The IMF provided $1.38 billion Rapid Finance Instrument Facility. The World Bank Group (WBG) prepared its comprehensive lending arrangement for Pakistan, an initial support of $240 million was provided. Over the next 15 months, the WBG promised providing $2 billion in new financing while $1 billion from the already approved funds was repurposed. The Asian Development Bank (ADB) also provided $500 million worth Counter Cyclical Support Facility and $305 million as Emergency Assistance Lending (EAL) within FY20.

Risks to the current account reduced after the above-mentioned external assistance. However, there were limits to such assistance from abroad. Ultimately, the government had to bridge the growing financing gap through non-debt inflows that were hard to find in pandemic times. Unfortunately, the government also expected a return of a significant number of Pakistani workers from abroad, particularly those working in the Gulf countries.[8] This could mean bad news for remittance inflows. A fear of financial contagion for many countries which were trading partners of Pakistan resulted in an uncertain outlook for exports and the foreign direct investment (FDI) to Pakistan.

During February 2020, just when the pandemic outbreak started in Pakistan, Dr Husain had explained that if the economic slowdown resulting from Covid-19 prolongs this could have an impact on the economy and CPEC projects. He was particularly concerned that in such circumstances, there may be a short absence of Chinese workers who were involved with CPEC projects. He explained if that happened, Pakistan's own skilled labour force would have to step up and keep these projects running smoothly. The sustainability of these projects was important to receive future investment flows.[9]

REIMAGINING NATIONAL PLANNING AND BUDGETING

As the second half of 2020 approached, the government needed to continue supporting expansion of the Ehsaas Programme—social safety nets programme—across the country. Only time will tell if the Rs 1.2 trillion relief package will be adequate to mitigate the pains of the poorest. Nearly 24 per cent of Pakistan's 210 million population was below the poverty line and Covid-19 was expected to push another 15 million into poverty.[10] Until now, 7.3 million beneficiaries had received cash support of Rs 12,000. This number could increase in case of a prolonged lockdown and lay-offs by the private sector. Additional assistance was being planned to be targeted towards 4.3 million women beneficiaries.[11] A Rs 75 billion package was announced for daily-wage workers—an initiative aimed at targeting around 6 million beneficiaries.

A conscious response from the government was needed to address social exclusion. At the time of writing this text, there had been some delays related to outreach and messaging to explain to the poor how to access relief package, biometric verification of beneficiaries, and targeting in the informal sector and far-flung areas. The recovery of small businesses required support over medium to longer term. The State Bank had cut the policy rate, expanded refinance schemes, and introduced temporary regulatory measures to help financial system's soundness. A Rs 5 million collateral-free loan facility was made available for micro and small businesses. Refinancing facility was also available for firms which do not lay-off workers. The government promised to cover three-month electricity bills for 3.5 million small and medium enterprises (SMEs). However, it is important to mention that most of the initiatives explained above experienced some delays in the roll out as banks needed more convincing to take such a risk. The SMEs which could receive assistance needed to be targeted, and the needy were faced with information gaps about how to access help. Regarding support to the SMEs, commercial banks were found reluctant to quickly process loans, anticipating a slower recovery and high risk.

By June 2020, the federal budget for FY21 was introduced. This budget realised that one-off measures may not be adequate to revive employment prospects in the private sector. Therefore, the budget for FY21 aimed at helping firms in reducing their cost of doing business. Some relief measures under GST on goods and trade taxes were announced. However, more needed to be done as firms complained about high burden of tax compliance costs, lack of a harmonised GST regime across provinces, and an uncertain tariff structure for electricity and gas.[12]

This supported select industries and services to repurpose or scale-up in the face of the pandemic. Hospitals operating at small and medium scale were allowed relaxation in trade taxes and reduced rate for credit uptake from banks. Firms producing personal protective equipment also saw relief in taxes. The trade taxes faced by such producers or even hospitals importing from abroad were rationalised. In the interest of ensuring food security, the agro- and food-processing enterprises were also supported.

One of the business segments which was found disappointed by the government's relief efforts were the private enterprises in IT and ICT space. Several online essential services were now important for the social and mental well-being of society. Online shopping and financial transactions saw a boost during the pandemic. It was in this context that the private sector wanted more liberal incentives for the e-commerce sector, something which was not announced.

It is likely that in the coming days the government may leverage e-commerce in the battle against Covid-19 and its aftermath. In this regard, e-commerce policy (already approved) could see priority implementation. The drive to digitalise the economy-wide business transactions also requires better cross-border data transfer rules; liberalisation of online payment mechanisms; adoption of cashless payment modes for payments towards utilities; improvements to intellectual property regime; tax, tariff, and investment framework in digital space; essential cyber security measures; and raising standards of human resource in IT and ICT. Any future free trade agreements should also include provisions regarding e-commerce.[13]

OPPORTUNITIES AMID THE PANDEMIC

The early days of the pandemic outbreak led to a fall in global crude oil prices, presenting an opportunity to hedge the uncertainty by locking in low oil prices.[14] Inflation had started to slow down and this was likely to take away some pressures on the demand-side and help augment purchasing power. The IMF had also announced that it will shield Pakistan's economy from any unanticipated balance of payments (BOP) problems.[15] It was expected that Pakistan may request for some relaxation in the time allowed to implement the structural reforms under the IMF's Extended Fund Facility (EFF).[16]

The volatilities related to the current account stabilised on the back of low import demand and falling oil prices. Going forward, it was important that opportunities presented by Covid-19 for exporters may be harnessed. Textile and garments exporters could repurpose production items and supply the necessary safety wear for doctors and paramedics. The demand for surgical goods and pharmaceuticals was also projected to increase. The Rupee depreciation also made Pakistani exports more competitive. Likewise, the automobile and auto-parts sector expected to repurpose in favour of producing ventilators and related accessories.

Covid-19 had also mitigated the immediate political threats to the PTI government. The government now had an opportunity to improve the health sector service delivery and prove its good governance. The regional integration process has once again been initiated with the South Asian Association for Regional Cooperation (SAARC) emergency fund being operationalised.[17] Many believed that this could prove to break the ice between India and Pakistan. Afghanistan and Pakistan also came closer with the latter having opened borders to transport transit goods five times per week. Opening up trade in health services with neighbours was now looking like an idea whose time had come.[18]

Covid-19 also provided an opportunity to the government to put in place measures which could reduce digital inequality and help the 'freelance' and e-commerce sectors. With social distancing measures in place, people found tremendous value in paying bills online, making online funds transfer, and ordering essential items online. This behaviour not only led to an exponential increase in usage of digital tools but also made more people aware of and reliant on the conveniences provided by the digital economy.[19] A greater use of online banking channels to complete transactions improved resilience of the financial sector in Pakistan.

In the days that followed, Dr Husain helped the government come up with its first e-commerce policy. He also emphasised at various forums the need to better understand a fair competition regime for online businesses. On this subject, he thought that an active role of the Competition Commission of Pakistan was critical. Furthermore, he stressed upon improving the consumer protection in Pakistan's online environment.[20]

PATHWAYS TO MACROECONOMIC AND STRUCTURAL REFORM

Covid-19 impacted Pakistan's progress towards the IMF programme in three ways. First, the schedule of regular review and monitoring of the macroeconomic performance altered. The reviews were now bound to take place after slightly longer intervals.[21] Second, as the State Bank expected to purse quantitative easing,[22] therefore, some performance criterion and indicative targets were being expected to slightly change to accommodate monetary and fiscal expansion. In our assessment, the criteria[23] which could see some flexibility during the coming months include: ceiling on net domestic assets, net foreign currency swaps, primary budget deficit, and budgetary borrowing from the State Bank. In our view, the IMF will not be flexible to allow ease in the ceiling on amount of government guarantees. This could also slow down the projects planned under the second phase of CPEC.

Likewise, some relaxation in indicative targets is possible. This could include ease in floor on social sector spending (possible diversion of resources to health sector), and floor on net tax revenues by the FBR (lower collection expected due to negative GDP growth rate). In our view, there may not be flexibility to alter ceiling on power sector payments arrears due to fall in oil prices. The IMF would like to see the government continue on the path of power sector reform and address the circular debt issue. Furthermore, to help the exporters it is likely that the FBR will expediently process the refund payments.

There may be some alterations to the structural benchmarks[24] depending upon the severity of the Covid-19. First, the government had committed not to grant tax amnesties during the programme period. We have, however, seen that to revive aggregate demand, the federal government had to announce a construction sector package which includes a tax amnesty component. Second, due to the heightened pressures on the Cabinet, and inability of the parliament to meet physically, there have also been some delays in the amendments to the State Bank of Pakistan Act. Third, with regards to reform of loss-making state-owned enterprises, there is a possibility that the privatisation programme may be expedited in case government faces issues with regard to the financing of budget deficit. Fourth, the government has already sought four months relaxation to comply with the remaining actions desired by Financial Action Task Force (FATF). It is likely that a further extension may be allowed on sympathetic grounds, however, there will be increased monitoring of measures to counter illicit financing during Covid-19 times.[25] Finally, while the IMF has directed to avoid the practice of issuing new tax exemptions, it is likely that sectors, such as health services, and producers of personal protective equipment may receive a tax relief, including rationalisation of customs duties for inputs.

Pakistan remains committed to the reforms agreed under the EFF. The IMF authorities will, however, resume discussions on the next review of the EFF once Covid-related pressures ease.[26] For the time being, a key priority for the IMF will be to keep Pakistan's public debt within sustainable limits. The April 2020 IMF country report does inform that Covid-19 could be a risk to debt sustainability. However, debt levels can be brought downwards in the later half of FY20 through help from bilateral creditors, including China, Saudi Arabia, and UAE.

The government had also formally approached the G-20 countries for debt relief. The country's $1.8 billion repayment due by December 2020 was deferred by 15 months. This repayment was owed to eleven G-20 economies (including Japan).[27] Such a development helped in keeping debt-to-GDP ratio within limits. It was expected that this ratio will hover around 90 by end of FY20. However, the government was also advised to make arrangements to boost non-debt inflows to cover for expected external financing gap of $1.5 billion in FY21.

With Dr Husain's support, a key achievement of the PTI government has been to get the public finance management law passed. This will demonstrate Pakistan's commitment to reforms in the coming days. The Public Finance Management Act 2019 was enacted 'to strengthen management of public finances with the view to improving definition and implementation of fiscal policy for better macroeconomic management, to clarify institutional responsibilities related to financial management, and to strengthen budgetary management'.[28] Apart from making the budget formulation process more transparent, this Act called for limiting the supplementary grants and restriction on movement of public money into scheduled banks' accounts, fully revealing to the parliament any tax exemptions and strengthening rules regarding supplementary budgets, appropriate of budgets, and surrender of savings. One sincerely hopes that the fate of this Act will be better than Fiscal Responsibility and Debt Limitation Act 2005—which has been repeatedly violated by several governments in the past.

Notes

1. Sohail Sarfraz, 'Ishrat for effective use of CNIC to detect tax evasion,' *Business Recorder*, December 3, 2019.
2. 'Pakistan: First Review Under the Extended Arrangement Under the Extended Fund Facility and Request for Modification of Performance Criteria,' International Monetary Fund, December 23, 2019.
3. 'Survey on Impact of Covid-19 (Coronavirus) on SMEs,' SMEDA, April, 2020.

4. Vaqar Ahmed and Cathal O'Donoghue, 'External Shocks in a Small Open Economy: A CGE-Microsimulation Analysis,' *Lahore Journal of Economics* 15, no. 1 (2010a): 45–90.

5. Vaqar Ahmed and Cathal O'Donoghue, 'Case Study: Global economic crisis and poverty in Pakistan,' *International Journal of Microsimulation, International Microsimulation Association* 3, no. 1 (2010b): 127–129.

6. Vaqar Ahmed, Ahsan Abbas, and Saira Ahmed, 'Public Infrastructure and Economic Growth in Pakistan: A Dynamic CGE-Microsimulation Analysis,' in *Infrastructure and Economic Growth in Asia. Economic Studies in Inequality, Social Exclusion and Well-Being*, eds., John Cockburn, Yazid Dissou, Jean-Yves Duclos, and Luca Tiberti (Springer, 2013).

7. Mehtab Haider, 'Creditors pledge Rs708b for Pakistan to fight Covid-19,' *The News*, April 28, 2020a.

8. Vaqar Ahmed, Guntur Sugiyarto, and Shikha Jha, 'Remittances and Household Welfare: A Case Study of Pakistan,' Asian Development Bank, Economics Working Paper Series, no. 194 (February 2010).

9. Fakhar Durrani, 'Will coronavirus affect CPEC and Pak economy?' *The News*, February 7, 2020.

10. 'Oil: To hedge or not?' *Business Recorder Research*, March 11, 2020.

11. Hafiz A. Pasha And Shahid Kardar, 'Revisiting economic impact of coronavirus,' *Business Recorder*, April 14, 2020.

12. Vaqar Ahmed and Mustafa Talpur, 'Towards a Fair and Just Fiscal Policy in Pakistan,' Policy Review, Sustainable Development Policy Institute, July 2015; and Vaqar Ahmed and Mustafa Talpur 'Corporate Tax Reforms in Pakistan,' Sustainable Development Policy Institute, 2016.

13. Vaqar Ahmed, M. Javed, R. Tabassum, A. Javed, M. F. Ferracane, and W. Anukoonwattaka, 'National Study on Digital Trade Integration in Pakistan,' United Nations Economic and Social Commission for Asia and the Pacific, Bangkok, 2021 (unpublished).

14. 'Oil: To hedge or not?'

15. 'Statement by IMF Managing Director Kristalina Georgieva on Pakistan,' IMF Press Release no. 20/113.

16. Imran Ali Kundi, 'IMF allows exclusion of corona prevention expenses' from fiscal deficit,' *The Nation*, March 7, 2020.

17. Dipanjan Roy Chaudhury, 'PM Modi proposes emergency covid-19 fund for SAARC nations,' *The Economic Times*, March 16, 2020.

18. Rabia Manzoor, Shehryar Khan Toru, and Vaqar Ahmed, 'Health Services Trade between India and Pakistan,' *The Pakistan Journal of Social Issues*, Volume VIII, 2017.

19. 'Corona and Pakistan's on-demand economy,' *Business Recorder Research*, March 19, 2020.

20. Ghulam Abbas, 'CCP to prepare rules for online businesses,' *Pakistan Today*, April 22, 2020.

21. In the past, these reviews were supposed to take place every quarter.

22. Practice of purchasing government securities to inject capital into the economy.

23. A complete list of performance criteria is available in Table 11 of the IMF Country Report No. 19/380.

24. A complete list of structural benchmarks is available in Table 12 of the IMF Country Report No. 19/380.

25. Malik Muhammad Ashraf, 'Welcome moratorium by FATF,' *The Nation*, April 10, 2020.

26. 'IMF representative terms performance of Pakistan's economy satisfactory,' *The News*, April 21, 2020.

27. Pakistan can still access those non-concessional loans which are allowed under the IMF Debt Limit Policy.

28. Excerpt from the Act.

CHAPTER 2

Debt Management in Pakistan: Challenges and Prospects for Future

ALI SALMAN AND BEENISH JAVED

OVERVIEW

Over the years, the rising public debt in Pakistan has manifested itself as one of the most important macroeconomic challenges for economic managers. This chapter provides an overview of the trend of public debt in the past two decades. A unique feature of the chapter is its utilisation of frameworks for debt analysis by Pakistan's two most distinguished economists: Dr Ishrat Husain and Dr Hafiz A. Pasha, both with extensive policy experience, who presented their papers at various national debt conferences organised by the Policy Research in Macroeconomics (PRIME). In addition, it evaluates the progress on medium-term debt management strategy 2015/16–2018/19. Lastly, the chapter concludes with a way forward for a prudent debt management.

HISTORICAL ANALYSIS OF DEBT

Before 2000, Pakistan was heading for an external debt trap. The public debt-to-GDP ratio stood at 100.3 per cent in 1999.[1] However, in September 2001, external debt under the Paris Club was rescheduled. As a result, the crisis was averted as foreign public debt declined from 50.9 per cent of GDP in 1999 to 23.4 per cent in 2007. The domestic debt also fell from 47.4 to 28.3 per cent during the same time. Overall, public debt fell from 98.3 to 51.6 per cent. However, the situation deteriorated afterwards (see Figure 1) as we saw a continuous rise in the public debt, including external and domestic debt.

Noticeably, after 2010, public and domestic debt witnessed a sharper increase relative to external debt. Many factors have been responsible for this trend, some prominent ones include: soaring fiscal deficit, rise in circular debt, and increased debt-servicing. In contrast, currency devaluation, debt-servicing, CPEC-accrued debt, and IMF loans have largely been responsible for an increase in external debt in recent years. As of December 2019, public debt-to-GDP ratio stands at 77.3 per cent.[2]

It is pertinent to note that the depreciation of currency adds to the debt burden by increasing foreign-denominated debt. As Pakistan transitioned to a market-determined exchange rate, the year 2019 saw the rupee sustain a plunge of nearly 12 per cent against the US dollar and 3 per cent during FY20, causing an increase in foreign-denominated debt and debt-servicing. During FY19, currency depreciation accounted for 39 per cent of the increase in public debt. Between June 2019 and June 2020, total public debt increased by Rs 3,689 billion of which Rs 399 billion or 10.8 per cent has been because of currency depreciation.

Figure 1: Trend in Public Debt (1999–2019)

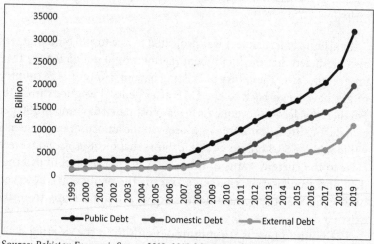

Source: *Pakistan Economic Survey 2018–2019*, Ministry of Finance

DEBT RISKS IDENTIFIED BY DR HAFIZ PASHA

During PRIME's second National Debt Conference in 2015, former finance minister Dr Hafiz Pasha made an alarming projection regarding debt-related indicators for the next four years. Table 1 summarises these predictions and presents the status of the relevant indicators.

Table 1: Public Debt Risks Identified by Pasha (2015)

Projections in 2015	Status in 2019[3]
External Debt will rise to $90 billion	External Debt stands at $106 billion
Debt-to-Revenue ratio will rise to 750%	Debt-to-Revenue ratio stands at 667.4%
Exports would have to increase to $36 billion in order to retire debt without the IMF's assistance	Exports stand at $20 billion as of July–April
Current Account Deficit will rise to 4% of GDP	Current Account Deficit stands at 4.03% of GDP
Amortisation payment will rise to $8.3 billion	Amortisation payment stands at $10.6 billion[4]

Source: Ministry of Finance

Pakistan's external debt was projected to rise to $90 billion. It was also predicted that the incumbent regime would not go for the IMF programme after the expiry of existing bailout. However, the country might have to go back to the IMF after general elections in 2018. Further, the debt-to-revenue ratio was postulated to climb to 750 per cent during fiscal year 2018–19. Moreover, the amortisation payments will double to $8.3 billion.[5] Table 1 shows that most projections were close to the current status of those indicators. The level of external debt and amortisation payments exceeds the predictions, however, indicating that the government is acquiring more loans to retire existing debt.

The point to note is the mushroom growth in the external debt-servicing burden. Dr Hafiz Pasha made some new predictions. The external debt-servicing burden was projected to increase by almost 77 per cent in 2019–20. Earlier, it grew by 46 per cent in 2018–19. Now a larger part of the external financing need is for meeting the debt-servicing obligation, whereas up till 2018–19 it was for financing of the current account deficit. This implies that following the success in reducing the latter by 75 per cent the pressure will continue for external borrowing to finance the rapid growth in the debt-servicing burden.

The implication is that, following the very substantial reduction in the current account deficit, a floor has been reached to the external-financing requirements. As debt-servicing increases with the rise in the size of external debt, there will continue to be growth in future years in the external financing gap. There is also a growing concern about the composition of external borrowing. During the first six months of 2019–20, the share of short-term borrowing increased sharply. This includes the $400 million from the short-term deferred oil payment facility of Saudi Arabia, $400 million short-term funding by IDB also for oil import, and the $1.3 billion of 'hot money'. With a combined total of $2.1 billion, 25 per cent of external debt comprise of short-term borrowings. This increases future liquidity risks due to the exit of 'hot money' in the event there is a negative development on the external front.[6]

The bottom line is that there is no scope for complacency with the big reduction in the current account deficit. External financing needs remain large because of growing external debt repayment obligations. If these are not financed fully by inflows of external assistance then there is the risk of a decline in reserves and a return to instability in the value of the rupee.

AN INSIGHT INTO DEBT SUSTAINABILITY BY DR ISHRAT HUSAIN

There is a contentious debate about the sustainability of debt in Pakistan. In order to shed light on debt-related issues and some of the misconceptions surrounding it, PRIME held its fourth National Debt Conference in 2017. In the conference, Dr Ishrat Husain, former Adviser on Institutional Reforms and Austerity, was invited as a keynote speaker. He shared his valuable insights on key debt sustainability indicators. According to Husain, a lot of criticism is based solely on the misunderstanding of the debt.[7] Hence, it is not advisable to examine the debt burden in terms of absolute amounts or per capita terms rather an appropriate way is to assess other indicators that relate total public debt to total revenues (see Figure 2), total foreign exchange earnings or foreign exchange reserves (see Table 2). The debt debate has become highly politicised, which is why there is need to explore the data and examine realistically rather than emotionally. In order to delve into the question of whether or not the debt is sustainable, this chapter makes use of the sustainability indicators highlighted by Husain.[8] In this regard, Figure 2 shows the sustainability trend of public, external, and domestic debt in terms of total revenues.

A smaller ratio of public, domestic, and external debt to total revenue depicts greater sustainability of debt and vice versa. Unfortunately, Pakistan's debt sustainability indicators deteriorated overtime, most noticeably after 2017 where the ratio of public, domestic, and external debt witnessed a sharp increase (see Figure 2). The indicator worsened as a result of an increase in public, domestic, and external debt with a simultaneous fall in government's total revenues owing to rising fiscal deficit.

Figure 2: Debt Sustainability Indicator as a % of Revenue

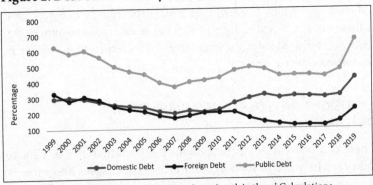

Source: Pakistan Economic Survey (Various Issues) and Authors' Calculations

According to Husain, lumping domestic and external debt together is analytically incorrect.[9] While both create debt-servicing liability for the budgetary purposes and therefore affect the fiscal balances, the risk profiles of the two are quite different. Domestic debt has to be paid in rupees which can be printed or the State Bank can acquire those obligations on its balance sheet by creating reserve money. It involves creating possible inflationary pressures but there is no risk of default which is a real threat in case of foreign currency denominated debt. Thus, it is pertinent to focus on total debt-servicing capacity, especially that of external debt as an indicator of sustainability. As this has to be paid in foreign exchange, the capacity is much dependent on the current and future earnings of foreign exchange and the level of reserves. In addition, the ratios of external debt and liabilities (EDL) to GDP, foreign exchange earnings or official reserves is also important to monitor because if these ratios are on a downward moving path over time, there is not much cause for alarm.[10] In this regard, Table 2 shows the external debt sustainability indicators for the last five years.

Table 2: External Debt Sustainability Indicators

Indicator*	2015	2016	2017	2018	2019
ED/FEE (times)	1.0	1.1	1.2	1.3	1.3
ED/FER (times)	2.7	2.5	2.9	4.3	5.1
ED/GDP (percentage)	18.8	20.7	20.5	22.3	25.9
ED Servicing/FEE (percentage)	8.5	8.5	12.4	10.8	17.2
EDL/GDP (percentage)	24.1	26.5	27.4	30.3	37.5
FER/EDL (percentage)	28.7	31.2	25.6	17.2	13.6

Source: Debt Policy Coordination Office, Ministry of Finance

It is pertinent to mention that Dr Husain stressed on proactive management of the external account as the foreign exchange earnings ratio was troublesome in 2017.[11] However, the situation only worsened from there onwards. External public debt-to-GDP ratio increased to 25.9 per cent at the end of June 2019 compared to 18.8 per cent at the end of June 2015, depicting an increase in the external debt burden. Apart from increase in the external public debt stock, reduction in GDP size in US dollar terms contributed towards increase in this ratio. Similarly, external public debt to foreign exchange reserves ratio

---

* External Debt (ED), External Debt Liabilities (EDL), Foreign Exchange Earnings (FEE), Foreign Exchange Reserves (FER)

increased and recorded at 5.1 times during FY 2018–19 compared with 2.7 times during FY 2014–15. Moderate growth in external public debt and depletion of Foreign Exchange Reserves (FER) owing to challenging the balance of payment situation led to an increase in this ratio over the years. Growth in external debt-servicing mainly driven by repayments of Eurobonds and commercial loans outpaced the growth in Foreign Exchange Earnings and accordingly external debt-servicing to foreign exchange earnings ratio increased to 17.2 per cent in FY 2018–19 compared with 8.5 per cent in FY 2014–15. The EDL to GDP ratio rose over the last five years depicting an increase in external debt liabilities and shrinking national income. Moreover, the declining FER to EDL ratio reiterates the fall in official reserves and an increase in external debt liabilities during the period under review.

Another important indicator of external debt sustainability is the composition of external debt, i.e., the break-up between Medium- and Long-Term (MLT) and Short-Term (ST) loans. If it is heavily dominated by MLT loans then the risk is relatively lower and vice versa.[12] Table 3 shows the composition of government's external debt. As evident, a majority of the external debt comprises of medium- to long-term loans which implies that the risk is lower than anticipated.

Table 3: Composition of External Debt

Government External Debt ($ in Million)	FY16	FY17	FY18	FY19	FY20
Long Term (>1 year)	50,026	55,547	62,525	66,536	66,236
Short Term (<1 year)	1,688	882	1,617	1,264	1,571

Source: Debt Policy Coordination Office, Ministry of Finance

From the above analysis it seems like the current level of external debt is somewhat sustainable and not as alarming as expected. Nonetheless, a proactive management of external account is necessary since the sustainability of external debt is contingent upon the level of foreign exchange earnings and reserves. That said, it is pertinent to analyse the strategies in place for proactive management of debt. The next section evaluates the progress of the medium-term debt management strategy 2015/16–2018/19.

CONTOURS OF DEBT MANAGEMENT STRATEGY

According to the IMF, 'Public debt can be regarded as sustainable when the primary balance needed to at least stabilize debt under both the baseline and realistic shock scenarios is economically and politically feasible, such that the level of debt is consistent with an acceptably low rollover risk and with preserving potential growth at a satisfactory level.'[13]

In other words, a country's public debt is said to be sustainable if the government is able to meet all its current and future payment obligations without exceptional financial assistance or going into default. In addition, the policies needed to stabilise debt should be feasible and consistent with maintaining the growth potential and should be associated with an acceptably low level of solvency and liquidity risks.

The contours of public debt management are complex, involving management of budgetary requirements, development of an efficient secondary debt market, keeping a balance between cost and risk, and maintaining the debt at sustainable levels.

The prime responsibility for managing debt lies with the ministry of finance. Its subsections, such as the Economic Affairs Divisions (EAD) and Finance Division (FD), maintain the record of all the relevant information regarding debt. Specifically, the EAD tracks debt-servicing, aid flows, and allocation of funds received in grants, aids, and borrowings. In contrast, the FD is liable for formulating the debt policy. Its export finance wing plays a crucial role in formulating medium- to long-term policies taking into account the nexus between debt-related variables, such as borrowings and debt-servicing. The SBP also keeps record of debt-related data whereas the Central Directorate of National Savings maintains information on the public domestic debt accrued through the National Savings Scheme.

MEDIUM-TERM DEBT MANAGEMENT STRATEGY (2015/16–2018/19)

The fundamental objective of the Medium-Term Debt Management Strategy (MTDS) 2015/16–2018/19 was to propose financing at the lowest possible cost while taking into account the possible risks. The strategic guidelines for the period 2016–2019 were as follows:

- Rollover risk is to be reduced through increasing the maturity profile of domestic debt by focusing on medium- and long-term financing instruments.
- Interest rate risk is to be minimised through monitoring the share of domestic debt re-fixing and time for total portfolio re-fixing.
- Concentration of principal repayments is to be avoided by pursuing a smooth redemption profile, particularly in the domestic debt.
- Benefit from favourable terms and conditions by availing concessional loans from development partners.
- Keep in view cost-risk trade-offs when maintaining a foot in international capital markets through issuance of Pakistan International Sukuks or Eurobonds.
- Foreign currency funding in US dollar is to be preferred given the balance of payment requirements and external debt profile.

Precisely, foreign currency risk was to be managed by bringing the external debt share between 20 to 35 per cent over the medium term. While refinancing risk was to be managed by bringing the share of domestic debt maturing in the next 12 months between 50 to 65 per cent and public debt between 35 to 50 per cent. The average time to maturity (ATM) was to be maintained between 1.5 to 2.5 years for domestic debt and 3 to 4.5 years for public debt. Lastly, interest rate risk was to be managed by keeping the share of domestic debt re-fixing in 12 months between 50 to 65 per cent and public debt between 40 to 55 per cent whereas average time to re-fixing (ATR) was to be maintained between 1.5 to 2.5 years and 3 to 4.5 years for domestic and public debt, respectively.

In order to analyse the progress of the MTDS, it is imperative to evaluate the performance of public debt risk indicators overtime. Table 4 compares the public debt risk indicators of the last four years. Between 2016 and 2019, the refinancing indicators have improved with respect to domestic and public debt as reliance on long-term debt increased. However, the external debt-related refinancing risks rose. The external debt indicators have deteriorated as short- and long-term foreign debt maturing in FY19 increased to 158.7 per cent of the total liquid foreign currency reserves by June 2019.

In terms of interest rate risk, the upper range for 'Domestic Debt Re-Fixing in 1 Year' and 'Public Debt Re-Fixing in 1 Year' was envisaged at 65 per cent and 55 per cent, respectively, while these indicators stood at 66.6 per cent and 55.5 per cent at end June 2018. This resulted as the borrowing through short-term domestic debt instruments (which requires interest rate re-fixing in the short term) as well as borrowing contracted from foreign commercial banks on floating rates (mainly to fund external debt maturities and to finance the current account deficit) increased. While the external debt's average time to re-fixing decreased from 8.2 years to 6.1 years during the period under review.

Public debt portfolio's exchange rate risk witnessed an increase between 2016 and 2019 as the percentage of total public debt stock denominated in foreign currencies rose from 28.6 to 34.8 per cent. Short-term external public debt maturities as percentage of official liquid reserves stood at 158.7 per cent at the end of June 2019 compared with 31.9 per cent at the end of June 2016. The higher proportion of external public maturities falling within a year compared with the level of official liquid reserves resulted in an increase in this ratio.

It is relevant to mention here that contrary to the objectives of debt management strategy, the debt market still has a very low participation of new players. The non-bank institutions still remain reluctant to trade in long-term debt instruments on a large scale. More recently, a declining interest was seen in the case of corporate investments and mutual funds to participate in long-term debt instruments. Even the banks' participation in longer-tenure T-bills remained non-existent as they tried to minimise their interest-rate risk.

Therefore, we can say that the MTDS (2016–19) has not been very promising as various thresholds were breached during the period under review. Nonetheless, the PTI government is still ambitious to bring down the public debt-to-GDP and debt service-to-revenue ratios to sustainable levels. It aims at bringing down the public debt-to-GDP from 74.2 per cent (FY19) to 50 per cent by 2032–33.[14]

Table 4: Public Debt Risk Indicators

Risk Indicators*	Public Debt Risk (June 2016–19) as %											
	2016			2017			2018			2019		
	DD	FD	PD	DD	FD	PD	DD	FD	PD	DD	FD	PD
Refinancing Risk Average Time to Maturity (ATM)–Years	2.1	8.9	4.1	2	8.4	3.8	1.6	7.6	3.6	4.2	7	5.2
Debt Maturing in 1 Year (% of total)	51.9	11.3	40.3	55.6	8	42.1	66.3	12.4	48.9	36.8	17.2	29.9
Interest Rate Risk Average Time to Re-Fixing (ATR)–Years	2.1	8.2	3.8	2	7.5	3.5	1.6	6.6	3.2	1.7	6.1	3.2
Debt Re-Fixing in 1 year (% of total)	52.8	23.4	44.4	55.6	8	42.1	66.6	32.2	55.5	64.9	36.1	54.9
Fixed Rate Debt (% of total)	61.6	82.6	67.6	54.6	77.7	61.2	44.3	72.5	53.4	71.9	68.3	70.6
Foreign Exchange Risk Foreign Currency Debt (% of total debt)			28.6			28.4			32.2			34.8
ST FX debt (% of official liquid reserves)			31.9			27.7			80.6			158.7

Source: Debt Policy Coordination Office, Ministry of Finance

* Domestic Debt (DD), Foreign Debt (FD), Public Debt (PD)

Going forward, following are the main priorities with respect to public debt management over the medium term:

- Government's objective is to bring and maintain its public debt-to-GDP and debt service-to-revenue ratios to sustainable levels through a combination of greater revenue mobilisation, rationalisation of current expenditure, and efficient/productive utilisation of debt.
- For domestic debt market development, the government is planning to introduce various new instruments with the objective to meet government financing requirements at the lowest possible cost while providing additional avenue to the investors in-line with their investment horizon and risk appetite/preference.
- Government intends to broaden the universe of Shariah compliant securities (domestic as well as international).
- Lengthening of maturity profile of domestic debt through enhanced mobilisation from medium- to long-term government securities will remain a priority to reduce the refinancing and interest rate risks of domestic debt portfolio.
- The government will continue to seek long-term concessional loans for development purposes.

DEBT SERVICE CAPACITY AND DEBT SUSTAINABILITY

According to the World Bank-IMF Debt Sustainability Framework for Low-Income Countries, if the ratio of debt service to revenues is 14 per cent or below then the risk of public debt distress is low and if it lies between 14 to 18 per cent then it is medium and if it falls between 18 to 23 per cent then it is high.[15] In order to assess the sustainability of debt according to the stated criteria, Table 5 depicts the share of debt-servicing in total revenue receipts for the last ten years. As evident, debt-servicing consumes a major proportion of total revenues. It is pertinent to note that the share has increased in the last five years, jumping to a staggering 57.9 per cent, thus threatening the sustainability of debt.

Table 5: Share of Debt Servicing in the Federal Budget

Year	Share of Debt Servicing in Total Revenue Receipts
2010–11	38.3%
2011–12	38.6%
2012–13	42.8%
2013–14	40.3%
2014–15	39.6%
2015–16	37.7%
2016–17	39.4%
2017–18	39.1%
2018–19	57.9%
2019–20	59.4%

Source: Federal Budget (Various Issues), Ministry of Finance

CONCLUSION

Over the years, serious concerns have been raised regarding hasty borrowings from domestic and foreign entities and its manifestation in the form of debt overhang and the consequences for the economy. The debt burden is badly affecting the investment climate and dampening growth prospects. It is also exerting a downward pressure on the exchange rate and is contributing to a dismal tax collection. Although debt can be conducive to growth and development, it can be detrimental if not put to optimal use—as has been the case in Pakistan. For the most part, twin deficits have been responsible for the mounting debt burden. In particular, the burgeoning budget deficit has been the underlying factor in excessive government borrowings.

The analysis reveals that Pakistan's public debt plight has not witnessed an improvement. In actuality, the public debt-to-GDP ratio stands at 77.3 per cent as of December 2019, breaching the threshold of the Fiscal Responsibility and Debt Limitation (FRDL) Act 2005. The public, external, and domestic debt increased in absolute terms while the revenues and foreign exchange reserves remain low. The external debt-servicing has increased significantly, thus exerting pressure on official reserves. Moreover, the objectives of the debt management strategy have also not been met in its entirety as various thresholds were breached during the period under review (2015–2019). Although debt-servicing and risk indicators have shown slight deterioration over the past few years, the external debt composition, however, has witnessed an improvement with 75 per cent falling under the medium-to long-term loans. Thus, the actual risk is lower than the general perceptions surrounding debt sustainability. However, this must not gloss over the sustainability risks associated with domestic debt. It is true that the central government can print money to pay back domestic lenders, however, it is also fraught with serious risks, including high inflation and crowding out of the private sector from the lending market. Combined with an alarmingly high level of revenue allocation to debt-servicing in the last two years, Pakistan's debt situation remains very fragile with high dependency on external sources of capital.

STRATEGIES FOR IMPROVING DEBT MANAGEMENT

The analysis above is not specific to the current government. Most administrations in the past have shown a weak resolve to streamline debt management in Pakistan. In this regard, there are certain policy recommendations that may assist in improving the discourse of debt management:

- *Informed Political Discourse*

  Pakistan needs to well-inform the political discourse on debt which is often misguided.

- *Fiscal Consolidation*

  The government should discipline its fiscal needs by enhancing its revenue generation capacity and limiting its current expenditures. The former could be attained by broadening the tax base and streamlining the tax procedures while the latter is possible through shifting priorities to areas having capacity to generate employment and improve the overall economic outlook.

- *Improve Policy Coordination*

  Debt management should be carried out keeping in view the fiscal and monetary policy. The fiscal policy determines the borrowing requirements. Therefore, improvement in public debt management requires a sound fiscal policy framework as mentioned above. On the same lines, coordination between debt management and monetary policy is also important. In this regard, the ministry of finance should make agreements with the SBP to clarify decision-making rules pertaining to domestic debt management.

- *Privatise loss-making SOEs*

  One of the major outflows of government spending in Pakistan is in the form of subsidies/guarantees to loss-making State-Owned Enterprises (SOEs). These bleeding SOEs need to be privatised so as to reduce the burden on the national exchequer.

- *Empower Debt Management Office*

  Given the lack of coordination between various debt management agencies, there is need to improve the scope and powers of Debt Management Office (DMO) so that it is able to execute its function of managing debt in a cohesive manner. The DMO should comprise of an independent board with representatives from various agencies, such as the finance ministry, the SBP, and other private-sector stakeholders.

- *Prudent Utilisation of Debt*

  There is need for prudent utilisation of debt. Debt should be utilised for productive purposes, such as development of essential infrastructure and human capital so that the long-run pay-off from these investments could contribute in the retirement of debt.

- *Open Government Partnership*

  Demand-side accountability needs to be enhanced for better management of debt in Pakistan. One way to achieve this is through the Open Government Partnership (OGP) which is a multilateral initiative to promote transparency by bringing governments and citizens together. Pakistan has missed the deadline to submit its commitments under OGP four times. However, the PTI government may consider the initiative of overseeing the debt management through OGP.

- *Modify Borrowing Strategy*

The government needs to explore cheap and efficient avenues of financing. Reliance on short-term money market borrowing needs to be reduced through development of domestic capital markets for long-term government securities which would also assist in altering the composition of domestic debt.

Notes

1. Debt Policy Coordination Office, 'Debt Policy Statement 2006–07,' Ministry of Finance.
2. 'Pakistan's Debt and Liabilities Summary,' State Bank of Pakistan.
3. 'Debt Policy Statement 2019–20,' Ministry of Finance.
4. Hafiz A. Pasha, 'Inflow of external financing.' *Business Recorder*, February 18, 2020.
5. 'Pak external debt may rise to $90 bn in next four years,' *The News*, December 13, 2015
6. Pasha, 'Inflow of external financing.'
7. Ishrat Husain, 'Analysis of Pakistan's Debt Situation: 2000-2017,' Fourth National Debt Conference (Islamabad: PRIME Institute), 2017.
8. Ibid.
9. Ibid.
10. Ibid.
11. Ibid
12. Ibid.
13. 'Review of the Debt Sustainability Framework for Market Access Countries,' IMF Policy Paper, January 2021.
14. 'Debt Policy Statement 2019–20.'
15. 'Joint World Bank-IMF Debt Sustainability Framework for Low-Income Countries,' World Bank and IMF, March 6, 2020.

CHAPTER 3

Monetary Policy Reforms in Pakistan

ZAFAR HAYAT

INTRODUCTION

This chapter is dedicated to building the case for monetary policy reforms in Pakistan.[1] To this end, the second section takes stock of the empirical evidence that underscores the counter-productive performance of monetary policy in Pakistan in achieving price stability and economic growth. The evidence indicates that the State Bank of Pakistan (SBP) undermined both the objectives because its policy was formulated to directly stimulate growth rather than trying to achieve it through price stability. The third section highlights empirical evidence on macroeconomic successes of other central banks that reoriented their monetary policy focus on price stability duly complemented by supporting monetary policy framework, inflation targeting (IT). The fourth section discusses the four key principles that help lay down the foundation for conducting an appropriate monetary policy under such frameworks. Furthermore, the fifth section evaluates the SBP Act 1956 to determine whether it adequately provides for the key principles of a good monetary policy and infers that none of the four principles are adequately catered to by the statutes. Lastly, the sixth section concludes that as a first step a natural recommendation that follows for monetary policy to yield desirable results is to reform the monetary policy framework by amending the SBP Act 1956 to provide for the fundamental principles of good monetary policy governance.

ROLE OF PAKISTAN'S MONETARY POLICY: WHAT DO THE EMPIRICS INDICATE?

The prime purpose of modern central banks' monetary policy is to ensure price stability as it helps in achieving inclusive and sustainable economic growth. This section brings forth findings of recent empirical literature to shed light on whether the monetary policy in Pakistan has played an enabling role in achieving and maintaining price stability to pave the way for sustainable economic growth. The empirical evidence, however, depicts a concerning picture. As subsequently discussed, historically, the SBP's monetary policy has not only failed to achieve price stability or inclusive economic growth but, on the contrary, produced counter-productive results, i.e., undermined both price stability and growth.

Empirical evidence shows that Pakistan's monetary policy remained the most relevant and relatively robust source of inflation bias—technically the inflation exceeding optimal or desirable levels for a society[2] in the country than any other sources. Hayat, Balli, and Rehman identified stabilisation and non-stabilisation sources of inflation bias (excess inflation) from the literature,[3] constructed their proxy variables, and analysed them through tests of a series of bivariate and multivariate long-term relationships to determine their relevance and relative robustness in explaining excess inflation in Pakistan. Firstly, they found that the SBP's temptation to exploit inflation output trade-off to serve its preference for growth-stimulation (without realising and acknowledging the limitations of monetary policy in this respect) has been the most relevant and robust source of inducing excess inflation in the economy. The second most relevant and robust source of excess inflation is the SBP's preference for stabilisation of shocks to real growth vis-à-vis inflation stabilisation in the long-term. Monetary surprises are yet another source of excess inflation. This source, however, remained only partially relevant as it explained inducing excess inflation in the economy but lacked in exhibiting as much consistency as the other sources did. Surprisingly, as per their study, government borrowing, which in Pakistan has generally been blamed by the SBP as the major source of excess inflation, turned out to be irrelevant and fragile in the long-term.

In another relevant study, Hayat, Balli, Obben, and Shakur empirically investigated the extent to which the SBP, using its monetary discretion, induced excess inflation without offsetting real growth gains in the long- and short-runs, both directly and indirectly.[4] They first developed a framework to quantify monetary discretion and the corresponding behaviours it caused in inflation and growth. Secondly, they ascertained not only the direct long- and short-term effects of monetary discretion on inflation and real growth but its indirect effects on the latter via the former. Their findings indicate that in the long-run, the SBP's use of monetary discretion induced significantly higher inflation without creating real growth gains. They found that short-term direct impact of monetary discretion on inflation and real growth is mixed—both positive and negative— with varying lags, however, the gains induced by monetary discretion were miniscule, far-outweighed by the losses the SBP's discretionary monetary policy induced in terms of excess inflation.

Recently, Hayat, Ahmed, and Balli went a step further to empirically examine the ability of the SBP's discretionary monetary policy in terms of achieving its dual objectives across the boom and bust cycles of the economy.[5] The findings of this research are robust to alternative methodologies, specifications, and extended-sample analysis. Their results indicate that the direct effects of the SBP's discretionary monetary policy distributed asymmetrically across the dual objectives as it created significantly higher inflation but growth, and across cycles as the effect on inflation is more pronounced in boom than busts while vice versa is the case with real effects. Indirectly, the SBP's discretionary monetary policy significantly hindered real growth both under the boom and bust cycles of the economy. The indirect detrimental effect nevertheless is relatively smaller under busts than booms.

Overall, these findings indicate that the monetary policy in Pakistan, whether intended for growth-stimulation or growth-stabilisation, significantly defeated the very objective of monetary policy of achieving sustainable growth through stable prices. The authors argued that since the effects of monetary discretion are largely and significantly translated to inflation rather than growth per se, a firm shift in the focus of monetary policy from direct growth-stimulation and growth-stabilisation to stabilisation of inflation at low levels may help build credibility and would eventually improve the effectiveness of monetary policy. For example, it would help anchor inflation expectations, hence limiting the translation of monetary stimulus to realised inflation vis-à-vis growth. Other than the recent literature cited above, several studies in the past have also indicated that inflation in Pakistan has essentially been a monetary phenomenon.[6]

On the role of the SBP's monetary policy, it is important to mention that, historically, growth has been one of the major statutory objectives of the policy. As against its stated goal, the literature indicates that instead of playing a positive role by paving the way for sustainable real economic growth through price stability, in general, the role of monetary policy in Pakistan remained unfavourable. Hayat, Balli, and Rehman estimated desirable, neutral, threshold, and undesirable inflation rates for Pakistan.[7] This research found that inflation from 1 to 3 per cent is desirable as it significantly enhances real growth. Inflation from 4 to 5 per cent is neutral, although the inflation in this range positively impacts the growth, however, this impact is insignificant. The 5 per cent inflation is the threshold-rate of inflation since any inflation rate in Pakistan beyond this level negatively affects the real growth.

These findings point to a very unfavourable monetary policy by the SBP because during the past six decades most of the time (65–70 per cent) the inflation undermined real growth as it rose to detrimental range (>5%). Further, their research also found that the more the inflation departs from price stability-consistent lower levels, the greater are the adverse effects on real economic growth.

Moreover, instead of real and nominal economic stabilisation, Pakistan's monetary policy remained a significant source of destabilisation and created long-lasting distortionary cycles.[8] They argued that since the population of Pakistan is extremely vulnerable to the outcomes of a poor monetary policy (higher inflation and low growth), a big chunk—i.e., approximately 40 per cent being below the poverty line and another 20 per cent close to it—has thus paid and continue to pay a big toll of monetary policy mismanagement.[9] This phenomenon of monetary policy mismanagement and counter-productiveness in Pakistan is deep-rooted, and theoretically and empirically valid not only in short- and long-run[10] but also directly/ indirectly, and in boom and busts.[11]

With all this empirical evidence in place, a natural recommendation for the SBP, thus, is not only a restraint from direct stimulation of growth but a full-fledged focus of monetary policy on price stability (low and stable inflation). The question, however, arises that are there compelling success stories that a central bank's reorientation in its primary focus on price stability and adoption of supporting monetary policy frameworks that led to better macroeconomic outcomes? Acknowledging the need for price stability, back in the late 1980s and early 1990s, central banks increasingly reoriented their focus towards price stability and in several cases adopted supporting monetary policy framework, commonly known as IT. The next section highlights empirical evidence to gauge if IT has led to improved macroeconomic outcomes.

MACROECONOMIC OUTCOMES OF INFLATION TARGETING (IT)

This section takes stock of the literature that empirically researched whether inflation targeting led to improved macroeconomic outcomes, especially in terms of key macroeconomic indicators, such as inflation, growth, interest rate, and exchange rate.

Inflation

Since the IT monetary policy framework primarily focuses on achieving price stability, it is important to learn whether IT led to improved outcomes in this area. The price stability performance of IT could be assessed through several complementing dimensions, including performance in terms of average inflation, volatility of inflation, inflation persistence, and inflation expectations. By and large the literature indicates that the inflation targeters (ITers) performed credibly well on all these aspects.[12]

With regards to the inflation volatility, Levin found that the overall inflation variance in both ITers and non-ITers is roughly similar.[13] They, however, further argued that shocks to inflation in the IT countries under the sample period have been larger compared to the non-IT countries, which is indicative of the relatively better performance of ITers.[14] Inflation persistence is yet another dimension of inflation found in the empirical literature through which the performance of IT has been assessed. For instance, Burdekin and Siklos[15] found a significant reduction in inflation persistence after the adoption of IT for a subset of countries, including New Zealand, Canada, Spain, Finland, United Kingdom, and Sweden.[16]

Lastly, inflation expectations are an important dimension to assess the inflation performance of the IT strategy. Johnson analysed the change in the behaviour of expected inflation for a set of 11 countries.[17] The panel included five IT countries (New Zealand, Australia, Canada, Sweden, and United Kingdom) and six non-targeting industrial countries (Germany, Netherland, France, Italy, United States, and Japan). The study concluded with a strong evidence of a large reduction in expected inflation after the announcement of the inflation targets. Similarly, Gavin concluded that IT central banks by announcing their objectives effectively anchor expectations.[18] This, in turn, makes it easier for them to achieve the objective of price stability.

Real economic growth

Arestis and Sawyer found evidence that adoption of IT helped to improve the trade-off between output gap and inflation variability,[19] which in their view might have occurred due to a relatively higher degree of monetary policy transparency and flexibility in the institutional framework. Truman[20] along with Hu[21] found that IT has resulted in a significant positive relationship with growth and a significant negative relationship with inflation. Levin, Natalucci, and Piger documented that IT has improved the trade-off between inflation and output volatility in the IT countries.[22] Corbo, Landerretche, and Schmidt-Hebbel, Neuman and Von Hagen, and Petursson,[23] among others, have also come up with similar conclusions.

Concalves and Salles explored the question if IT matters for developing countries[24] while addressing the issues with Ball and Sheridan's methodology.[25] The overall number of countries which were analysed was 36 out of which 13 were the countries that had already adopted IT. It was found that the IT countries witnessed significant decreases in inflation and output variability as compared to those with alternative monetary policy regimes. A similar finding was reached by Roger in his analysis as well.[26]

Mollick, Cabral, and Carneiro found that IT has led to improved output growth both in the developed and developing countries during 1986–2004, marked as globalisation years.[27] They noted that, since IT ensures economic growth along with price stability, it is more pro-poor. For example, Son and Kakwani argued that the growth associated with low levels of inflation is pro-poor because this type of growth benefits poor proportionately more than the non-poor and that higher level of inflation is related to anti-poor growth.[28] Attention has been drawn by Hayat towards this crucial point that since a bigger chunk of Pakistan's populace is either living below the poverty line or is close to it,[29] price stability may be beneficial, as on one hand inflation would be low, and on the other hand, economic growth would be achievable on a sustainable basis.

Interest rate

Interest rates are the primary policy instruments used by central banks in the conduct of monetary policy.[30] Several studies have used interest rates in order to assess the performance of IT strategy. Ball and Sheridan did not find any significant evidence in terms of reduction of interest rates variability that can be advocated to IT.[31] Kahn and Parrish, nevertheless, observed that short-term nominal interest rates are lower and less volatile in the post-adoption period compared to the pre-adoption period in the IT countries.[32] With respect to the real interest rates, they observed that the IT countries have witnessed an increase in the real interest rates, reflecting tight monetary policy. A similar finding was reached by Neumann and Hagen that on average the short-term interest rates and its volatility have fallen in the IT economies after its adoption.[33] Whilst comparing the variability in short-term interest rates before and after the adoption of IT, Petursson also found a general decrease in variability after the adoption of IT,[34] a result consistent with the earlier findings of Kahn and Parrish[35] and Neumann and Hagen.[36]

Exchange rate

Vulnerability in terms of exchange rate shocks is one of the concerns—especially from developing countries' perspective—because an increase in imported prices when passed on to domestic prices may affect the performance of the IT in terms of achieving its inflation targets. However, this depends on whether the adoption of IT increases or decreases the exchange rate pass-through. In order to explore the effect of IT adoption on exchange rate pass-through, Coulibaly and Kempf[37] found that not only the contribution of exchange rate shock to price fluctuations in emerging targeters is more important than the non-targeters but in the former case the pass-through has declined after the adoption of IT.[38] This finding is consistent with Taylor who argued that exchange rate pass-through is lower in low-inflation environment because firms expect a deviation from inflation to be less persistent and therefore, passes on less of an exchange rate induced increase in price of imported inputs to the selling prices.[39] A step further, evidence of a considerable decline in exchange rate pass-through in Indonesia and Thailand at the domestic level to the prices of tradable and non-tradable goods was also found by Siregar and Goo[40]—except in case of tradable goods for Indonesia.

In terms of the variability of exchange rate, Petursson found results consistent with the theoretical arguments that price stability at lower levels is positively related to exchange rate stability.[41] He concluded that IT has decreased exchange rate volatility on average, specifically in countries with a floating exchange rate regime before they adopted IT. It was argued that the increased volatility in the exchange rate in some of the IT countries is due to the fact that prior to IT, those countries practised a fixed exchange rate regime. Lin[42] extended the analysis of Lin and Ye[43] to see the effects of IT on exchange rate volatility and international reserves while using the propensity score-matching methods. He found significantly different impacts on the developing and advanced countries. As a result of the adoption of IT, developing countries showed significant improvements in nominal and real exchange rates and international reserves stability while such significant improvements were lacking in the latter.

To conclude, there is ample empirical evidence that support the notion that adoption of an IT monetary policy framework leads to improved macroeconomic outcomes. What essentially makes the difference when it comes to the IT monetary policy frameworks are the unique governance principles embedded and institutionalised in IT central bank's statutes. Following and implementing these principles in letter and spirit, the central banks are encouraged to conduct monetary policy in a disciplined and accountable way, eventually leading to achievement of broader goals. The key principles underlying such monetary policy frameworks are discussed in the next section.

MONETARY POLICY GOVERNANCE UNDER AN IT FRAMEWORK: KEY PRINCIPLES

Generally, the governance framework of a modern central bank consists of three interlinked key concepts that define the power structure and its objectives, decision-making processes, and how the account is rendered to relevant stakeholders. From monetary policy perspective, all these concepts are primarily meant to establish statutory focus of the central bank on the following key principles: (i) the central bank's objective, (ii) its autonomy, (iii) its decision-making structures pertaining to monetary policy and Fit and Proper Test (FPT) of professionals, and (iv) its accountability and transparency.

The best central bank practices, especially the ITers indicate that the objective of the central bank is precise and clear, with supremacy over any other objective. Under an IT monetary policy framework, the central banks' statutes predominantly specify 'price stability' as the primary objective of the monetary policy. The reason for this objective is clear. If the central banks could ensure price stability, it eventually paves the way for sustainable financial and economic growth as the economic agents find it convenient to take rational saving and investment decisions. The price stability objective also allows putting in place supporting accountability mechanisms which otherwise are not possible without clarity in the objective. For instance, a central bank with dual objectives of price stability and growth might not be held accountable for not ensuring price stability as it may argue that price stability was compromised because of the policy preference for the growth objective.[44]

Once price stability is clearly stated as the primary objective of the central bank's monetary policy, it is natural that for its achievement, autonomy is granted at least at the operational level to insulate the central bank from governmental, political, or other pressures that could influence the conduct of monetary policy and may distract from the objective. It is for this reason that the central banks are made fully autonomous and insulated from potential or perceived political and government pressures. It is important to emphasise that the autonomy is not absolute but comes with a certain accountability. This is essential because in the absence of accountability, absolute autonomy may be damaging. The blueprint of procedural arrangement encapsulating these principles is done transparently, the other integral principle. For instance, what inflation rate(s) would constitute price stability and in case of non-achievement of the prime objective, what would be the accountability mechanism for ensuring achievement of the objective on an ongoing basis, and what sort of penalties would the authority be subject to in case of negligence.

Since efficient discharge of all the functions require special expertise, the bare minimum of the FPT for essential positions and the scope and structure of responsibilities is to be vividly specified in a transparent way in the statutes. This helps in ensuring induction of adequately qualified relevant professionals with relevant specialisations, relevant demonstrated research excellence, relevant experience, and no conflict of interest. Their decision-making process is made adequately transparent for public scrutiny. The transparency in the FPT and the decision-making process works as a constant check on the government and the central bank in the recruitment process and subsequent periodic performance management and evaluation against the stated objectives.

After understanding the unfavourable role that monetary policy has played in Pakistan in the second section and having learnt the key principles of monetary policy governance in this section, it is important to critically assess whether the SBP Act 1956 has adequately incorporated these key principles. If not, not only that insofar the poor monetary policy in Pakistan had led to detrimental outcomes but going forward, in its absence, the policy would continue to do more harm than good. The next section critically evaluates the SBP Act 1956 against the four key principles of a good monetary policy governance framework.

MONETARY POLICY GOVERNANCE IN PAKISTAN: AN EVALUATION AGAINST THE KEY PRINCIPLES

The SBP Act 1956 is the statutory document that lays out the monetary policy framework and governance structure.[45] This section of the chapter focuses only on determining whether the Act adequately provides for incorporation of the key principles that support good central bank governance with respect to monetary policy. The four key principles, namely; (i) the central bank's objective, (ii) its autonomy, (iii) its decision-making structures pertaining to monetary policy and FPT of professionals, and (iv) its accountability and transparency are critically evaluated one by one.

Price stability as the primary objective

The SBP Act 1956 is not only vague about the objective of monetary policy but also seems to have the issue of duality. In its preamble, the Act states that: 'Whereas it is necessary to provide for the constitution of a State Bank to regulate the monetary and credit system of Pakistan and to foster its growth in the best national interest with a view to securing monetary stability and fuller utilisation of the country's productive resources.' From this text, it appears that the SBP has two broader objectives, including securing 'monetary stability' and 'fuller utilisation of the country's productive resources'.

Hayat argues that there is no tangible way to exactly define 'monetary stability' for the purposes of monetary policy conduct and evaluation.[46] For instance, monetary stability is commonly referred to as the stability in prices, interest rate, and exchange rate. Assuming this definition, the main problem the existing framework poses is that it is hard to quantify monetary stability to provide an objective basis for conduct, evaluation, and communication of monetary policy. For the purposes of objectivity, if monetary stability is to be gauged by stability in some measure of money, say growth in broad money (M2), several issues emerge. For example, what growth rate of M2 would stabilise prices, interest rate, and exchange rate at the desirable levels to be used as an indicator of monetary stability, and in turn, an indicator of accountability?

On the flip side this notion would also imply opacity as it is hard to determine any unique combination of inflation, interest, and exchange rates that, on one hand, would help achieve monetary stability while, on the other, a sustainable economic growth. Instability in money demand function is yet another dimension which over time led the central banks to abandon monetary targeting as it cannot provide an efficient direct anchor for monetary policy than inflation. Thus, it is evident that the SBP Act 1956 does not meet the requirement of putting in place the basic tenet of mandating 'price stability' as the primary and overriding objective of monetary policy.

Autonomy of the SBP

The IMF staff's legal doctrine on the central banks legal frameworks emphasises four integral aspects of autonomy in the context of best central banking practices viz. institutional autonomy, functional autonomy, personal autonomy, and financial autonomy.[47] The SBP Act 1956 has gaps with respect to all these dimensions. For instance, in terms of institutional autonomy, a central bank's legal framework should explicitly prohibit the members of its decision-making bodies from seeking or taking instructions from any public or governmental authority, and from any other body (including private economic interests), however, currently there is no such provision in the Act. In this respect, the Act should also clearly state that no government, parliament, or any other entity, except the judicial courts, may annul, stay, block, suspend, or amend the central bank's decisions.

For functional autonomy, a central bank should have a clear legal framework that is applicable to it. Central bank autonomy is not an end but is instrumental in achieving the primary objective of the central bank. As discussed above, modern central banks predominantly use inflation as an anchor to stabilise prices at low levels (price stability). The SBP Act, however, insofar has dual unclear objectives rather than having a clearly defined objective of the 'price stability'.

As regards the personal autonomy, security of tenure for the members of a central bank's decision-making body or bodies safeguards its autonomy. For instance, the minimum term of office for central bank decision-making officials should be longer than the electoral cycle and more than one authority should be involved in the appointment and dismissal of the members of a central bank's decision-making body or bodies (so-called 'double veto' procedure). As per the SBP Act, the terms of office of the governor, deputy governors, and other non-executive monetary policy committee members is three years, extendable to another three years. This feature incentivises the incumbent officials to please politicians by serving their interests to seek reappointment for another term.

Finally, in terms of financial autonomy, the SBP should always be sufficiently capitalised (including through retained earnings and reserves); should be subject to limits on the provision of monetary financing of the government; and be prohibited from financing quasi-fiscal activities. Currently, this is not the case, for instance, the SBP is actively involved with quasi-fiscal activities, such as export refinance and SME-financing. Moreover, the SBP Act authorises the government to direct the SBP to inject equity in troubled banks, which is a non-core central bank activity. Such direction is not compatible as it infringes on the institutional autonomy of the SBP.

In a nutshell, in its current state, the SBP Act 1956 does not lay down the basis for key ingredients of the principle of autonomy for sound governance as it lacks on all the four counts.

Decision-making structures and FPT of professionals

In its existing form, as per the SBP Act 1956, the SBP's executive management is concentrated in the position of the governor. Section 10 (1) defines the governor as the SBP's chief executive officer and tasks this position with the direction and control of 'the whole affairs of the bank'. Currently, as a matter of practice in the SBP, the governor is assisted by deputy governors and several management committees, including the corporate management team. This team comprises the governor, deputy governors, the SBP's heads of clusters/groups/departments, and the directors of the SBP's subsidiaries. This is, however, important to note that these are not decision-making bodies, and therefore there is a need to establish a decision-making structure to take the executive, regulatory, and policy decisions in a collegial manner. Moreover, regarding the board, Section 9 (2) of the SBP Act states that:

> The Board shall consist of—a. the Governor; b. Secretary, Finance Division, Government of Pakistan; and c. eight directors, including at least one from each province, who shall be eminent professionals from the fields of economics, finance, banking and accountancy, to be appointed by the Federal Government. Those appointed to the Board shall have no conflict of interest with the business of the Bank.

This section of the Act does not go well with the fundamentals/essentials required for a credibly independent central bank. For example, as noted by Hayat, the governors of credibly independent central banks are technically sound high-profile charismatic individuals (no less than PhD by qualification—generally with specialisation in monetary policy with demonstrated research capabilities in allied areas in esteemed international journals—and relevant experience).[48] As per the current wording of the section, however, the governor of the SBP or any other board member could be, say, an eminent accountant or an eminent economist with a PhD but specialisation or proven experience in monetary policy is not required. Further, it is also important to note that as a matter of practice at the SBP there are sub-committees of the SBP board, which perform several specialised functions. For example, HR committee, investment committee, audit committee, publication review committee, enterprise risk-management committee, and financial law and reform committee. Therefore, there is a need to have at least one high-profile member at the board level with relevant specialisation, experience, and demonstrated research excellence in each of the areas to guide appropriate policy/decision-making. But in its current form the law does not cater to such needs.

Another important aspect is that of the conflict of interest provision. Although the Act says that 'those appointed to the board shall have no conflict of interest with the business of the bank', however, the Act is self-contradicting this principle by placing secretary finance in the board with voting rights. Furthermore, Hayat notes that several members of the board, including the governor are appointed from the market with clear association with the financial sector.[49] Thus, glaringly compromising on the principle of avoiding conflict of interest due to lack of clarity in the Act as to what this principle implies or constitutes, and not tying the hands of the government/politicians in any respect to force them to ensure that the professionals being inducted for crucial positions have no conflict of interest with the bank's business as such.

Apart from the general governance of the bank, as regards the specific decisions related to monetary policy, the SBP Act, Section 9D vests the responsibility with the monetary policy committee, comprising of the governor as chairman and (deputy governor in his absence); three senior executives of the bank to be members nominated by the governor; three members of the board; and three external members (economists) appointed for a term of three years by the federal government on the recommendation of the board subject to the reappointment for another term. As per Section 9E, the monetary policy committee shall, without prejudice to its powers and functions and those of the bank, support the general economic policies of the federal government and formulate policies accordingly.

Both sections 9D and 9E lack in terms of setting a clear objective for the monetary policy committee and do not spell out any fit and proper criteria in line with the best practices for senior executives of the bank, the three members of the board, or the external members. Historically, Pakistan's experience with all these members indicates that none of them had either specialised in monetary policy or had demonstrated research capabilities in the area to assimilate research advancements to guide and steer policy-related research to enrich monetary policy decision-making. Even the recent and current experience with the external members of the monetary policy committee in Pakistan indicates that although these are professors, they have no specialisation or demonstrated research excellence in the areas of monetary and exchange rate policies. The Act also provides that the term of office of external members is three years, hence, the members have a clear incentive to make the government/politicians happy—by serving their interests—for reappointment.

Accountability and transparency

The best practices require an autonomous and independent central bank to be accountable with respect to: (i) the objective of price stability, (ii) financial functions and objectives (through a supervisory board), and (iii) human and financial resource. The SBP Act 1956 does not provide any accountability mechanism for any of the highlighted dimensions. For instance, whatever the rate of inflation in the economy is and no matter to what extent does it hurt the society and economic growth, there is no way to take the SBP to task for its negligence with respect to non-achievement of price stability.[50] Similarly, the Act does not stipulate any accountability mechanism with respect to financial stability function of the SBP. With regard to accountability in terms of human resources induction ensuring FPT and their performance management/evaluation against the stated goals, there is no check and balance.[51] With respect to accountability against the use of financial resources, the SBP Act does not put in place any mechanisms that will hold a professional accountable for abuse of financial resources. For instance, recently, the SBP pumped a colossal $24 billion (or equal to Rs 3.7 trillion at the current exchange rate) into the interbank market during the interim periods of the last two IMF programmes to defend the exchange rate.[52]

The question is why is it the case that during the IMF programmes, the SBP buys dollars from the interbank market to build reserves without having to have the need to defend the exchange rate while the market has enough potential to supply dollars. But as soon as the IMF programme is over or is in abeyance, the SBP reverses the policy. Instead of continuing to buy dollars from the interbank market, it starts selling billions of dollars because now it has to defend the exchange rate. How come the entire dynamics of the economy changes the moment vigilant monitoring from the IMF is no longer in place as the IMF programme is in abeyance or has come to an end? The severity of the negligence in the use of precious foreign exchange reserves post-IMF programme in 2016 is non-trivial because it plunged the entire country into a very severe economic crisis, for which the entire nation is bearing the consequences: higher current account deficit, debt, inflation, and lost reserves and economic growth, so on and so forth. Despite all this waste and negligence, none of the SBP's officials could be questioned or taken to task because for such purposes no accountability mechanism has been embedded in the Act.

The SBP Act 1956 does not adequately provide for the principle of transparency. This normally takes the form of laying down basis in the statutes in terms of: (i) obligatory information disclosure about monetary policy (quantified primary objectives; macro econometric model; macroeconomic forecasts; quarterly and medium-term forecasts for inflation; monetary policy strategy; detailed minutes; individual voting records; and policy adjustments with explanations), (ii) publication of detailed profiles of senior officials (in this case should be governor and deputy governors, board, members of monetary policy committee, executive directors, and directors) to facilitate their public scrutiny, (iii) financials/audited accounts and financial stability reports, and (iv) freedom of information (FOI), where the central banks are normally subject to disclose specific information/records requested by the public (perhaps with selective disclosures to non-sensitive information). As highlighted by Hayat, in terms of the principle of transparency the SBP lacks in all these dimensions.[53]

CONCLUSION

Monetary policy plays an instrumental role in achieving sustainable economic growth by maintaining price stability. The SBP's monetary policy, however, could not yield desirable results due to unclear focus on price stability and ambition for direct stimulation of economic growth. Countries with their central banks' monetary policy focus on price stability and supportive monetary policy governance frameworks benefited in terms of macroeconomic outcomes in the form of achieving price stability, stability in interest rates and exchange rates, and a sustainable real economic growth. In Pakistan, such benefits could not accrue because of statutory inadequacy of fundamental principles of good monetary policy governance. Unless the statutes ensure putting in place a monetary policy governance framework clearly delineating the key principles of a good monetary policy governance, viz., the price stability objective, autonomy of the SBP, collegial decision-making and accountability and transparency, and subsequently implement in letter and spirit, the policy will tend do more harm than good to the country.

* * *

It is an honour to be invited by the SDPI to write in this anthology in honour of Dr Ishrat Husain, whose role towards modernising the SBP will always be remembered. The views expressed in this chapter build on my specific research on Pakistan's monetary policy and relevant experience for more than a decade and reflect my personal views rather than that of my current or past employers. I also owe a word of thanks to my colleague, Saher Masood, for the review and the SDPI editorial team for their comments.

Notes

1. This chapter was first authored in February 2020.
2. Zafar Hayat, Faruk Balli, and Muhammad Rehman, 'Does Inflation Bias Stabilize Real Growth? Evidence from Pakistan,' *Journal of Policy Modeling* 40, no. 6 (November–December 2018): 1083–1103.
3. Zafar Hayat, 'Pakistan's Monetary Policy: Some Fundamental Issues,' *The Pakistan Development Review* 56, no. 1 (Spring 2017): 31–58.
4. Zafar Hayat, Faruk Balli, James Obben, and Shamim Shakur, 'An empirical assessment of monetary discretion: The case of Pakistan,' *Journal of Policy Modeling*, Elsevier 38, no. 5 (2016): 954–970.
5. Zafar Hayat, Jameel Ahmed, and Faruk Balli, 'What monetary discretion can and cannot do under boom and bust cycles? Evidence from an emerging economy,' *Journal of Economic Studies* 46, no. 6 (October 2019): 1224–1240
6. See Abdul Qayyum, 'Money, Inflation, and Growth in Pakistan,' *The Pakistan Development Review* 45, no. 2 (Summer 2006): 203–212; Mohsin S. Khan and Axel Schimmelpfennig, 'Inflation in Pakistan: Money or Wheat?' IMF Working Paper No. 06/60 (April 2006); M. Ali Kemal, 'Is Inflation in Pakistan a Monetary Phenomenon?' *The Pakistan Development Review* 45, no. 2 (Summer 2006): 213–220; Madhavi Bokil and Axel Schimmelpfennig, 'Three Attempts at Inflation Forecasting in Pakistan,' IMF Working Paper No. 05/105 (May 2005); M. Aslam Chaudhary and Naved Ahmad, 'Sources and impacts of Inflation in Pakistan,' *Pakistan Economic and Social Review* 34, no. 1 (Summer 1996): 21–39; and Jonathan D. Jones and Nasir M. Khilji, 'Money Growth, Inflation, and Causality (Empirical Evidence for Pakistan, 1973—1985),' *The Pakistan Development Review* 27, no. 1 (Spring 1988): 45–58.

7. Hayat, Balli, and Rehman, 'Does Inflation Bias Stabilize Real Growth? Evidence from Pakistan.'

8. See Hayat, Balli, Obben, and Shakur, 'An empirical assessment of monetary discretion'; and Hayat, Ahmed, and Balli, 'What monetary discretion can and cannot do under boom and bust cycles?'

9. The Recent IMF staff report points to fixed exchange rate and loose monetary policies as a source of the ongoing higher debt and repayment crisis. See: https://www.imf.org/en/Countries/PAK.

10. See Hayat, Balli, Obben, and Shakur, 'An empirical assessment of monetary discretion'; Hayat, 'Pakistan's Monetary Policy'; and Hayat, Balli, and Rehman, 'Does Inflation Bias Stabilize Real Growth? Evidence from Pakistan.'

11. Hayat, Balli, Obben, and Shakur, 'An empirical assessment of monetary discretion.'

12. For example, in terms of average inflation, Vittorio Corbo, Oscar Landerretche, and Klaus Schmidt-Hebbel ['Assessing inflation targeting after a decade of world experience,' *International Journal of Finance & Economics* 6, no. 4, Special Issue: Exchange Rates and Monetary Policy Issues (October 2001): 343–368] found that on average the ITers have met the targets for inflation. The average deviation from its target in case of ITers was merely 12 basis points. Similarly, A. G. Haldane, *Targeting Inflation* (London: Bank of England, 1995); Frederic S. Mishkin and Adam S. Posen, 'Inflation Targeting: Lessons from Four Countries,' Economic Policy Review, Federal Reserve Bank of New York, vol. 3 (August 1997): 9–110; Kenneth N. Kuttner and Adam S. Posen, 'Does Talk Matter After All? Inflation Targeting and Central Bank Behavior,' Federal Reserve Bank of New York Staff Report No. 88 (1999); Ben S. Bernanke, Mark Gertler, and Simon Gilchrist, 'Chapter 21: The financial accelerator in a quantitative business cycle framework,' *Handbook of Macroeconomics* vol. 1, Part C (1999): 1341–1393; Stephen G. Cecchetti and Michael Ehrmann, 'Does Inflation Targeting Increase Output Volatility? An International Comparison of Policymakers' Preferences and Outcomes,' NBER Working Paper No. 7426 (December 1999); and Manfred J. M. Neumann and Juergen von Hagen, 'Does Inflation Targeting Matter?' *Federal Reserve Bank of St. Louis Review* 84 (July 2002): 127–148 are some of the other studies with similar findings of a considerable reduction in inflation after the adoption of IT.

13. A. Levin, F. Natalucci, and J. Piger, 'The macroeconomic effects of inflation targeting,' *Federal Reserve Bank of St. Louis* 86, no. 4 (2004): 51–80.

14. Thorarinn G. Petursson ['Inflation Targeting and its Effects on Macroeconomic Performance,' SUERF Conference Proceedings and Studies, no. 5 (2005)] also found that inflation variability (using standard deviations) has reduced after the adoption of IT by the ITers. Carlos Goncalves and Joao M. Salles ['Inflation targeting in emerging economies: What do the data say?' *Journal of Development Economics* 85, no. 1–2 (2008): 312–318] found that adoption of IT significantly reduced the inflation volatility.

15. Richard C. K. Burdekin and Pierre L. Siklos, 'Exchange Rate Regimes and Shifts in Inflation Persistence: Does Nothing Else Matter?' *Journal of Money, Credit and Banking* 31, no. 2 (May 1999): 235–247.

16. Several other studies have also reached similar conclusions such Kuttner and Posen, 'Does Talk Matter After All?'; Mervyn King, 'The Inflation Target Ten Years on,' *Bank of England Quarterly Bulletin* (Winter 2002); Levin, Natalucci, and Piger, 'The macroeconomic effects of inflation targeting'; and Petursson, 'Inflation Targeting and its Effects on Macroeconomic Performance.'

17. David R. Johnson, 'The effect of inflation targeting on the behavior of expected inflation: evidence from an 11 country panel,' *Journal of Monetary Economics* 49, no. 8 (2002): 1521–1538.

18. William T. Gavin, 'Inflation Targeting: Why it Works and How to Make it Work Better,' Federal Reserve Bank of St. Louis Working Paper (2003).

19. Philip Arestis and Malcolm Sawyer, 'A critical reconsideration of the foundations of monetary policy in the new consensus macroeconomics framework,' *Cambridge Journal of Economics* 32, no. 5 (February 2008): 761–779.

20. Edwin M. Truman, *Inflation Targeting in the World Economy* (New York: Columbia University Press, 2003).

21. Yifan Hu, 'Empirical Investigations of Inflation Targeting,' IIE Working Papers Series WP No. 03-6 (2003).

22. Levin, Natalucci, and Piger, 'The macroeconomic effects of inflation targeting.'

23. Corbo, Landerretche, and Schmidt-Hebbel, 'Assessing inflation targeting after a decade of world experience'; Neumann and Hagen, 'Does Inflation Targeting Matter?'; and Petursson, 'Inflation Targeting and its Effects on Macroeconomic Performance.'

24. Goncalves and Salles, 'Inflation targeting in emerging economies.'

25. Laurence Ball and Niamh Sheridan, 'Does Inflation Targeting Matter?' National Bureau of Economic Research, Working Paper 9577 (March 2003).

26. Scott Roger, 'Inflation Targeting Turns 20,' *Finance and Development* 47, no. 1 (March 2010).

27. André Varella Mollick, René Cabral, and Francisco G. Carneiro, 'Does Inflation Targeting Matter for Output Growth? Evidence from Industrial and Emerging Economies,' *Journal of Policy Modeling* 33, no. 4 (July 2011): 537–51.

28. Hyun Son and Nanak Kakwani, 'Economic growth and poverty reduction: Initial conditions matter,' United Nations Development Programme, International Poverty Centre, Working Paper 2 (August 2004).

29. Hayat, Balli, Obben, and Shakur, 'An empirical assessment of monetary discretion.'

30. Gordon H. Sellon and Stuart E. Weiner, 'Monetary policy without reserve requirements: analytical issues,' *Econometric Reviews* 81 (1996): 5–24.

31. Ball and Sheridan, 'Does Inflation Targeting Matter?'

32. George Kahn and Klara Parrish, 'Conducting monetary policy with inflation targets,' *Economic Review* 83, no. Q III (1998): 5–32.

33. Neumann and Hagen, 'Does Inflation Targeting Matter?'

34. Petursson, 'Inflation Targeting and its Effects on Macroeconomic Performance.'

35. Kahn and Parrish, 'Conducting monetary policy with inflation targets.'

36. Neumann and Hagen, 'Does Inflation Targeting Matter?'

37. Dramane Coulibaly and Hubert Kempf, 'Does Inflation Targeting decrease Exchange Rate Pass-through in Emerging Countries?' Banque de France Working Paper No. 303 (November 2010).

38. A similar result was also reached by Frederic S. Mishkin and Klaus Schmidt-Hebbel ['Does Inflation Targeting Make a Difference?' *NBER Working Paper No. 12876* (January 2007)] but their sample did not include emerging inflation non-targeters as control group (Coulibaly and Kempf, 'Does Inflation Targeting decrease Exchange Rate Pass-through in Emerging Countries?').

39. John Taylor, 'Low inflation, pass-through, and the pricing power of firms,' *European Economic Review* 44, no. 7 (2000): 1389–1408.

40. Reza Siregar and Siwei Goo, 'Effectiveness and commitment to inflation targeting policy: Evidence from Indonesia and Thailand,' *Journal of Asian Economics* 21, no. 2 (2010): 113–128.

41. Petursson, 'Inflation Targeting and its Effects on Macroeconomic Performance.'

42. Shu Lin, 'On the International Effects of Inflation Targeting,' *The Review of Economics and Statistics* 92, no. 1 (February 2010): 195–199.

43. Shu Lin and Haichun Ye, 'Does inflation targeting make a difference in developing countries?' *Journal of Development Economics* 89, no. 1 (2009): 118–123.

44. See Hayat, 'Pakistan's Monetary Policy,' for discussion on this point.

45. For a constitutional status and evolution of the SBP from a historical perspective prior to the enactment of SBP Act, see http://www.sbp.org.pk/70/his.asp.

46. Hayat, 'Pakistan's Monetary Policy.'

47. See Ashraf Khan, 'Monetary and Capital Markets Department Central Bank Legal Frameworks in the Aftermath of the Global Financial Crisis,' IMF Working Paper WP/17/101 (May 2017).

48. Hayat, 'Pakistan's Monetary Policy.'

49. Ibid.

50. This issue of absence of accountability of the SBP has frequently been raised, see Khaleeq Kiani, 'Autonomy with accountability,' *Dawn*, December 17, 2018.

51. For instance, Mehtab Haider, 'Brain drain,' *The News*, April 2019, indicates that at technical level there is not even a single employee at the SBP that has specialisation in monetary policy with relevant demonstrated research excellence.

52. Shahbaz Rana, 'SBP poured $24b into inter-bank market between two IMF programmes,' *The Express Tribune*, January 20, 2020, highlights this fact.

53. Hayat, 'Pakistan's Monetary Policy.'

CHAPTER 4

Foreign Investment Climate in Pakistan

BUSHRA YASMIN

INTRODUCTION

Foreign Direct Investment (FDI) has been considered as one of the major contributors in economic development by means of improving infrastructure, enhancing technical skills and entrepreneurship abilities of domestic workers, bridging the financial gaps in government revenues and foreign exchange earnings, and providing the global market access. Although the volume of the FDI in developing countries has tremendously increased over time, its distribution has remained widely dispersed among different regions of the world. As Latin America and the Caribbean were among the largest recipients of FDI until the mid-1980s, the trend turned in favour of Asian and Pacific countries in the late 1980s. These regions received 85 per cent of the FDI flows to the developing countries in the 1990s. Having a glance at the recent global trend in the FDI, this has been declining with a 13 per cent global fall in the first two quarters of 2018 due to repatriated foreign earnings accumulated by the United States Multinational Enterprises, as reported in UNCTAD report.[1] In particular, the FDI to developed regions declined by 27 per cent while for the developing countries it remained stable with an upsurge of about 2 per cent in year 2018. At the regional level, the FDI rose by 11 per cent in Africa and up to 4 per cent in the developing Asia while in Latin America and the Caribbean it declined to 6 per cent. Overall, the FDI flows to the Asian developing countries—world's largest FDI recipient—increased by 3.9 per cent in 2018 where South Asia received an increase by 3.5 per cent.

PAKISTAN'S EXPERIENCE OF FDI

Pakistan adopted a number of measures to attract FDI with the advent of deregulation, privatisation, and liberalisation policies at the end of 1980s, and the amount of foreign investment consequently increased from $10.7 million in 1976–1977 to $1,296 million in 1996–1997, growing at the compound rate of 25.7 per cent. In the wake of liberalisation programmes, the country observed a phenomenal increase in foreign investment when FDI in the power sector grew by 146.5 per cent in 1995–1996.[2] Realising the potential role of FDI in accelerating economic growth, Pakistan pursued wide-ranging structural reforms that helped it in becoming an attractive destination for Multinational Enterprises (MNEs). After incentivising foreign investment, Pakistan received reasonable amount of FDI worth $5 billion in year 2007–2008. In terms of its contribution in the GDP, the FDI was 3 per cent of GDP in year 2007–2008 which, however, could not be sustained due to the financial crunch, terrorism, and energy crisis and ended up at 1 per cent of the GDP by 2014–2015. Comparatively, the FDI increased sharply from $988 million in 2014–2015 to $2,305 million in 2015–2016 and further increased to $2,749 million, and $3,471 million in years 2016–2017 and 2017–2018, respectively. Generally, the growth-oriented initiatives, including higher development expenditures, low inflation, and CPEC-related investment supported this upsurge in inflows of direct investment. Particularly, the political instability, poor law and order, and inconsistent economic policies that earmark the 1990s and early 2000s were put down with rigorous efforts on the ease of doing business and related measures. The incentives, like 100 per cent foreign ownership of capital and no limit on remitting profits and dividends, supported the FDI inflows positively. However, a reduction of 51.7 per cent was again observed in year 2019 due to weak international scenario.

Overall, the figures on foreign investment in Pakistan show a low growth trajectory. China has remained a major FDI partner to Pakistan but its contribution declined from 60.5 to 31.2 per cent in 2019 due to a sharp decline in power sector's investment by completion of early harvest projects. The other major partners are UK, Hong Kong, and USA that have contributed 12 per cent, 10 per cent, and 5 per cent, respectively. In the backdrop of CPEC, the sectors which attracted more investment are the construction sector, oil and gas exploration, and financial businesses as these are growing sectors under various CPEC projects and the Special Economic Zones (SEZs). The manufacturing sector and large-scale physical infrastructure attracted major FDI that brought along a package of capital, technology, skills, and market access. With a special focus on the telecommunication and power sector, the CPEC project is being considered a 'game changer' for the economy of Pakistan. A long-term plan of $60 billion investment by China for years 2017–2030 is a huge opportunity for the economy to flourish. The largest investment under the project is in the energy sector worth $22.8 billion which includes 17 projects. The other focused sector is the highway which links China to the Arabian Sea and another $5.2 billion is proposed on highway development. Similarly, the railways project is worth $8.2 billion. The spurt in the growth rate of the economy is expected to be up to 2 per cent point as potential economic impact of CPEC.

Initially, the highly regulated nature of Pakistan's economy deterred the inflows of FDI. Specifically, FDI was discouraged due to significant ownership of the public sector, strict licensing for industrial investment, financial constraints, segmented financial markets, and non-competitive trade regime with import licensing, high tariffs and bans. However, Pakistan instigated a more liberal foreign investment policy under the Structural Adjustment Program (SAP) at the end of the 1980s. The new industrial policy in 1989 emphasised on the inclusion of the private sector in the investment endeavours and accordingly a number of policy and regulatory measures were taken to improve the business environment in general and to attract the FDI in particular. A Board of Investment (BOI) was set up to support in generating investment opportunities along with the provision of investment services. Particularly, a 'one-window facility' was established for investors to overcome difficulties they face while setting up new industries.

In a nutshell, Pakistan has been following the liberal investment regime in order to attract FDI by putting various efforts to bolstering investors' confidence and improving investment environment for foreign investors along with local ones. Pakistan gradually adopted the strategy of liberalisation with promotion and facilitation in terms of low investment restrictions and simple administrative procedures to pull foreign investment. Till 1997, Pakistan pursued an investment policy which was favourable for the industrial and manufacturing sectors. However, the establishment of the BOI to generate FDI opportunities and introduction of 'one-window facility' to support setting up of new industries with lesser restrictions in the 1980s moved the country towards a liberal foreign investment policy. Subsequently, the first Investment Policy, framed by the BOI in 1997, opened other sectors for inviting foreign investment, including infrastructure, social, and services sector that proved a major step towards globalisation and world markets' integration of Pakistan's economy. The BOI also instituted an online registration procedure for foreign firms entering and operating in Pakistan which provides support to foreign investors by guaranteeing the entitlements specified in the policy framework. Besides, the Protection of Economic Reforms Act 1992 (PERA) and Foreign Private Investment (Promotion and Protection) Act 1976 (FPIA) proved to be a guard for providing protection of fiscal incentives to foreign investors in setting up their business. Similarly, the Investment Policy[3] was formulated specifically to attract foreign investment by improving the investment climate. Afterwards the Government of Pakistan has worked on reforms in promising sectors by adopting a number of measures in the pursuit of this cause. Several new sectors and regions have also been opened up for investment. Malaysia, UAE, and other gulf countries have taken interest in the new initiatives offered by the current government.

This is pertinent to mention that after the 18th Amendment, the provinces of Pakistan have been given the power to institute their own BOIs following the one-window policy and related facilitation measures. However, the duplication of the same institutions sometimes creates confusions among the stakeholders, especially when the powers are not explicitly identified. The establishment of an Investment Council on the pattern of Economic Coordination Committee (ECC) has been suggested to be formulated to promote inter-provincial coordination to handle foreign investors effectively.

ESTABLISHMENT OF SPECIAL ECONOMIC ZONES

The establishment of export-processing zones and development of Special Economic Zones, aimed at transforming trade corridors into economic corridors, have been regarded a main pillar to establish industrial clusters which can attract foreign investment. These can offer long-term benefits in the form of global supply chain, employment opportunities, output growth, technology transfer, and import substitution. The establishment of SEZs are widely used both in the developed and developing countries to attract foreign investment. The new liberal investment policies and increasing investment competition in the world markets with the establishment of SEZs have emerged as a booster to the FDI. According to World Investment Report, out of the overall 5,400 established SEZs, more than 4,000 are in developing Asian countries with China as the major host of about 2,500 SEZs.[4] Pakistan has been focusing on improving industrial collaborations after reaping potential benefits from early harvest project from CPEC. Pakistan has more than 80 established industrial estates to promote industrialisation and, although very few of them meet success, yet there is a huge potential for further industrial cooperation in the fields of engineering, automotive industry, information technology, textiles, chemicals, and small and medium enterprises.[5] The establishment of the M-3 Industrial City near Faisalabad is the largest industrial estate in Pakistan and is a success story as well. This industrial estate provides a huge magnitude of international infrastructure and attracts substantial local and foreign investment. The Allama Iqbal Industrial City is one of the most recent and largest SEZs which have the advantage of being adjacent to the M-3 Industrial City which comprises of a large number of projects, including textile, pharmaceuticals, information technology, chemicals automotive, service complex, etc. A number of national and international companies are interested in this project.

In order to facilitate the business community and investors, the Government of Pakistan announced comprehensive and business-friendly incentives for the investors from China and other countries which in turn are expected to promote the industry and employment and will help in improving the ease of doing business in Pakistan.

The country has improved its position at the ease of business index by jumping at 136th position in 2018 from 147th in 2017 out of the total 190 countries with an improvement of 11 places. The said position was further improved with a plunge of 28 places, standing at 108th position in World Bank's Ease of Doing Business Index 2020, according to the *Economic Survey*.[6] This helped the country attract a substantial FDI in July–March 2020 which increased by 137.3 per cent. The other measures include tax incentives/exemptions to facilitate the local and foreign investors. The special tax holidays for investment in SEZs, with possible extension, has been considered a favourable step into that direction. This is in addition to the exemption on the custom duty on import of machinery. Other fiscal incentives include 25 per cent accelerated depreciation allowance, reduction of 20 per cent in the corporate tax rate on profits from the FDI, and 20 per cent credit on tax payable for the first two years for enlistment in the stock exchange. On the same count, tax-to-GDP ratio needs to be increased to 16 per cent that is currently 13 per cent by widening the direct tax, which is 34 per cent of the total tax revenues and 4.5 per cent of GDP currently. As an outcome, the stock of FDI inflows as percentage of GDP has increased from 6.8 per cent in 1995 to 13.4 per cent of GDP in 2018 in Pakistan.

Similarly, a number of other incentives include no restriction on the repatriation of dividends, royalties and capital, no minimal requirement of capital except in banking sector, Intellectual Property Rights (IPR) law enacted in 2012, and 100 per cent shareholding for legal entities in Pakistan while the opportunities are widely extended for foreign investors in the construction sector, railway rolling stock and signalling system, truck, automobiles, power generation machinery, renewable energy, information technology besides other traditional sectors.[7]

CURRENT SCENARIO AND THE ROLE OF BOI

Compared to other countries of South Asia, despite incentivising foreign investment by adopting various facilitation measures, Pakistan still lags in terms of investment flows due to political instability, corruption, uncertain investment environment, and the resultant lack of investors' confidence. Due to this, the country faced a decline to $2.4 billion investment in 2019. Comparatively, India's investment rose by 6 per cent to $42 billion in the manufacturing, communication, and financial services sector, and Bangladesh and Sri Lanka witnessed a record rise in the inflows the same year.

A highly regulated nature of the economy that remained a major hindrance in the way of foreign investment earlier was eased by adopting a number of incentives, as discussed above. And this is established by the fact that Pakistan has been vigilantly pursuing investment-friendly policies. And despite facing a myriad of challenges, like political instability, security concerns, energy crises, corruption, and low growth the investment outlook is not that bleak if we look at the figures in year 2020. Pakistan managed to attract $289 million in February 2020 as compared to $223.1 million in the previous month. The oil and gas industry alone pulled $177 million while the financial services, power sector, and communication received $194,575 and $471 million, respectively.

Moreover, the BOI and other stakeholders are considering following a 10-point agenda to attract more investment to Pakistan which comprises of industrial relocation under CPEC to cater for non-Chinese companies, offering incentives to backward linkages, SEZs, fast tracking of CPEC projects, promoting industrial cooperation in use of technology, and revisiting the priority sectors for investment as reported in the *Economic Survey of Pakistan*.[8]

ROLE OF ISHRAT HUSAIN IN PROMOTING REFORMS FOR FDI

The role of Dr Ishrat Husain cannot be ignored in sensitising the need for reforms to improve the investment climate of Pakistan. He asserted on the need of balanced and deep-rooted structural reforms along with the move towards privatisation, deregulation, and liberalisation measures.[9] The financial sector reforms, tax regulations, tariff rationalisation, import deregulation, and other related measures are stressed to remove bottlenecks from foreign investment. The abolition of quotas and withdrawal of subsidies in agriculture, textile, and other tradable goods are also put forward as good indicators of institutional reforms. The measures taken up in the light of Dr Husain's recommendations helped in promoting regional global integration, easing business environment, and removing the structural bottlenecks from the economy.

In particular, he focused on strengthening the industrial sector by promoting ease of doing business and suggested to regulate the tax collection system which has remained a hindrance in the way of investment in Pakistan. He stressed on the effective mechanism to support SEZs under CPEC which is expected to play a powerful role in attracting investment. In an effort to attract foreign investors, he identified a number of factors that can be safe and secure the investment climate in Pakistan for the foreign investors. Regarding the economy of Pakistan as more resilient to the exogenous political and financial shocks, Husain highlighted the open and unrestricted trading regime of Pakistan where foreign investors can earn a decent return on their investment. Besides the liberal foreign exchange regime, along with lucrative offers in terms of authority in repatriate profits, debt service payments, remittances, dividends, royalties, fees for technical services, and other legitimate payments to head offices and suppliers overseas are some other highlighted factors to attract foreign investment.

SUSTAINABILITY OF FDI AND THE WAY FORWARD

Turning to the sustainability concerns, Pakistan faces adverse impacts of Covid-19 which has put global growth and investment at risk. Despite the number of measures taken by the government to improve the investment climate, the outbreak of the virus can curtail foreign direct investment. According to the *Asian Development Outlook 2020*, the economic growth in Pakistan is expected to decline to 2.6 per cent with a rise in inflation to 11.5 per cent this year.[10]

At the start of 2020, Pakistan managed to attract foreign investment in the debt market due to the high rate of return in T-bills which encouraged investors to transfer their funds to Pakistan than to the developed world with zero return. On a good note, the FDI and workers' remittances also remained unaffected in the first quarter of the fiscal year. And because of lucrative investment opportunities in fixed-income securities due to high interest rate, the portfolio investment almost doubled in treasury bills and Pakistan Investment Bonds but the pace has slowed down and foreign investment declined to Rs 337 billion in March 2020 after the outbreak of Covid-19. Globally, the conservative drop in the global FDI from 15 to -15 per cent in early March 2020 is expected to contract further from -30 to -40 per cent in 2020 and 2021, according to UNCTAD's revised forecasts.[11]

Keeping in view the rising number of cases of coronavirus in Pakistan, the curve has not flattened, yet the country has faced a serious challenge in terms of diverting Public Sector Development Program (PSDP) to other more immediate needs. There is a strong likelihood of a fast V-type recovery given the strong and timely policy measures taken by the government. So far, the country is at the crossroads in choosing between lockdowns or opening businesses given the already weak outlook of production and jobs. In a plea to international donors and international financial institutions, the government has urged for a global solution to the global problem and has requested debt reliefs for keeping the economy away from deep recession. Furthermore, the government has requested potential investors not to put their projects on hold and even allowed lucrative incentives, including tax amnesty for the real estate sector.

In the current era of the fourth industrial revolution of technological evolution, the world has seen a progressive move towards digitising. This progress actually helped countries equipped with sound technologies and patent tools in handling Covid-19 more effectively. The integrated databases to track and predict Covid-19 cases, mobile tracking, mapping of potential carriers, and various forms of artificial intelligence have been of great use in dealing with the pandemic—an area where Pakistan requires interest of both multilateral donors and private investors.

With a scanty 1 per cent of GDP going to the health spending and the country standing at 150 out of 189 countries in Human Development Index, the situation seems to be very demanding. The existing health delivery system appears to be incapable of dealing with the challenge imposed by the pandemic. However, health sector goals can be met with blended finance, including public-private partnerships.

Trade in health services is another important area where the pandemic has opened up opportunities. While the trade in traditional sectors is under threat due to the slowdown,[12] new sectors, such as healthcare and pharmaceuticals, could gain and these advantages could be amplified with the use of online trading and payment mechanisms. The technological infrastructure in healthcare has emerged as a need of not only this time but also for the future sustainability of macroeconomy. On the other hand, domestic resources are to be diverted to the e-health, e-learning, and e-delivery. The promotion of foreign investment in these sectors can be a big task ahead for the BOI.

There are also reasons to believe that FDI levels could come back on track faster than expected. This view is held by those who believe that foreign investment is a long-term binding commitment between governments of businesses and may not be affected by the pandemic. Secondly, the virus outbreak information management system has been reinforced and an inclusive hospital information management system has been ensured for an early detection of outbreaks. Finally, the government is trying to liberalise, promote, and facilitate investors at a provincial level, offering new transactions in line with the opportunities offered by the global shocks. In particular, the investment in e-health services, e-business, and e-commerce firms can be potential sectors to take ahead by attracting foreign investors.

Notes

1. 'World Investment Report: Special Economic Zones,' UNCTAD, 2019.
2. Ashfaque H. Khan and Yun-Hwan Kim, 'Foreign Direct Investment in Pakistan: Policy Issues and Operational Implications,' EDRC Report Series No. 66 (July 1999).
3. 'Foreign Direct Investment Strategy 2013-17,' Board of Investment, Government of Pakistan, 2017.
4. 'World Investment Report: Special Economic Zones.'
5. 'Pakistan Economic Survey 2019–20,' Ministry of Finance, Government of Pakistan, 2019.
6. Ibid.
7. 'Foreign Direct Investment Strategy 2013-17.'
8. 'Pakistan Economic Survey 2019–20.'

9. Ishrat Husain, 'Why should Investors Choose Pakistan as their Destination?' Remarks delivered at Euromoney Seminar on Pakistan: Investment Destination held at Dubai on September 21, 2003.
10. 'Asian Development Outlook (ADO) 2020: What Drives Innovation in Asia?' Asian Development Bank, April 2020.
11. 'World Investment Report: Special Economic Zones.'
12. World Trade Organization has predicted a plunge of 13–32 per cent in world merchandise trade during 2020 as a result of Covid-19.

CHAPTER 5

The Role and Importance of Institutions in Development

SHAKEEL AHMAD

The political and economic institutions of a country are undoubtedly at the centre of policy decisions on resource distribution, public service delivery, and investment for growth and development. Many economists have attempted to shape this argument into a formal theory, with slight variations over time.

Ranging from the economic branch of new institutional economics where Douglas North defined institutions as the rules, laws, and norms that govern individual behaviour and social interactions, to the more recent work by Daron Acemoglu and James A. Robinson that explains differences in countries' prosperity through its economic and political institutions, the role of institutions in economic development has been explored by many economists.[1]

In their famous book, *Why Nations Fail: The Origins of Power, Prosperity and Poverty*, Acemoglu and Robinson used a range of country case studies to conclude that 'inclusive and pluralistic' institutions that are based on incentives for shared resources and distribution of power allow nations to prosper faster. On the other hand, nations that are gripped with 'extractive institutions' that benefit only a small sub-section of society by exploiting resources and accumulating wealth are bound to lag behind.

Ishrat Husain, too, has alluded to these theories in his extensive work on governance and institutions. In his book, *The Economy of An Elitist State*,[2] he remarks on the interaction between the market and the state, arguing for the markets to allow distribution of resources but the state to govern it through the right set of rules and regulations, along with incentives that are: a) the same for everyone, and b) do not favour one group over the other. Husain's explanation of Pakistan's faltering economic progress since the early 1990s centres on poor governance that has resulted in highly inequitable distribution of resources. He talks about the political and bureaucratic inertia that inhibits any meaningful long-term reform and that the increasingly lower standards of civil institutions are largely to be blamed for the rise of the military, disconnect of the general public from access to institutions, and ultimately the ability of the powerful to capture the lion's share of state's resources.

While analysing the different political and economic eras of Pakistan, he concludes that reforms, whenever introduced, were largely as a result of the conditions put forward by the IMF. As soon as the economy stabilises, the reforms are left half-way due to lack of the political will and commitment. He notes that reforms are often painful and create both winners and losers. Hence, without any sound political commitment, it is impossible to hope for any long-term structural reforms. It is this inertia that has caused civil institutions, like the Planning Commission to wither over time, losing the authenticity, standards, and quality they once upheld. He argues for the inter-linked framework of policies, institutions, and strong leaders to inculcate good governance and implement sound economic policies.

Whether the debate is structured through the lens of civil service reforms or the role of economic and political institutions, Husain argues that the key variable is good governance without which inclusive and sustainable growth cannot be achieved. He quotes the World Bank's definition of governance: 'the manner in which power is exercised in the management of a country's economic and social resources' whereas good governance entails the 'checks and balances' that controls the abuse of power by institutions and confines their role within the mandate given to them while also ensuring that they work for the greater good of the country.

Husain's analysis hits the nail on the head; the unequal distribution of power and the expanding role of institutions outside their mandate has continued to distort the market forces in Pakistan. However, as we theorise this hypothesis, some key questions need to be answered in the context of what can be learned from the work of Ishrat Husain.

First, if institutions were to be placed at the centre of the conversation here, how should they be defined and if that definition needs to be revisited in the context of a struggling economy like Pakistan. Second, those characteristics need to be defined that we seek in institutions that corroborate with the notion of good governance, be it motivation and incentive structure for civil servants, or an environment that allows risk-taking and experimentation to facilitate change and a process of creative destruction. This chapter will attempt to answer these while drawing on examples from literature and work of economists like Ishrat Husain.

DEFINING INSTITUTIONS

Institutions are not mere organisations or civil service bodies that run the state machinery, rather they reflect deeply embedded values and norms and rules of business that govern behaviour and interactions. Husain separates institutions from governance as he argues for the need to have good governance for institutions to play their due role. He cites the example of countries like South Korea, Hong Kong, Singapore, and Taiwan to demonstrate the appropriate role of the state institutions, which is to act as a facilitator for market competition and to provide the required infrastructure for market expansion rather than occupy the space of private players in the production and distribution of goods and services. The key here is for good governance to carve out the role of state institutions and the division of power. Contradictory to this definition, Douglas North defined institutions as:

> humanly devised constraints that structure political, economic and social interactions. They consist of both informal constraints (sanctions, taboos, customs, traditions, and codes of conduct) and formal rules (constitutions, laws, property rights).[3]

For countries like Pakistan, it is often the rules of business, both formal and informal that are so heavily skewed in favour of the powerful, that they end up creating what Acemoglu and Robinson define as 'extractive institutions'. It is these very rules of business that in the words of Ishrat Husain eliminate the access of the public from civil institutions, reducing accountability, transparency, and quality assurance. These extractive institutions embody distorted incentive structures and choice sets, tipping the distribution of power and resources in favour of a selected few. The prime examples are military and judiciary in Pakistan that have started to operate beyond their allocated boundaries, distorting market powers and failing to perform their attributed responsibilities effectively.

In an ideal scenario, the formal and informal constraints and incentives that institutions embody should evolve with time, shaping the path that an economy takes as institutions interact with market forces. Instead of controlling market forces through an artificial and overarching management of economic forces, the institutions should manage it through an evolving set of choices and incentives that are not biased in favour of one group.

As North argues when economies evolve along the path of higher specialisation, mass production, and division of labour, the nature of transactions and exchange also changes.[4] For the volume of trade to grow and organisations to expand and increase investment, it is important that institutions play their due role in contract enforcement, protection of property rights, and in lowering costs of information. If institutions fail to do so through evolving but impersonal and unbiased 'rules of business', economies will not be able to expand as private players will be discouraged to invest.

The increasing use of technology and innovations in today's agile business models is an example of the crucial role that institutions must play in providing property rights and enforcing rules that do not favour one group over the other.

Pakistan, along with some other developing countries, has struggled with sustainable economic growth because of ballooning institutions capturing space that should either be left to the market forces or managed by other effective institutions.

THE STATE AND THE GOVERNMENT IN PAKISTAN

Wallis and North defined the state as the 'the organization that organizes all other organizations'.[5] If the government is in charge of doing so, then the state and the government are one and the same. However, in some countries including Pakistan, there are also many other entities that operate behind curtains without legitimate sanction of the government, creating what they term as a 'weak state or weak government'. Weak governments develop when powerful private entities run the state with public offices just being the face of it.

If this arrangement of interlocked public offices and private entities was to be viewed from the lens of private exchanges, then in a weak government privately set rules and regulations would govern most transactions. For a modern prosperous economy, the exchange between entities must be impartial and impersonal to address this problem of privately set rules and regulations. In other words, the rules of business must be the same for every type of transaction and exchange between entities. This brings us back to the earlier conclusion: impartial institutions that embody the same rules of business for everyone are essential for sustainable economic development.

To further draw parallels with the current state of institutions in Pakistan, we can once again draw on the work of North that theorises different types of social interactions in different regimes. He coined the term 'natural state' for countries where special privileges can be granted to dominant coalitions or powerful entities, secure property rights are not guaranteed to everyone, and the allocation of resources, rights, and privileges is arbitrary.

So, how can 'natural states' transition towards a more prosperous economy where unbiased rules govern all transactions? North answers this by putting forward three conditions: judiciary plays its role in legally monitoring all transactions between the rich and the powerful, perpetual organisations in both public and private spaces allow for impersonal exchanges coupled with strict enforcement of contracts and property rights, and lastly, an organisation embedded in the state structure that keeps a check on the power and control of the military.

Here, Husain's argument aligns itself very closely with the work of North as he too stressed upon three key institutions in Pakistan for inclusive development: judiciary, legislative bodies, and the executive—the judiciary to provide property rights and contract enforcement, legislative bodies to structure the right regulatory framework, and the executive body to formulate policies and manage public service delivery.

In his essay, 'Why Institutional Capacity Matters and Where Reforms Should Start', Husain has suggested seven steps across different layers of institutions and policymaking bodies to foster good governance.[6] This includes reform of the electoral process; democratic governance model of political parties; higher fiscal, administrative, and legal powers of local governments; civil service reforms in police, public services, land management, and administrative services; better access to and management of judiciary, access to information for the general public to hold civil servants accountable; the parliament playing its role in controlling the power of executive bodies; and lastly, decentralised authority in federal and provincial governments to improve accountability. Collectively, all these reforms target institutions on five levels: management of free markets, delivery of public services, judicial management and protection of people's rights, accountability and transparency, and promoting and encouraging equity through the right set of incentives for all.

This theoretical framework for analysing the importance of institutions in the context of the state and the role of government as public offices is a strong foundation for realising the development challenges of Pakistan. To use the terminology of North, Pakistan is a 'natural state' where institutions are not representing impartial rules of business for all. To progress from this state, the analysis of North agrees with Husain's arguments that the judiciary has to play its role in enforcing contracts and property rights; the power and space occupied by the military has to be checked and the executive needs to develop unbiased rules and regulations for everyone.

Hence, institutions must play a fundamental role in ensuring that personal recommendations and social interactions do not influence the rules that guide transactions. So how will these impersonal rules of business develop and institutions evolve in a manner that Pakistan is able to progress from this natural state? In the following sections, we discuss the characteristics of public institutions that can push through meaningful change and reform.

CIVIL SERVANTS AND REFORM OF PUBLIC INSTITUTIONS

Ishrat Husain has discussed extensively the need for comprehensive and long-term civil service reforms that are backed by political will and commitment. However, a key element in this debate is missing—the role and attitude of civil servants without whom reforms will continue to fail and institutions will not evolve in the manner that Pakistan needs it to. Human interactions will eventually impact the rules of business and to the extent that these can be impartial depends upon the attitude adopted by civil servants.

History provides us with numerous examples of reform and modernisation of institutions but any meaningful change can only seep through if those who must implement it—the civil servants—are determined to make them successful. It is often the lack of intrinsic motivation that creates an inertia as public officials see change as a threat to their jobs and their way of doing business. If working for efficient, innovative, and agile institutions is personally rewarding to civil servants, and therefore intrinsically satisfying, there is bound to be greater acceptance for developing impartial rules of business.

Unfortunately, in most cases extrinsic motivation is more influential in public offices, as employees perform just for an external reward or to avoid a punishment. Although, a well-structured incentive programme can be used to leverage the extrinsic motivation of employees but for any meaningful change, intrinsic motivation should be more influential to guide civil servants in their choices and attitude towards reform and adaptation.

There is a strand of literature that discusses how intrinsic motivation can be built, if at all possible. There is no clear conclusion if or not intrinsic motivation could be built. Like leadership, personality traits play an integral role for someone to be intrinsically motivated or not. Nevertheless, to some extent, intrinsic motivations could be developed through teachings, counselling, and especially through a societal ecosystem which values ethical standards, empathy, and living for a purpose. It could be a long process of training and society interaction which would be more useful in the initial stages of one's life. Both intrinsic and extrinsic motivations supplement each other and may produce higher results when applied in tandem.

Public service motivation is a key area of development for both developing and developed countries alike. Numerous studies and consultations with practitioners have been done on the issue to identify the extrinsic and intrinsic motivational factors that the public sector should seek in its employees. In conditions of budget shortage and a very different management style, the public sector cannot compete with the private sector for its human resource. Some researchers argue that perhaps it should not even do so because of the varying requirements of work. Civil servants choose public sector because of their motivation to work for altruistic good. Hence, by definition, intrinsic motivation should overshadow extrinsic factors for civil servants.

Perry and Wise defined public service motivation as 'an individual's predisposition to respond to motives grounded primarily or uniquely in public institutions or organizations'.[7] Another study by Perry identifies four factors that motivate individuals to select public sector: the attraction of designing and influencing public policies, commitment and motivation to work in the interest of the public and perform in civil duty, self-sacrifice, and the quality of compassion.[8] Yet, in another study by Brewer, Selden, and Facer II, public service motivation is classified in four different orientations that are aimed towards helping others: samaritans (working for individuals in need), communitarians (drawn to activism for the community), patriots (working for their country), and humanitarians (working for the greater interest of humanity).[9]

All these studies show that employees of public sector are more altruistic than their counterpart in the private sector and hence, it is this intrinsic motivation that draws them to the public sector. A study data of public sector employees in Britain found that if extrinsic rewards are very high in the public sector a lot of people will get attracted to it without having any intrinsic motivation to work for the public sector, and consequently, would be less committed to their work and their organisation. However, as all public sector employees cannot be intrinsically motivated enough or inclined to be committed to their job, a combination of extrinsic and intrinsic rewards are needed. The bottom line is that the public sector should seek to hire candidates that possess altruistic qualities like the ones defined above to have a motivated workforce.

In a study done by the UNDP Pakistan to assess factors that motivate civil servants in Pakistan, it was found that a majority of civil services opt for a career in government because of incentives like job security and the status that comes with it—factors that constitute extrinsic motivation in literature.[10] At the same time, the study also found that intrinsic motivation of employees can be tapped through better HR practices that inculcate strict adherence to performance-based criteria and elimination of nepotism and undue political influences from public offices. This shows that inconsistency in policies and impartial rules of business eventually lead to lower motivation in civil servants. And hence, as the study's survey revealed, two-thirds of young employees said they'd be willing to switch sectors if they find a good opportunity. This briefly reflects the state of institutions in Pakistan that are governed by civil servants with little motivation to adapt to change.

Has the public sector of Pakistan failed to tap into human resource with the right set of qualities and who are more intrinsically motivated to work for the greater good of the country and the society rather than extrinsic rewards? Or is it that once they enter the workforce, the poor regulatory environment, biased HR policies, and undue political influence diminishes their motivation and they, too, adapt to the 'business as usual'? Whichever resonates more closely with the current state of HR in the public sector, the truth is that civil servants have little motivation to fight the existing practices that are damaging public institutions.

In an interesting survey done by Buurman, Dur, and Van den Bossche, respondents were asked to choose between a lottery, donation to a charity, or redeemable gift voucher. Interestingly, it was found that civil servants at the start of their career were more likely to choose the option of donating to a charity. However, those employees who were at later stages of their career were increasingly less likely to pick the altruistic option and feel that they are already contributing enough to the society by working on low pays.[11]

INNOVATION AND RISK-TAKING IN PUBLIC SECTOR

With rapid change in technology and the norms of doing business, adaptivity is essential for institutions to remain relevant. And this quality can only be inculcated through a workforce that is willing to adopt risk-taking behaviour, experiment with new ideas, and to think outside the box.

This is a challenge that affects public offices in perhaps many countries. The short-term gains or losses are more heavily priced and attractive in political institutions than they are in private institutions. The risk of losing tax-payers' money, political reputation, or voters' confidence is big enough to discourage policymakers from taking any risk. However, the risk-averse attitude causes institutions to become obsolete overtime and lose their relevance, quality, and standards. Given the pace at which new technologies are being introduced, public institutions need to quickly adapt and use them to increase productivity.

Risk-averse behaviour is also highly linked to behavioural and personality attributes. Some individuals are by nature less likely to be risk-takers and perhaps they make a better fit for the public sector. However, a large workforce might also lose the zeal to take risk because that attribute is not encouraged by the leadership. Risk-taking behaviour is also a cultural trait that must be integrated by the leadership through the right set of incentives. In public institutions of Pakistan, risk-taking is largely discouraged and management offers little to those who dare to do it. As the fear of punishment also overrides the possibility of reward, most individuals are unwilling to change their ways.

Pakistan is a classic case of how institutions have become highly unproductive and inefficient due to their inability to be agile, readily accept change, and improve output. The incentive structure in public offices is also often not designed to encourage risk-taking behaviour as the political cost of failure is extremely high. Due to the inappropriate incentive structure, public officials in Pakistan are largely uninterested and unwilling to take risks and to experiment with new technology and new ideas as they either fear being rendered obsolete or it is simply seen as having more demerits than merits.

Linking this back to the starting point of our discussion on what constitutes institutions and the characteristics that define them, it is essential to realise that adapting to modern ways of doing business and incorporating higher use of technology means shrinking space for corruption and irregularities. Hence, technology offers a very important tool to develop impartial rules of business that can push institutions of Pakistan to transition from their existing 'natural state' to a 'modern state' as defined by North.[12] However, the unmotivated and risk-averse attitude of public sector employees has created an inertia that constantly revolts to the introduction of any reform that might rock the boat.

Having said this, technological innovation will itself not automatically transform the way public institutions operate. It will need a combination of intrinsic motivation aka the purpose to serve the masses as well as a system of checks and balances. Without these, technological innovation may lead to a situation that is called 'gamming'. In such situations, the functionaries may game the system in a way that it maintains the status quo. I have had personal experiences where, despite automation of services, I had to request friends and acquaintances for a legal public service. Because at the end, even technological solutions and operating models are to be implemented and operated by humans. Without a minimum level of intrinsic motivation to serve people, the state of institutions may not change even with automation and technology-led solutions. Yes, it can be of help to some extent.

Now the question is how to build intrinsic motivation. This is a million-dollar question. Put it differently. What even if intrinsic motivation could be cultivated? Based on my personal experience I see at least two factors that could influence intrinsic motivation. First is the work environment. A condition where peers, especially senior colleagues, demonstrate motivation to serve which influences the behaviour of others and, especially those who are new in the system. But such enabling conditions do not develop on their own. This requires a sense of purpose to be inculcated in the mind of every worker. It requires a minimum level of collective capital that practices and exemplifies such behaviours. The second is essentially the way the society is groomed. This starts straight from one's home and parents.

A society which does not vigorously preach and practice 'values' cannot produce a high level of intrinsic motivation in its population. It is a capital and frame of mind which must be seeded at the very start of one's life. It is not just the teaching of it in textbooks but rather the practical demonstration of it by every member of the society where such values are shared, refined, and sustained.

* * *

Ishrat Husain is, without a doubt, a leading expert on institutions in Pakistan. What makes him different from his contemporaries is the unique combination of his theoretical and practical work. We know about his teaching and research work as well as his engagement with the government and different development agencies. This gives him a big advantage in grounding his theoretical and research experience to the realities of life. His work on institutions in Pakistan provides great insights of how Pakistan's governance and institutional ecosystem could be aligned to the needs of the modern Pakistan. At the same time, it provides an incredible foundation to further expand on his work and explore the role of some of the key formal/public institutions as well as the role of informal institutions. The latter become more important when we want to study the questions related to intrinsic motivation, especially in public organisations. This will allow studying the question of governance in Pakistan in a broader manner: in a way that looks at the entire society to understand incentives, the way these incentives are created and the way behaviours are framed, nourished, and sustained.

Notes

1. See Douglass C. North, 'Institutions,' *The Journal of Economic Perspectives* 5, no. 1 (Winter 1991): 97–112; and Daron Acemoglu and James Robinson, *Why Nations Fail: The Origins of Power, Prosperity, and Poverty* (London: Profile Books, 2012).
2. Ishrat Husain, *Pakistan: The Economy of An Elitist State* (Karachi: Oxford University Press, 1999).
3. North, 'Institutions,' 97.
4. Ibid.
5. J. J. Wallis and Douglass C. North, 'Defining the State,' Working Paper (Mercatus Centre, George Mason University, 2010).

6. Ishrat Husain, 'Why Institutional Capacity Matters and Where Reforms Should Start,' The Wilson Center, 2018.

7. James L. Perry and Lois R. Wise, 'The Motivational Bases of Public Service,' *Public Administration Review* 50, no. 3 (May/June 1990): 367–373.

8. James L. Perry, 'Measuring Public Service Motivation: An Assessment of Construct Reliability and Validity,' *Journal of Public Administration Research and Theory: J-PART* 6, no. 1 (January 1996): 5–22.

9. Gene A. Brewer, Sally Coleman Selden, and Rex L. Facer II, 'Individual Conceptions of Public Service Motivation,' *Public Administration Review* 60, no. 3 (2000): 254–264.

10. 'Motivation of Public Service Officials. Insights for Practitioners,' UNDP Global Centre for Public Service Excellence, 2014.

11. Margaretha Buurman, Robert Dur, and Seth Van den Bossche, 'Public Sector Employees: Rise Averse and Altruistic,' IZA Discussion Papers No. 4401 (Bonn: Institute for the Study of Labour, 2009).

12. North, 'Institutions.'

CHAPTER 6

Role of Public Sector Development Programme in Economic Development

Hamid Mahmood

It is an honour to be contributing to this volume which aims to honour the work of Ishrat Husain. As I recall, he has been called to help the country in some of the most testing times. In delivering his duty, he has contributed to reform various aspects of the economy. One such area is the reform of Public Sector Development Programme (PSDP). In essence, one of the key drivers that have contributed towards economic growth, along with other factors, is the PSDP which helps towards transformation of the economy using limited resources. The goals for PSDP are often many, including employment generation; prioritisation of sectoral investment across infrastructure and social sector development; protecting the vulnerable segments of society; and achieving the development objectives planned for economic growth in line with the five-year plan and vision of the government in power.

Global development paradigm is shifting away from public sector growth and employment, towards knowledge-base and entrepreneurship. Economically viable PSDP-financed projects help boost economic growth by bridging infrastructure and skill gaps besides putting in place an enabling environment for the private sector. In this respect, the PSDP aims to compliment overall growth policy of the government. It also supports other productive policies, such as industrial and trade policy.

One of the key challenges of our times is the Covid-19 pandemic which has tested the PSDP and its efficiency. The pandemic outbreak has not only exposed the vulnerabilities in the economy but also impacted different sectors and vulnerable population. For some industries, the impact is quite significant which will hurt the balance of payments position (through channels of uncertain exports and imports) and government's fiscal position (through uncertain revenue position).

Before the pandemic, Pakistan was facing a low-demand milieu due to the stabilisation measures under the IMF programme which led to a reduction in the current account deficit and a transition towards growth recovery. These gains eroded quickly due to the impact of Covid-19 and immediate lockdowns across the country. Keeping in view the above factors, one of the positive changes noticed globally was decrease in the oil prices which helped the government in reducing the current account deficit and mitigating, to some extent, the impact through Covid-19 since a large part of the import bill is in the form of energy inputs, including oil and gas.

The Cabinet, of which Dr Ishrat Husain a very important part, took drastic steps for countering and minimising the impact of the pandemic. These steps include prime minister's package of Rs 1,200 billion to protect industries, financial sector, and vulnerable population, including elimination of import duties on imports of emergency health equipment; relief to daily-wage workers (Rs 200 billion); cash transfers to low-income families (Rs 150 billion); accelerated tax refunds to the export industry (Rs 100 billion); financial support to SMEs (Rs 100 billion) and resources for an accelerated procurement of wheat (Rs 280 billion); financial support to utility stores (Rs 50 billion); relief in fuel prices (Rs 70 billion); support for health and food supplies (Rs 15 billion); electricity bill payments relief (Rs 110 billion); an emergency contingency fund (Rs 100 billion); and transfer to the National Disaster Management Authority (NDMA) for the purchase of necessary equipment to deal with the pandemic (Rs 25 billion). The PSDP's projects were unfortunately adversely affected due to non-implementation of development activities for almost six months and low utilisation of public funds. The drop in overall government resources also decreased the PSDP's size to Rs 650 billion for 2020–2021 from Rs 701 billion in the previous year.

The government, in addition to the stimulus package, has also earmarked Rs 70 billion in the PSDP for the next fiscal year for helping to mitigate the effects of Covid-19. This was supposed to help in understanding the trend through survey analysis, financial package in different sectors of the economy depending on the loss from Covid-19, and changing the socioeconomic patterns helping towards economic activity in the country which will be dependent on economic policies announced by the government from time to time for reducing the impact of Covid-19.

In line with this intervention, the role of the PSDP became more significant through intervention in social sectors by increasing the share by 3 per cent in the next fiscal year in the area of health, education, and social protection programmes. As per Dr Husain's advice, the government opened the construction industry where 40 sub-industries are supported by 68 per cent share of infrastructure projects under the overall PSDP, helping to create employment.

The focus of the government in the medium-term should ideally be on the protection of vulnerable population below the poverty line, upgradation of rural and urban health facilities, construction of new hospitals in-line with the best practices globally, increasing awareness of education standards, and quality and financial inclusion of the population either through the PSDP funds or others in line with the policies of the government. Although, Covid-19 and its impact on the socioeconomic fabric of society is understandable, it is also important to highlight the weakness that is persistent in the PSDP's policies and operation from a practical viewpoint. The challenges confronted with the operation of the PSDP are many and if corrected will help in streamlining the development funds towards the development activity in no time and mitigate the impact of Covid-19 and other such emergencies in future.

Dr Husain offered guidance and funds authorisation as per precedence (was based on demand from the ministry) has been done away with and now authorisation is issued in one go, the Principal Accounting Officers (PAO) of the ministry are accountable for effective utilisation and effectiveness of the schemes. This reform has increased the utilisation of the PSDP funds by more than 10 per cent in fiscal year 2019–2020 and is also supported by Public Finance Management Act (PFMA), helping to streamline financial accounting system with the objective of bringing professional and significant impact of resources on economic growth in the country.

Having been highlighted by several researchers and commentators, common issues such as lack of effective PSDP operations include a large chunk of resources taken by recurrent expenditures (salaries and pension, defence-spending, debt-servicing, etc.); duplication of projects; politically-motivated projects; weak monitoring and evaluation of ongoing projects; and weak project design and evaluation. The objective should be ideally to bring about efficiency in development expenditure supported by other policy measures where the given input has large outcomes for development, promoting both employment and growth in the country, especially in the face of crisis emanated by the pandemic.

One of the important challenges faced by the PSDP is a low fiscal face. To fund more development budget, increased debt had to be procured in the past. The other critical issue with fiscal management is the 18th Amendment and 7th National Finance Commission (NFC) award which increased the share of provinces in the divisible pool and abolished the concurrent list. Both actions have given a higher share to the provinces and new allocation of functions to the provinces. The revenue contribution by provinces has not grown at a scale anticipated at the time of enactment of the 18th Amendment.

The federal government is still expected to undertake vertical programmes for the provinces in the areas of education, health, SGDs programme, which after the 18th Amendment should have in principle been shifted to the provinces. The 18th Amendment should be reviewed for improvements in light of new challenges confronted by Covid-19, security challenges at the border, debt-servicing, SGDs programme, etc., where provinces can help in contributing the revenue share for the above key areas of intervention in future. In the sectors mentioned above, provinces should reduce their reliance on the federal budget.

The last eight years have witnessed a drop or stagnancy in the PSDP's portfolio, which has often been inflated by including SGDs programme, temporary displaced persons' (TDP) rehabilitation, security enhancement, and block allocations, etc., which is directly dealt with by the finance division and other ministries. Therefore, in real terms, the PSDP's portfolio managed by the Planning Commission has dropped considerably and the above discrepancies add on average 36 per cent to the PSDP. In other words, 36 per cent of the PSDP's portfolio is actually not a development portfolio and not even close to the definition of development-spending. Therefore, this tendency needs to be done away with to protect the true essence of the PSDP.

This has also brought out the fact that whatever research is done on development-spending and its impact on economic growth is doubtful since data is taken of budget allocations and often missed revised estimates; actual surrender of savings; re-appropriations; supplementary grant; technical supplementary grant, etc., operated within the fiscal year which automatically changes even the share of sectors in the PSDP at the end of fiscal year.

This can be corrected by introducing a real-time data portal and reducing the role of above-mentioned components of budget for a clear understanding of the PSDP's portfolio. In the global context, public sector development programmes undergo proper scrutiny from the parliament with the help of independent research organisation, etc., before approval of design and implementation of the projects.

Even many approved schemes are outsourced and brought into the framework of public-private partnership, helping to implement and streamline project objectives-based on evidence-based research outcomes and result-based management framework. In the context of Pakistan, it has been observed in the past, there is clear politicisation of schemes before evaluation and towards approval, weak analysis based on no real-time data support and weaken prioritisation. It is time to realise that technical teams dealing with projects' approval need to be professionally trained and given scientific training, involving the private sector from approval to implementation of the schemes for a positive impact of the schemes.

The role of the Planning Commission needs to be reimagined. The Economist and Planners Group—a civil service cadre of the Ministry of Planning, Development & Special Initiatives—needs to be trained properly and empowered. The objective of this group was to bring evidence-based research into the plan formulation process and help five-year, annual, and perspective (vision) plans.

Going forward, the Planning Commission could act as a secretariat of the Council of Common Interest (CCI) which represents all provinces. Besides this, as per the decision of the Executive Committee of the National Economic Council (ECNEC) in 2006, Economist and Planners Group needs to be expanded with seats in all ministries, organisations, and foreign offices abroad which will also help in evaluating foreign aid and investment proposals.

The monitoring and evaluation of the PSDP's schemes is another weak area. There is a monitoring wing in the ministry but staff is ad-hoc, employed through various schemes of the PSDP where the officers employed are contractual and lack necessary powers for effective monitoring.

The government needs to ensure and bring in the framework for proper recruitment of the monitoring wing in the ministry on a permanent basis along with necessary professional training locally and from abroad for ensuring professionalism and desired outcomes. The monitoring framework should be linked with Pakistan Space & Upper Atmosphere Research (Suparco), which could use satellite monitoring and help in proper scrutinisation of projects. More than 65 per cent share of the PSDP includes infrastructure which can be monitored through satellite imaginary.

The financial operations of the ministry's development budget have been streamlined to a large extent after the introduction of SAP system (financial accounting system) which directly disburses funds in the assignment account. Public Finance Management Act 2019 has reduced the traditional role of Deputy Financial Advisors (DFA) and block funds authorisation, however, the role of Accountant General of Pakistan Revenues (AGPR) and capacity building of staff in various ministries, having schemes in the PSDP, still needs to be streamlined in line with changes mentioned above. When the funds are authorised, it takes about on average 15 days by other ministries to issue a sanction letter and on average about 15 days more by the AGPR for final cheque issuance to the contractor or signatory of projects. Therefore, in total, it takes around more than one month after authorisation for funds to reach the contractor to start the project. Therefore, it is advisable that the role of other ministries and the AGPR may be minimised for issuance of sanction and procedure formalities which will help in full utilisation of funds and effectiveness of the PSDP's schemes in the long run.

The reform of the PSDP cannot be a one-off exercise. As the economy evolves, systems and processes that govern the PSDP would also require innovation. For this, an internal unit responsible for organisational evaluation and learning is important. Such a unit will continue to collect information on the current demands on the PSDP and how to deliver them in the best possible manner, considering the international experience and best practices.

Part

STATE OF
SUB-NATIONAL ECONOMY

CHAPTER 7

Envisioning Inclusive Growth in Punjab

M. Aman Ullah

ECONOMY OF PUNJAB

Punjab lies at the centre of the national economy and accounts for almost 55 per cent of the country's annual production of goods and services (see Figure 1). The weight of the province in entirety ensures that the performance of the national economy remains strongly correlated with that of Punjab's economy. Thus, the key issues of fiscal deficits and current account deficits are equally worrying for province as they are for the national economy. In terms of performance, the share of Punjab in the national economy has gradually increased over the last five years, suggesting that the growth in the province has been faster than that at the national level.

**Figure 1: GPP of Punjab and GDP of Pakistan, 2013–2018
(Rs million at fixed cost prices)**

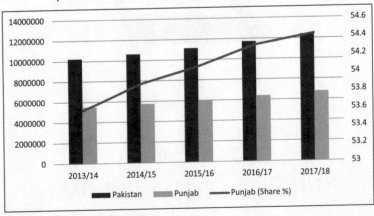

Source: Punjab Bureau of Statistics

CONTRIBUTION TO THE PERFORMANCE OF THE NATIONAL ECONOMY

Figure 2 shows that the performance of Punjab's economy moves in tandem with the national economy, and with the exception of 2012–2013, it exceeds the national GDP growth rate for all reported years.

As a share of value-added of the respective national sector, Punjab contributes significantly in all sectors. The contribution of Punjab during 2017–2018 in national agriculture value added was 41 per cent, in manufacturing was 58 per cent, and in the services sector was 57.4 per cent.

Figure 2: Growth rate of Punjab GPP and Pakistan GDP, 2010–2018 (per cent)

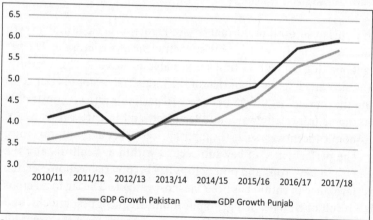

Source: Punjab Bureau of Statistics

PERFORMANCE OF THE ECONOMY

The Gross Provincial Product (GPP) of Punjab has increased at an average rate of almost 4.70 per cent annually from 2010 to 2018. The growth in GPP was slightly higher than the average growth rate of the GDP of Pakistan, which averaged 4.4 per cent per annum over the same period.

Figure 3: Sectoral Growth Rates in Punjab, 2010–2018 (per cent)

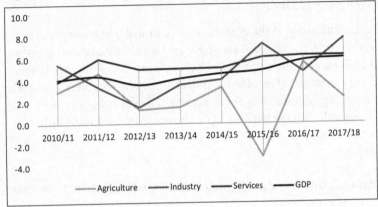

Source: Punjab Bureau of Statistics

In terms of sectoral performance (see Figure 3), agricultural growth rates were highly volatile with a coefficient of variation of 112 per cent, making it about six times as variable as the GPP. This volatility was also much larger than that of the industrial sector (44 per cent) and the services sector (15 per cent). In part, this reflects constraints on inputs (especially water and fertiliser) and in part a response to economic incentives, such as support prices of key agricultural crops.

The performance of key sub-sectors within agriculture, and the growth in key crops and other crops has been variable, however, the performance in cotton has been the most variable. The lag in all crops is a result of climate change implications, frequent pest attacks, and depressed commodity prices. Cotton ginning has been the worst hit sector. Production in the industrial sector, led predominantly by large-scale manufacturing (LSM), saw a broad-based increase since 2010, with the exception of a slight dip in 2016–2017. The mining sector has been volatile, facing issues of regulation and contracting.

The LSM sector is expected to gain momentum from the development work on projects under CPEC going forward, especially now that the work on Special Economic Zones (SEZs) has already started. However, there needs to be a strong policy to make this happen.

The performance of the services sector has been the least volatile among the three main sectors of the economy. The construction, wholesale and retail, and finance and insurance are the better performing sectors and are likely to continue a positive growth trajectory.

CONTOURS OF ECONOMIC GROWTH IN PUNJAB

For inclusive development[1] in Punjab, people-centric growth strategy—which not only documents specific targets, priorities, and plans but also highlights the issues, challenges, opportunities, and workable solutions for sustainable growth—has been formulated. For the first time ever, in-house preparation of the Punjab Growth Strategy (PGS) is being undertaken by Planning & Development (P&D) Board, Government of Punjab.

The Punjab Growth Strategy 2023 presents the five-year socioeconomic plan of the government to address some of the fundamental issues and structural anomalies faced by the provincial economy as well as setting of strategic actions required to trigger the main growth drivers of the economy. Under PGS 2023, the Government of Punjab is focusing on key priority areas, including water scarcity, agriculture, export competitiveness, industrialisation, education, health, private sector development, and climate change among others, along with a special focus on the development of deprived regions, especially South Punjab.

The development priorities of Punjab have been aligned with the PGS 2023 and the government is focused towards the five main pillars of growth: (i) Increased focus on agriculture and SME sectors due to clear comparative advantage of Punjab, (ii) emphasis on private sector development as the main engine of growth, (iii) human capital formation and its upgradation for industrial development, (iv) setting the most optimal allocation of public sector investment for Punjab in terms of growth outcomes, and (v) ensuring adequate resource requirements and sources of finances that support not only the development plans of Punjab but also take into account regional equalisation as a precondition to attain sustainable growth.

With macroeconomic pressures at the national level and the squeezing of development budget in the provinces with certain looming liabilities over the next five years, the Punjab government in terms of public investments is focusing on stabilisation and then aim for rapid higher growth in the following years. The size of the Annual Development Programme (ADP) for the FY 2019–2020 was Rs 350 billion. The current government has emphasised the need for developing the province's human capital rather than just focusing on infrastructure development. The salient features of the ADP 2019–2020 are as under:

- Projects are distributed across the province to achieve equitable development in all regions.
- Priority has been given to schemes that ensure better performance of Punjab against key Sustainable Development Goals (SDGs) indicators.
- The development schemes that create and enhance urban clusters and ensure the provision of requisite services are prioritised.
- Punjab's agrarian land is transforming into arid land due to variations in climate conditions, thus the priority is given to the agriculture and irrigation sectors (special focus on small dams).

SUSTAINABLE DEVELOPMENT GOALS

The Government of Punjab intends to further augment its existing approaches towards mainstreaming, acceleration, and policy support for Agenda 2030. Based on the Provincial SDG Framework, measures will be taken to develop a competitive environment in the province where all stakeholders should work together for the achievement of SDGs in a true letter and spirit. Following are the key points of the Government of Punjab's approach to keep SDGs aligned with the Punjab Growth Strategy 2023:

i. Strengthening the legislative patronage of SDGs in the province will be a priority area for creating a momentum. Close liaison between Parliamentary Task Forces/Committees and SDGs support institutions will be developed.

ii. The Government of Punjab is committed to invest in SDGs, however, financing needs of implementation of SDGs is the biggest challenge worldwide. The financing gap to achieve the SDGs worldwide remains $5–7 trillion annually, of which around $2 trillion is the gap for developing countries.

iii. Proactive role of institutions and civil service is vital for the realisation of the SDGs. Therefore, efforts will be made to bring institutional innovation capable to buy-in from all the stakeholders of the SDGs.

iv. The importance of local governments for the SDGs implementation is universally acknowledged. Therefore, the government will take the SDGs to local governments as per the new local government system.

v. Monitoring, evaluation, and review of progress towards the SDGs will be strengthened mainly through institutions' capacity-building for statistical analyses and collection of relevant and accurate data against each SDGs indicator.

vi. Stakeholder engagement is vital for achieving the SDGs. The government will adopt bottom-up, participatory approaches across the levels of administrative, and financial decision-making in order to address specific development needs of the masses.

vii. Technological innovations, particularly the potential of ICTs will be harnessed for mainstreaming and acceleration of the SDGs. In this regard, partnership will be developed with academia and tech companies.

CHINA-PAKISTAN ECONOMIC CORRIDOR (CPEC)

The Government of Punjab has prioritised adequate resources for the timely completion of CPEC projects in the province. The newly-approved socioeconomic action plan under CPEC will also help Punjab in improving education, healthcare, poverty alleviation, and access to safe water supply. The government is in the process of preparing actionable socioeconomic projects for the welfare of our citizens and less developed districts.

Public-Private Partnerships

The Government of Punjab is working hard on capturing the potential of the public-private partnerships (PPPs) in public welfare projects. The PPPs now being envisioned as an additional development tool— aligned with Punjab Growth Strategy. Reforms are being introduced to remove bottlenecks and strengthen legal/administrative PPP framework in Punjab. The government aims to finance 10 per cent of the Annual Development Programme (ADP) through PPPs by 2023 and achieve an annual growth of 16 per cent per annum in private investments.

The Ease of Doing Business Reforms Agenda

The Government of Punjab in collaboration with the World Bank and multiple agencies is implementing targeted interventions envisaged under the Ease of Doing Business Reform Agenda. The agenda is being implemented in different sprints, each having a duration of 100 days approximately with a targeted set of interventions. Following reforms/interventions have been implemented:

- In order to provide ease in registering various types of business entities, a Business Registration Portal (BRP) was developed and operationalised which has reduced the time and cost since the need to visit multiple offices has been eliminated.
- A building permit issuance system has been automated by the Lahore Development Authority in order to provide ease to the general public regarding issuance of construction permits.
- Punjab Land Revenue Authority has simplified the procedure of registering property in Lahore.
- The Government of Punjab, State Bank of Pakistan, and 1-Link signed a Tripartite Agreement last year to launch a system of payment of taxes electronically, through alternate delivery channels.

Punjab Spatial Strategy 2047

The Government of Punjab has formulated the Punjab Spatial Strategy (PSS) to facilitate integrated planning in the development process by adding a spatial dimension to the process. The primary aim of the strategy is to equip Punjab with a long-term spatial planning framework. It will ensure integrated planning and its compliance will structurally transform Punjab into an economically developed and sustainable region.

Multiple Cluster Index Survey for Evidence Based Planning and Development

Multiple Indicator Cluster Survey (MICS) 2017–2018 team reached out to more than 53,000 households and conducted interviews with 74,000 women, 27,000 men, and 74,000 children across 36 districts in Punjab, which was a massive undertaking. The Survey Finding Report of MICS Punjab, 2017–2018, provides valuable data on many critical socio-economic indicators that will be useful for policymakers in Punjab to evaluate the current situation in these areas and to help them serve as a guideline for the formulation of relevant interventions for the betterment of citizens of the province in future.

Launching of Punjab Planning Portal

An online portal for the Smart Monitoring of Development Projects (SMDP) across Punjab has been launched by the Government of Punjab. This portal will increase efficiency and efficacy of public sector development projects of the province. The online system also ensures transparency and efficiency in the implementation of medium-term development framework along with the Annual Development Programme. The system will enable the management to not only make evidence-based decisions at the highest level but to monitor and manage the minutest details along with providing year-wise comparisons for analysis at the sector, department, division, and district level.

Community Development Programme

The Community Development Programme is a development initiative of Planning & Development Board to establish an effective and sustainable instrument to improve the living conditions and economic status of the disadvantaged communities.

Collaborations with Development Partners

Over the last few years, the size of donor and development partner engagement in Punjab has increased manifold. During the last year, the Government of Punjab managed a large portfolio of transactions ($4 billion), discussed and concluded several loan negotiations and tracked performance of large technical assistance programmes. The Government of Punjab also in the process of establishing donor coordination forums, tracking, and monitoring dashboards and building loan programmes and negotiation capacities. In addition to several small support programmes, the government is majorly benefitting from the technical and financial support from the World Bank, Department for International Development (DFID), Asian Development Bank (ADB), and Asian Infrastructure Investment Bank (AIIB), among others.

DR ISHRAT HUSAIN'S CONTRIBUTION TO REIMAGINING ECONOMIC DEVELOPMENT IN PUNJAB

With extensive and varied work experience, Dr Ishrat Husain attracted admiration, especially through his work on steering Pakistan's economy through difficult times. In his various interviews and lectures, Dr Husain presented 'strengthening of key economic institutions at the provincial and local levels' as one of the main pillars and drivers for achieving growth in Punjab.

The first institution to implement and follow this change suggested by Dr Husain was the Planning & Development (P&D) Board, Punjab. Realising that drastic change in the mandate, thrust, and terms of reference of the department is badly needed, the P&D Board made a shift from focusing on approval of schemes to a more holistic approach towards development, i.e. assessment of needs; policy formulation; programme and project preparation; monitoring implementation; and evaluation of policies and projects. The department also replaced the traditional way of preparing ADPs with the rolling out of Medium-Term Development Framework and Medium-Term Public Expenditure Framework, on which the annual budgets are anchored. Furthermore, today the P&D Board is the parent department of the Government of

Punjab to take a lead in the coordination of all economic policies and strategies with the federal government.

'Unification of provincial tax and revenue collection agencies' was another key reform suggested by Dr Husain, as the division between the Board of Revenue and Excise & Taxation Department in the collection of taxes and revenues was foreseen as an issue. Consequently, the Punjab Revenue Authority was set up based on modern organisational principles to entail elimination of multiple taxes, simplification of tax policy and procedures, reliance upon self-assessment, enforcement of audit on a selective basis, and a dispute-resolution mechanism that is quick and efficient. The governance structure of the authority is also different from the traditional department and has the autonomy with full accountability for the results.

Dr Ishrat Husain's third element of institutional reform where I believe the Government of Punjab needs to focus on is that the district governments should be given full administrative and financial powers to manage primary, secondary, and college education along with basic health units, tehsil, and district hospitals. The staffing of these entities should be drawn from local cadres of staff and supervisory bodies, consisting of government, private sector and communities, and should be responsible for supervision and oversight of these institutions. This will take immense political pressure of transfers from one district to another which occupies so much time of our legislators. At the provincial level, all the higher educational institutions, hospitals, and health institutes should also be supervised by autonomous boards. This may not be the most popular or politically correct viewpoint of Dr Husain but there is no doubt that de-politicisation and de-bureaucratisation of our educational and health institutions would be the greatest service we can render to the public at large.

Dr Husain's fourth ingredient has to do with the organisation of agriculture education, research, extension, and dissemination of new knowledge and techniques among our farmers. The Government of Punjab has been at the forefront in implementing this reform. The government has continued providing seeds, fertilisers, and insecticides to enhance productivity, and at the same time has been encouraging the private sector to take the lead. Leading researchers and experts at agricultural universities of Punjab are being encouraged to develop integrated approaches and synergies between education, research, extension, and dissemination.

The fifth element of the institutional reforms by Dr Husain is segregating overlapping functions, autonomy, and roles of government departments. I believe this reform is important in enhancing the efficiency of our government departments in Punjab. The Government of Punjab is reviewing the terms of reference of each existing department and separating policy, regulatory, and operational responsibilities. Policy formulation, budgeting, and monitoring should continue to be vested in the departments; regulatory functions should be transferred to independent regulatory bodies and operation and implementation to the autonomous bodies, authorities, corporate entities, or other structures fully endowed with adequate powers. The rules of business have already been amended to reflect the new processes.

FACTORS ASSOCIATED WITH THE WEAKNESSES IN PUNJAB'S GROWTH PROCESS

Firstly, Punjab's population has seen a relentless growth. Although, the growth rate has now declined, but due to past rates, the population of Punjab is now 110 million. At this population any size of fiscal effort is going to remain inadequate. This implies that Punjab will have to use its resources carefully, spending in areas that are the responsibility of the government, i.e., are pure public goods. It will have to make spending in such a way that most needy, marginalised, and the disadvantaged are targeted. It will have to weigh in the opportunity cost of continuing to invest in megaprojects versus improving the provision of basic services. Finally, it will have to restore meaningful austerity in governments' own expenditures.

A linked issue to the historic growth in population is the youth bulge faced by Punjab. Out of the 110 million people, 32 million are in the age bracket of 15–29 years. The challenge becomes more serious as 11.52 million people from the age group of 15–24 are considered idle in the economy. This creates a pressure on the government to take strong measures to increase productive employment opportunities. In the economy of Punjab, 90 per cent of the output of goods and services is produced by the private sector. Thus, employment opportunities will have to come from the private sector. The Government of Punjab will be facilitating the private sectors by: (i) reducing the cost of doing business, (ii) increasing the ease of doing business, and (iii) making strategic catalytic investments to trigger private sector-led growth. The government will also look at its procurement policies to ensure more SMEs can benefit from this and are able to contribute more.

Secondly, the top 10 cities of Punjab are rapidly urbanising. Over the last two decades the population sizes of the cities of Lahore, Faisalabad, Gujranwala, etc., have grown by more than 70 per cent. This has increased the pressure on urban facilities and has created a big shortage of houses. However, investments outside of Lahore have been minimal. The government will have to invest to upgrade other emerging cities of the province.

Thirdly, due to the past skewness in public investments, districts in Punjab are sharply segmented in terms of multidimensional poverty. The government will have to invest to bring about regional equalisation.

Fourthly, Punjab, due to its large population, has still not managed to provide adequate facilities and quality of health, education, water, and sanitation services to its citizens. Whereas part of this has been a result of limited resources but it has also been a result of inadequacy of governance. These factors are critical in building a productive human capital for the province. The province intends to tackle these issues on a war footing.

Fifthly, water is becoming a scare commodity in the country and its shortage will be most damaging. The federal government has already initiated a drive to improve water storage by committing to building new dams. However, in the shorter term, water conservation and efficient use can also help Punjab and the country in countering the trends being observed in water recourses. The Punjab government will improve its water courses, promote drip irrigation as compared to flood irrigation, and initiate string awareness campaigns to improve the use of water resources and eliminate wastage.

Sixthly, Punjab will need to emerge as a stronger place to support private sector development. It will have to support its potentially vibrant but, at the moment, depressed SMEs sector and support the integration of Punjab firms in the global value chains at favourable points. Easing regulation and improve enforcement for boosting domestic commerce is also very important. The government must take a strong view in its industrial policy to initiate the process of industrialisation in Punjab. It will have to invest in human resource development and allow for entrepreneurship and IT sector-led growth to fuel the economy.

The key elements underpinning the development of the private sector are the ease and the cost of doing business and the impediments to investment. Accelerating the growth of Punjab's GDP to a sustained rate of 6–6.5 per cent (or higher of 7 per cent as per growth strategy) a year will require a substantial increase in the province's investment rate. Most of the investment in the output-producing sectors will have to come from the private sector. The incentive to invest depends largely on profit, therefore, anything that impedes the investment process or increases the cost of doing business will discourage entrepreneurs from creating productive facilities, irrespective of the nature of business activity.

Finally, Pakistan is signatory to international commitments, such as SDGs and CPEC. These initiatives offer contingent opportunities, yet are inevitable threats, if Punjab does not respond to them appropriately. Hence, the government has developed its strategy that internalise the SDGs and CPEC in the decision-making process.

INSTITUTIONAL REFORMS TO OVERCOME WEAKNESSES IN PUNJAB'S GROWTH PROCESS

Punjab has more than 250 entities that have 40 departments. These departments have associated departments, companies, authorities, agencies, boards, and bodies. So, there is a plethora of institutional arrangements that not only deal with the administrative structure of Punjab but also the services that the Punjab government provides. But, unfortunately, they are not really geared towards generating significant improvement in Punjab's economy. It is pertinent that we bring the focus of these institutions towards economic reforms and economic growth. This would involve not only capacity-building but also a change in the mindset from controlled to development. Key reforms to uplift various sectors of Punjab's economy are the following:

Urban development and the provision of modern infrastructure is the priority of the Government of Punjab. Major initiatives, such as mass transit projects in various cities, Punjab safe cities project, Lahore Knowledge Park, and establishment of solid waste management companies in major cities are starting to have a spill over effect, creating economic activities and enabling growth around the areas of development.

Energy crises had plagued the economy since the past decade. To improve the energy situation, the province has invested significantly in developing the capacity for power generation by exploring solar and renewable sources along with traditional methods. Resultantly, major energy projects in Punjab have been completed with a record speed and efficiency. Moreover, the Government of Punjab is also focusing on providing an enabling environment to attract private sector investment in the energy sector.

The government has placed a much greater focus on agriculture research to address ailments faced by the sector and continues to support reforms, such as productive use of energy by the sector, upgradation of value chains of high value-added products, better land use and environment management, strengthening the Punjab warehouse receipt financing system, supporting the establishment of high-tech mechanisation service centres, and capacitating farmers' cooperatives.

Jobs and competitiveness programmes target improvement in the investment climate and promotion of investment and jobs in more inclusive and sustainable industrial estates in Punjab. On investment climate reforms, the programme supports reforms to reduce the cost and risks of doing business, improve laws affecting labour, in particular to facilitate women's employment, promote PPP's and investments by foreign investors. This also includes support in compliance with GSP + labour conventions. The Government of Punjab, in collaboration with development partners and relevant provincial departments, has embarked upon an ambitious Ease of Doing Business (EODB) Reform Agenda to improve the sub-national doing business performance, business regulations and compliance, trade competitiveness, and investment promotion through various interventions.

For employment and skills development, the Punjab government continues to focus on supporting the youth through Punjab Skills Development Fund, development of technical education and vocational training institutes, better quality employment for low-income groups via Waseela-e-Rozgar and the Punjab Employment Opportunity Programme, self-employment loan schemes for the skills-graduates, and various other scholarship programmes. Punjab is on target on this objective.

For revenue mobilisation, Punjab faces a challenge in terms of an increasing tax gap due to tax policy and administrative shortcomings. To overcome this challenge, the Government of Punjab has developed a draft revenue mobilisation strategy which focuses on both tax and non-tax revenues, for enhanced fiscal space to broaden revenue base, including both tax and non-tax revenue, increased integration/use of IT software and different facilities, enhance efficiency and effectiveness of tax system, and encourage taxpayer's voluntary compliance and increase their satisfaction.

The Government of Punjab is undertaking huge investments in the area to improve its industrial competitiveness, calibrating it with CPEC as well. Annual Plans of Punjab are being developed to support a comprehensive industrial policy, domestic commerce strategy, spatial planning for the industry, developing a long-term engagement strategy with the Chinese, identifying industries of joint ventures and investments, and regulating the industrial space.

The establishment of industrial parks, one of the most important levers for industrial development that is available to Punjab government is the provision of industrial land. Punjab historically has invested in industrial estates, and two new institutions Punjab Industrial Estate Development and Management Company (PIEDMC) and Faisalabad Industrial Estate Development and Management Company (FIEDMC)were set up as a result of the Punjab Industrial Policy 2003. The Punjab Small Industries Corporation (PSIC) has also made significant investments in industrial estates for small and cottage industries. From just 4 large industrial estates in 2007, there are now more than 10 large industrial estates.

Under PGS 2023, we have planned to use spatial mapping to identify key infrastructure gaps in the deprived districts, especially the farm-to-market and connectivity roads, universities, stock of schools and hospitals, technical and vocational centres. These spatial gaps will be used to make targeted infrastructure investments in the deprived districts.

Over the next five years, the Government of Punjab also plans to attain close to 50 per cent colonisation in the already established industrial estates in Vehari, Rahim Yar Khan, and Bahawalpur by developing technical institutes in the industrial estates and creating employment opportunities for the local labour.

Note

1. Our understanding from inclusive development implies high pace of growth accompanied by considerations which include sustainability, employment creation, and poverty reduction.

CHAPTER 8

Towards Shared Growth: Perspectives from Sindh

Naeem Uz Zafar

BACKGROUND AND CONTEXT[1]

Sindh is the second largest economy in Pakistan.[2] Historically, the province's contribution to Pakistan's GDP has been between 30 and 32.7 per cent. Its share in the service sector has ranged from 21 to 27.8 per cent and in the agriculture sector from 21.4 to 27.7 per cent. In the manufacturing sector, Sindh has demonstrated an impressive share, ranging between 36.7 to 46.5 per cent. The manufacturing industries mainly include machine and capital equipment, cement, plastics, chemicals, textiles, and other goods. Agriculture along the Indus River and beyond also provides impetus to the manufacturing industries besides contributing to food security of the country. The main agricultural outputs include: cotton, rice, wheat, sugarcane, dates, bananas, and mangoes. The provincial capital, Karachi, is also the major financial and trade hub partially due to being a seaport city.

Sindh has a unique socioeconomic landscape, it houses Karachi, the biggest city of Pakistan which has various medium- and small-sized towns. This has created a dualistic structure which is a challenge for balanced growth. Barring Karachi, the remaining cities and towns in Sindh are characterised by lack of urban infrastructure, regional connectivity, and industrialisation—which do not augur well for reducing urban migration and progressing on balanced provincial growth. This dualism has led to weaker social outcomes for rural Sindh.

The higher per capita GDP of Sindh was majorly based on the economic activity in Karachi. This continued in the initial four decades after Independence but between the late 1980s and late 1990s geopolitical unrest in Karachi reduced its growth. The poor law and order and continued unrest affected Karachi's status as an investment hub.[3] Poverty levels in Sindh are high. According to Multidimensional Poverty 2015, 43 per cent of Sindh was poor and rural Sindh was 75.5 per cent poor. The province's economy requires growth at 6 to 7 per cent annually to provide 600,000 additional jobs to a young workforce entering the labour market every year. While public expenditure remains a major driver for growth in the province, however, this may not be enough to absorb the entire working-age labour force.

GLIMPSES FROM SINDH'S GROWTH STRATEGY

More recently, the Government of Sindh has been following growth strategy which is grounded in the local context, i.e., geography, regional endowment, infrastructure, economic potential, and socioeconomic disparity of the province. The strategy focuses on the regional sources of growth, strengthens social and economic equity, adopts fiscal measures for resource generation, and uses public-private partnership for improved efficiency and resource generation. It has clarity in prioritising and clubbing sectoral interventions in various regional clusters for a balanced growth of the province. For example, Thar Coal field is planned in conjunction with Keti Bandar Coastal Coal Jetty and Power Park; secondary cities' improvement projects connect divisional headquarters with the surrounding cities for creating an economy of scale; barrage improvement projects are dovetailed with off and on-farm water sector improvement projects; and arid area development put special focus on increasing the green cover and so on.

It is, therefore, crucial that growth strategy should improve secondary cities' liveability by investing in regional connectivity, urban and municipal infrastructure, and economic opportunities in Sindh. To accelerate growth in secondary cities, there is a need to identify growth sources, improve connectivity, integrate agriculture and water, and do climate change mitigation. Secondary cities' improvement projects should also create synergy secondary cities and poverty reduction strategies in the adjoining towns. We discuss some of these areas in detail below.

IRRIGATION, AGRICULTURE, LIVESTOCK, FORESTRY

Waterlogging and salinity, over-exploitation of fresh groundwater, low efficiency in delivery and use, inequitable distribution, unreliable delivery, and insufficient cost recovery are major problems in Sindh. The problem of water scarcity is compounded by water-intensive crops and inefficient irrigation system. The government is investing in the construction of main and branch canals, distributaries, and minors. It is investing in barrages to extend their lives so that the infrastructure may regulate water flow. It is investing in appropriate canal lining to improve water conservation and efficiency. And finally, it is investing in small dams and recharging projects to improve water availability in areas dependent on rainfall.

The Water Sector Improvement Project (WSIP) 2007 was implemented with the overarching objective to improve the efficiency and effectiveness of irrigation water distribution in three Area Water Boards: Ghotki Canal, Nara Canal, and Left Bank Canal. The WSIP is about to reach a successful end but only after paving the way for the Sindh Water and Agriculture Transformation project (SWAT). The major objective of the SWAT is to further augment the canal infrastructure work for the right bank canals of River Indus and climate-smart agriculture in Sindh.

The investment in irrigation led to added water availability, especially in tail areas and increased yield in all major crops of Sindh. According to the Pakistan Bureau of Statistics, Sindh's average wheat yield between 2010 and 2017 was 35.2 mounds/acre compared to the national average of 28.4. Similarly, for rice, sugarcane, and cotton, these numbers were 35.6, 600, 11.7 mounds/acre for Sindh and 23.5, 578, 7.4 for national average, respectively.

The government has invested in agriculture research, agriculture extension, quality seed, agriculture mechanisation, and production of hybrid seed of cotton and sugarcane at the Research Institute Ghotki. In the same way, there is a focus to improve date palm varieties at the Date-Palm Research Institute, Khairpur. The Horticulture Research

Institute is established at Sukkur. In the same way, Tissue Culture Laboratory has been set up in Tando Jam to produce disease-free and high-yielding bananas, and a pesticide-testing laboratory has been established at Tando Jam.

A major reason for the loss in horticulture value is lack of preservation and storage facility of fruits and vegetables. Lack of these facilities forced farmers to accept the dictated prices offered by the middleman. The creation of these facilities would help in achieving a balance between demand and supply of horticulture commodities, thus increasing income transfers to the rural economy. A large focus is also on making the output exportable. Therefore, in Mirpurkhas, an expo centre was established where mango promotion and export exhibition are held every year to increase mango exports.

Livestock is another major source of livelihood in various regions of Sindh, therefore, the government is focusing on establishing cattle colonies, introducing high-yielding 'Boer' goat breed, establishing model veterinary centres in the arid zone of Sindh, establishing Bhambhore dairy village and processing zone for meat animals with public-private participation at district Thatta, establishing mobile artificial insemination and extension service units, tagging livestock for traceability, and boosting exports.

Although the government invested in improving fisheries but the investment gap in this sector is substantial, especially considering the growth potential of this sector. Nevertheless, the major focus of the public sector is to help rehabilitation and renovation of the Karachi Fish Harbour—External Services, improvement of fish and shrimp hatcheries, establishment of fish biodiversity hatchery and a training and extension institute at the Manchar Lake, establishment and upgradation of floating jetties in Sujawal, Thatta, and Badin.

Climate change has already contributed significantly in temperature induced reduction in agriculture and resulting migration which is why Sindh is implementing 'Sarsabz Sindh' project for making the province green and environmentally friendly with a target of planting 100 million trees in the next five years and plantation of one billion trees under the 'Green Pakistan Program' with 50 per cent funding by the Govenrment of Punjab and 50 per cent by the Government of Sindh. In addition to afforestation under provincial and federal projects, mangrove forests have been planted in 50,000 acres in coastal belt.

SECONDARY AND INTERMEDIATE CITIES DEVELOPMENT

The government was fully aware of the dualistic state of development in Sindh and wanted to improve urban facilities in the secondary cities of Sindh. With this aim, in 2008, the government started the Sindh Cities Improvement Program (SCIP)[4] with the help of Asian Development Bank (ADB). The SCIP aimed to improve water supply, wastewater management, and solid waste management (SWM) services in clusters of secondary cities in Sindh.

The master plans or Urban Development Strategies (UDS) for Sukkur and Larkana have been successfully prepared and approved and UDS Sukkur has been formally notified by the Government of Sindh as well. The development master plans for 14 district headquarter towns and one tehsil headquarter are almost complete. The master plan will identify the potential areas of investment for economic as well as social development of these cities and towns. To operationalise the UDS, the provincial government has started working on two cities: Sukkur and Hyderabad. Major areas of intervention include: city planning and institution-building through systems development, municipal management, property tax collection, developing plans for outer growth, redevelopment of inner city markets, decongestion, landscaping, infrastructure overhaul of water, sanitation, inter and intra city communication network, mass transit regional connectivity for Hyderabad and Sukkur, dry port and an international airport for cargo services in Sukkur for improving linkages with agri-products and value chains.

EDUCATION SECTOR REFORMS

The total school enrolment in Sindh is around 4.5 million, of which the enrolment in primary schools was 2.9 million. As many as 1.4 million children in Sindh are studying at private schools, which is 31 per cent of the total enrolment. The major challenge is the high number of out-of-school children and low quality of education. At the end of primary education, only 50.3 per cent of children can read whereas only 21 per cent can solve simple mathematical problems. At the end of secondary education, only 56 per cent can read while only 25 per cent can solve age-appropriate mathematical problem.

Public-private partnership has been streamlined to improve school governance through Education Management Organization (EMO) and Adopt-a-School Program (AASP), Sindh Education Foundation (SEF). The SEF attained breakthrough on the issue of access—enrolment increased from 226,000 to 550,000 (112 per cent). The foundation also achieved significant improvement in the quality of education—this is reflected in the third-party validation, showing 10 per cent point improvement in mathematics, science, and language results.

The government is establishing 106 model schools under Sindh Basic Education Program (SBEP). These schools will not only provide quality education to the community children but will also provide educational and managerial leadership to schools in the neighbourhood. Out of 106 schools, 68 model schools have been established and are run under the EMO framework. These schools are located in the northern districts of Sindh. In a short time, enrolment in these schools has risen to over 35,000. The remaining schools will be made operational in the current fiscal year. Following the success of the model, around 200 such schools are being developed in the southern districts of Sindh. Besides EMO, about 500 schools have been given to the private sector management under AASP.

A similar project is done with the help of the ADB largely in the southern districts. The project has three outputs: construction of 160 to 200 new secondary school blocks and management of these schools under EMO, improvement in the teaching capacity in key subjects of English, mathematics, biology, chemistry, and physics, and strengthening secondary education examination system.

On the college and university front, in the last five years, 53 degree colleges were provided with missing facilities and 86 were rehabilitated and many were upgraded to the degree level. Heavy investment was undertaken in higher education by establishing new universities, new campuses, financing infrastructure, and introducing post-graduate courses. Twenty-five new university campuses have been established, four university colleges for engineering and technology have also been established, 12 state-of-the-art community colleges have been set up through Sukkur Institute of Business Administration, two universities of law have been established, tech centres of robotics, artificial intelligence are under construction, and the Thar Institute of Technology and NED Campus at Tharparkar are being established.

HEALTH SECTOR REFORMS

The devolution brought challenges and opportunities related to the provincial health system. The health system has chronic issues of redundancy, human resource, governance, overloaded tertiary healthcare, and disjointed preventive programmes. The Government of Sindh took a start by creating the required legal and policy framework.

The government began with a prioritised and focused approach and worked on increasing the budgets of big tertiary/specialised healthcare facilities, expanding capacity of tertiary hospitals, creating satellite centres of major facilities, upgradation and improvement of health units, development of tertiary healthcare, increasing the role of public private partnerships in the management of primary and secondary healthcare, and increasing universal health coverage through integrated primary healthcare.

Over the last decade, assistance has been provided to health institutions: National Institute of Cardiovascular Diseases (NICVD), Sindh Institute of Urology and Transplantation (SIUT), National Institute of Child Health (NICH), Indus Hospital, Jacobabad Institute of Medical Sciences (JIMS), Jinnah Postgraduate Medical Centre (JPMC), Gambat Institute of Medical Sciences, and many more. To expand the services for cardiovascular diseases, satellite units of the NICVD have been setup in nine districts (Larkana, Tando Mohammad Khan, Sehwan, Hyderabad, Sukkur, Nawabshah, Mithi, Khairpur, and Lyari). Fully equipped and functional chest pain mobile units have been set up at 10 locations in Karachi to rush people in distress to the NICVD. Renovation, rehabilitation, and addition of TB Hospital (Institute of Chest Disease) at Ojha Campus, Dow University of Health Sciences, Karachi, has been completed. Besides these, health facilities were upgraded at Shaheed Benazir Bhutto Accident Emergency & Trauma Services Complex, PMCH Nawabshah, IMS Gambat, SIUT

Karachi, Chandka Medical College Hospital Larkana, Peoples' Medical College Hospital Nawabshah, Liaquat University Hospital Hyderabad, Abbasi Shaheed Hospital Karachi, JIMS, Syed Abdullah Shah Institute of Medical and Health Sciences Jamshoro. While upgrading these facilities, special attention was given to improved surgical services, gynaecological services, and paediatric services.

To increase healthcare coverage at the district and sub-district level, 10 district headquarter (DHQ) hospitals are being expanded and rehabilitated and 7 taluka headquarter (THQ) hospitals are being upgraded to the level of DHQ hospital. Thirty-nine THQs are being renovated and rehabilitated. This work includes the establishment of 41 accidents-cum-emergency centres. The government is fully aware that investment in health facilities infrastructure will not bear fruit without improved service delivery. And improvement in service delivery requires significant improvement in governance. The government is increasing the role of the private sector in various healthcare system tiers. The government has made a long-term contract with People's Public Health Initiative (PPHI) and various other health management organisations (HMO) for better governance and better service delivery. The health department has made performance-based contracts with HMOs.

The government has endeavoured to reduce fragmentation and consolidate facilities at primary healthcare but a lot needs to be done. There is a strong realisation to consolidate the existing services into a well-coordinated and integrated provincial health, nutrition, and FP system. To achieve this, a comprehensive map of integrated public healthcare services is planned with the help of the World Bank Group. The plan will improve integrated supply side for antenatal care, natal care, post-natal care, new-born resuscitation, child health, nutrition services, family planning, control and management of communicable and non-communicable diseases, basic emergency/first aid, basic laboratory services, and health education at the primary health care level (PHC) level.

Specifically, improvement in the supply side will comprise of the provision of missing services and upgrading of existing services where necessary, functional integration between services to promote referral mechanism and ensure follow-ups, establishing durable relationship between mother-child dyad and services through front-line service provider, including services during pre-conception and to adolescent girls, and to improve human resource development of adolescent girls and young women. On the demand side, the plan will use Conditional Cash Transfers (CCT) for incentivising uptake of continuum of care services (by developing support structure between the community and service providers).

Under performance-based contract management agreements and other health services have also been initiated, such as: Aga Khan Hospital is managing the hepatitis-c diagnostics and treatment services at Shaheed Benazirabad and Larkana divisions. ChildLife Foundation is managing children emergency rooms in 10 government hospitals under a PPP agreement in Karachi, Nawabshah, Larkana, Sukkur, and Jamshoro. Regional Blood Transfusion Centers (RBTC) at Karachi is connected with four hospital-based blood banks at Jamshoro, Sukkur, Larkana, and Nawabshah are being managed under the PPP modality.

As a result of the investments and interventions in healthcare system, service delivery from major tertiary hospitals has improved tremendously and service delivery from PHC has improved significantly as evidenced by recent Pakistan Demographic & Health (PDHS) and Multiple Indicator Cluster Surveys (MICS) data.

ADDRESSING FOOD INSECURITY AND MALNUTRITION

Malnutrition and food insecurity are severe in the southern districts and in districts at the right bank of Indus. Program of Women and Children/Infants Improved Nutrition in Sindh (WINS) was conducted with the help of the European Union in Thatta, Dadu, and Shikarpur. It aimed at improving the nutritional status of children and pregnant and lactating women in Pakistan and strengthen the capacity to address high rates of malnutrition in selected districts of Sindh. Learning from WINS and after its conclusion in 2016, Program for Improved Nutrition in Sindh (PINS) was designed to reduce malnutrition as well as strengthen the system's capacity for quick reduction of malnutrition. The 10 priority focus districts include: Shikarpur, Thatta, Kambar Shahdadkot, Larkana, Dadu,

Jamshoro, Matiari, Sajawal, Tando Allahyar, and Tando Mohammad Khan. Other programmes complimenting this effort include Nutrition Support Program (NSP) and Accelerated Action Plan (AAP) for reducing malnutrition.

FROM SOCIAL SAFETY NET TO INCOME GENERATION

The provincial government started Union Council-Based Poverty Reduction Program (UCBPRP) in 2009 using the World Bank's 'poverty scorecard' tool to target assistance to poor households. The UCBPRP approach has now been replicated by the EU-funded Sindh Union Council and Economic Strengthening Support (SUCCESS) programme, where funds are allocated to Rural Support Organizations (RSPs) to carry out a similar programme of interventions in eight districts. Together the UCBPRP and SUCCESS programmes provide Community-Driven Local Development (CDLD)-based poverty reduction support in a total of 20 rural districts of Sindh.

The two programmes invested heavily in community mobilisation to create social capital of communities. Various schemes of micro-assets, revolving investment fund, community infrastructure, low-cost housing, and health insurance were initiated. The government renamed this programme to People's Poverty Reduction Program (PPRP) in 2018.

From sustained efforts of the PPRP and SUCCESS, the provincial government organised 1.5 million household of rural Sindh, created 13,511 village organisations, and established local support organisations in 672 union councils. Using these communities, almost Rs 3 billion were distributed under Community Investment Fund (CIF) to 235,831 households. Vocational training was provided to 60,000 individuals in different marketable trades and 17,027 houses were built under low-cost housing schemes.

While reduction in community's poverty was heartening, sustainable and substantial poverty decline was still an objective to be achieved. The Government of Sindh developed the Poverty Reduction Strategy (PRS) which focuses on addressing the rural and urban poverty of province in a customised way. The strategy makes the CDLD the foundation for poverty reduction approaches. It goes beyond micro-interventions and the social capital of communities is used to create a meso-level linkage between government and local communities. It is believed that without creating this link, communities will not be able to pull down the available social and economic services community benefit; also, without this link, the participative development process in the selection of development instruments will not take place.

The PRS clearly emphasises that the dimensions of urban and rural poverty are different, therefore, urban poverty requires different interventions to target poverty. The addition of the urban poverty dimension brings an opportunity to review urban/rural connections and create a cohesive approach for the development of the PRS and CDLD.

The strategy identifies: agglomeration as the key to rapid growth of both rural and urban centres—hence, growth centres are seen to be critical in poverty reduction as well, need of a catalytic approach to prioritise sectors and interventions, to reduce risk, create success, and reap maximum sustained benefits, and engagement of communities for sustained ownership of development process.

Broadly, reduction in rural poverty was planned through the development of Rural Growth Centres (RGCs), whereas for urban poverty, a general urban poverty program titled, Urban Income Enhancement Program, was planned. The programme will have key interventions for enterprise development and vocational skills training, targeted at individuals and households where there is viable capacity for employment or enterprise opportunity.

The PRS is planned to be implemented in a pilot project approach. Towns with feasible proximity with several villages are selected as the RGCs. This clustered approach is followed to exploit agglomeration and, thus, the economy of scale to create sustainability and ownership of development process. Two types of strategies are applied on the selected RGC: 'survival strategies' and 'income generating strategies'. Survival strategies are aimed at saving lives and are needed to address adequacy of basic living conditions, including water, sanitation, nutrition, shelter, and health services.

Income generating strategies focus on interventions to either increase household assets or improve chances of employment. Such strategies focus on areas such as increasing productivity and value in selected commodities in rural towns through ownership of the local communities, enterprise development, education, and vocational skills development.

KARACHI TRANSFORMATION STRATEGY

The Government of Sindh, with the help of the World Bank, conducted the Karachi City Diagnostic (KCD) to collect, curate, and present detailed data on the economy, liveability, and key urban infrastructure of the city and to provide an overview of the challenges and opportunities[5] faced by the Karachi Metropolitan Region. The diagnostic also presents requirements to bridge the infrastructure gap and improve the metropolitan region's economic potential.

The KCD led to the development of Karachi Transformation Strategy (KTS). The strategy estimates that Karachi needs around $9 billion to $10 billion in financing over a 10-year period to meet its infrastructure and service-delivery needs in urban transport, water supply and sanitation, and municipal solid waste. Accordingly, major investments have been undertaken to improve urban transport, municipal infrastructure and service delivery, solid waste management, district performance, and urban spaces. It should not go without saying that the importance of these projects increases further in the context of Chinese investment in the Special Economic Zone of Dhabeji. Quite likely, economic and industrial activity in Karachi will increase further with the functioning of this SEZ.

Roads and Urban Transport in Karachi

All urban transport projects were conceived in Karachi Transport Master Plan developed with the help of Japan International Cooperation Agency (JICA) in 2012. The plan comprises of the revival of Bus Rapid Transit (BRTs) of Green line, Blue line, Red line, and Yellow line, joining several residential districts of Karachi with the industrial area and downtown through north-south directions. The BRTs of Orange line, Aqua line, and Silver line will be running east-west. Finally, the plan suggested the revival of Karachi Circular Railway, which connects these

BRTs and literally all districts of Karachi with the airport and city's downtown. Under the transport sector, the government is gradually moving ahead in alignment with the Transport Master Plan[6] for Karachi. The government undertook projects in Karachi for speeding up major rehabilitation work. With these interventions, connectivity between east and central districts of Karachi has greatly improved.

Municipal Infrastructure, Services, and District Performance

To reform and capacitate Karachi Water & Sewerage Board (KWSB), the provincial government has undertaken the Karachi Water & Sewerage Services Improvement Project (KWSSIP) with the help of the World Bank. It is a 10-year project with an investment of $1.6 billion project in the form of a Series of Projects (SOP). First SOP of $105 million is underway whereas the second SOP of around $600 million is being developed. Under these SOPs and from other provincial investments, several schemes for adding water to the KWSB system and for improving the sewer disposal and treatment system are underway.

Solid Waste Management System (SWM)

Investment in sewerage system may go waste without investment in solid waste management. The Government of Sindh constituted a Solid Waste Management Board in 2014 for the collection and disposal of solid waste in Sindh, especially Karachi, but its institutional capacity, waste handling, transportation capacity, and landfill management capacity are weak.

In anticipation of uncertain rain patterns, the provincial government is cleaning up storm water drains. On long-term basis, the government is planning sizeable investment in the SWM of Karachi. Investments are planned for the development of the SWM backbone infrastructure at Jam Chakro dumpsite (with sorting facility and site improvement), development of advanced waste treatment in Dhabeji, construction/upgrading of selected transfer facilities, improving front end collection, and provision of equipment and machinery.

Competitive and Livable City of Karachi Project (CLICK)

Municipal functions are divided among the Karachi Metropolitan Corporation (KMC) (for the entire urban area of Karachi) and six District Municipal Corporations (DMCs). The adjoining rural areas are under the jurisdiction of a separate entity, namely the District Council. While the KMC is a legacy organisation, the six DMCs are fairly new. Moreover, political dynamics and frequent changes in the local government system have hampered the system's ability to provide services in a sustainable way. Just like the KWSB, these organisations are also dependent on provincial expenditure for their operations.

These municipal organisations need to improve their performance and their tax administration and system. To achieve these, the project CLICK is envisaged. It is a $240 million intervention aiming at institutional strengthening and infrastructure financing of local councils in Karachi, overhaul of urban immoveable property tax, and improving the ease of doing business. The project will finance performance-based grants to Karachi local councils so that their management capacity and institution are strengthened.

The Karachi Neighborhood Improvement Project (KNIP) is also being implemented. It is a $98 million project and it aims at enhancing public spaces in targeted neighbourhoods and at improving urban roads infrastructure.

DHABEJI SPECIAL ECONOMIC ZONE

The Dhabeji Special Economic Zone (DSEZ) is a priority project in CPEC which will facilitate potential investors of China and other countries to either start new enterprises or transfer their facilities to Pakistan. The Government of Sindh has earmarked 1,530 acres of land to be developed as DSEZ. The project is targeting investments from businesses in steel foundries, automotive and auto parts, chemical and pharmaceuticals, consumer electronics engineering, textile and garments, warehousing, building material, and fast-moving consumer goods.

Infrastructure for Thar Coal Field

Thar coal fields are spread over an area of 9,000 square km in the desert of Thar. The geological survey has divided this area into 12 blocks, based on available infrastructure and favourable geology. Coal mining and power generation is at various stages in three blocks of the coal field. The limiting factor for exploring coal in this area and subsequently using it for power generation was the absence of connectivity, infrastructure, and water. The government has now invested in over 335 km of road network for the coal field. The country saw transmission of 660 MWs Thar coal-fired electricity to the national grid in April 2019. Other initiatives include the establishment of Islamkot Airport, construction of Water Carrier from Left Bank Outfall Drain (LBOD) Spinal Drain to Nabisar and from Nabisar Reservoir to Thar coalfield block-II, installation of 150 tube wells on solar energy for assured supply of 100 cusecs of water for Thar coal, and Makhi Farsh Link Canal for providing 200 cusecs of water to Block-I power projects.

POWER GENERATION FROM THAR COAL

The three blocks where coal excavation is at different stages are: Block-I, Block-II, and Block-VI and they are included in CPEC. Block-II is at the most advanced stage. Phase-I of Block-II was given to Sindh Engro Coal Mining Company (SECMC), a public-private partnership having 49 per cent stakes of the Government of Sindh. The project was about producing 3.8 million tonnes coal per annum (MTPA) coal and 660 MW of electricity. The project was executed successfully ahead of the scheduled time and now the mine is already supplying 660 MW of electricity to the national grid using that coal. The SECMC has worked on the expansion of Phase-I and to install two more coal-based power plants of 330 MW, thus expanding coal power generation of Phase-I from 660 MW to 1320 MW. At Block-II, the SECMC has completed mine expansion studies for increasing the coal production.

Phase-II expansion will cater to power plants of Lucky Power Company (LPC), Siddiqsons Energy Limited (SPCL), and Bitra Power Company Limited (BPCL). Phase-III expansion will cater to power plants of Arif Habib Group and Liberty Thar Power Limited.

Thar Block-I was awarded to Sino Sindh Resource Limited (SSRL). The sand overburden of 10 million-billion cubic meter (BCM) is already achieved and mining operations are about to commence. It is hoped that coal production and power generation will start in 2021. This block will generate 1,320 MW of electricity.

Thar coal Block-VI is awarded to a joint venture between a British and Chinese firm. The Private Power & Infrastructure Board (PPIB) has approved issuance of letter of intent for 1,320 MW Captive Power Plant (CPP) subject to completion of requirements.

FERTILISER AND DIESEL PRODUCTION FROM THAR COAL

Thar coal can be employed for producing Synthetic Natural Gas (Syngas) or methane, the major input in production of fertiliser. The coal production of two mines of 7.6 MTPA can be employed in a phased manner to first produce 1,320 MW of electricity and then Syngas to produce 2.6 million tonnes of urea per annum. This proposal has already been submitted to the 9th Joint Coordination Committee meeting of CPEC held on November 5, 2019 in Islamabad. This proposal is financially attractive with very low risk, therefore, it makes every sense for two governments, China and Pakistan, to expand their cooperation in coal power generation and urea production, too.

Another strategic employment of Thar coal can be the production of diesel using indigenous coal. Back of an envelope calculation show that coal to liquid plant having a production capacity of 50,000 barrels per day (BPD) cost $5 billion. The required mine size for this production is 7.6 MTPA which roughly costs $1 billion, thus the total investment would be $6 billion. The production of diesel will be 18.25 million BPY. At $66/barrel, the internal rate of the return of project is more than 20 per cent.

KETI BANDAR

The project was recommended for inclusion in CPEC by the Senate in 2015. It is an important part of the government's strategy towards developing the energy sector. Situated 150 km from Karachi, it provides the best growth option for Thar coal and corresponding infrastructure. The proposed project includes construction of 1,320 MW power base on Thar coal and expansion of power generation to 10,000 MW, investment in power evacuation and connecting it to the national transmission lines, laying of a 350 km railway line for the transportation of Thar lignite from Islamkot to Keti Bandar, construction of a coal jetty, and related infrastructure. It is expected that jetty and port will not only facilitate the much-needed expansion of Thar coal mines but will also serve as a platform for future export and import of Pakistan and China.

EASE OF DOING BUSINESS

Pakistan's ranking in doing business index is based on the performance of Karachi and Lahore. Karachi has weightage of 65 per cent in the ranking whereas Lahore is weighted at 35 per cent. The Government of Sindh has worked to reform the regulatory atmosphere for Ease of Doing Business to enhance the ranking of Pakistan. The provincial government's efforts have resulted in improvements across various departments and agencies:

- Sindh Environmental Protection Agency (SEPA) has reduced environmental checklists process from 30 to 15 days.
- Karachi Water & Sewerage Board (KWSB) has reduced time for commercial connections from 61 to 21 days.
- Sindh Building Control Authority (SBCA) has reduced time to grant construction permits from 60 to 30 days.
- 50 per cent records in registries of Karachi digitised; time required to register property in Karachi reduced from 208 days to 17 days—a 92 per cent reduction.

Sindh Business Registration Portal now has links to four provincial departments: Sindh Employees' Social Security Institution (SESSI), Excise and Taxation and federal departments (FBR, NADRA, Securities & Exchange Commission of Pakistan [SECP]) for swift business registration. This integration will enable a potential investor to use the SECP platform and interact with provincial registration authorities and regulators in a seamless way. It will also simplify the procedure, reduce human interface, and improve doing business experience further.

PUBLIC-PRIVATE PARTNERSHIP

PPP Legal and Institutional Framework

The PPP Unit was formed in the year 2008 in the finance department with the technical assistance of the ADB. To provide legal framework and pave the way for institutional development, the Provincial Assembly of Sindh passed the Sindh Public-Private Partnership Bill, 2010 on February 18, 2010. This happens to be the first PPP law in Pakistan.

The PPP Act is an all-encompassing document, which provides legal cover to institutional framework (PPP Policy Board, PPP Unit, and departmental PPP Nodes). The PPP Act regulates the contractual relationship between the public and private sector. The PPP Act also covers processes regarding project approval and spending from Project Development Facility (PDF) fund and Viability Gap Fund (VGF). The Sindh Procurement Rules have been amended for PPP projects with inclusion of a separate section which specifically mentions procurement rules for projects in PPP mode.

As per the organisational framework of the PPP, a policy board was formed which is headed by the Chief Minister Sindh, a PPP Unit was established in the finance department creating a Departmental Public-Private Partnership (DPPP) Node in each agency/department, which seeks to implement a project on PPP basis.

From the very onset, the PPP programme is spread over all sectors of the government whereby many of these sectors are already part of the PPP process and yet more are becoming involved. In terms of activities, these range from the project screening, project design, appraisal mechanism, transaction advisory process, project procurement process, financial close and monitoring and evaluation during the execution phase of the project. Throughout these activities, the PPP Unit is actively involved.

The complex nature of PPP projects and intricate financial and risk structure requires a skill set of professionals from specialised areas, such as corporate/project finance, investment appraisal, corporate/commercial law, and technical field. Over the course of time, the PPP Unit has hired and retained market-based professionals on a contractual basis. It is pertinent to mention here that the Economic Intelligence Unit (EIU) published a report, 'Evaluating the environment for Public Private Partnership in Asia—The 2018 infra-scope' and has ranked PPP Unit Sindh as sixth best in Asia with the overall score of 67 out of 100. The index evaluates the PPP environment across five components: enabling laws and regulations, the institutional framework, maturity, the investment and business climate, and financing. The EIU edition of the Asia Infrascope comprises countries only, however, two exceptions are there, the Gujarat state (India) and Sindh province (Pakistan), which are sub-national governmental entities and which show the importance of subnational government-PPP programmes as potential models of best practices.

One of the most important components of institutional framework is the PPP Node, which were supposed to be formed in those departments of provincial government which seeks to implement PPP project. Accordingly, works and services, transport and mass transit, health, school education and literacy, energy, information and science and technology, and agriculture have formed such PPP Nodes.

PPP Support Facility—New VGF Fund

The PPP Support Facility (PSF) is the company which has been incorporated under Section 42 of The Companies Act, 2017 in December 2017. Its aim is to manage the new Viability Gap Fund (VGF), thereby enhancing corporate governance, transparency to improve the delivery of public infrastructure and social services by achieving better value and improving risk management of the VGF.

The VGF is dedicated for the PPP projects only. The provincial government provides financial assistance in the form of subordinated and concessional loan or through equity participation. The Sindh PPP Unit, since its inception, has undertaken several initiatives in various sectors, including energy, infrastructure, education, and health. In the power sector, the involvement of private sector in Thar coal excavation and power generation is a testimony to the PPP's success in the energy sector in Sindh. In the education sector, the PPPs were seen effective in Education Management Organization and Adopt-a-School Program of the Sindh Education Foundation.

LAW AND ORDER

For a routine business development of a society, maintenance of law and order is the key. Karachi suffered heavily with a severe law and order situation, political rifts, organised crimes, and terrorism. This resulted in low economic activity, uncertainty, and capital flight. It was necessary to restore law and order so that businessmen can plan and invest.

Accordingly, the Government of Sindh undertook various measures to reduce crime in general and heinous crimes, especially. These measures include legislation, equipping law enforcement agencies, working closely with other federal and provincial security agencies. Special emphasis is given to the restoration of law and order and the writ of law in Karachi for obvious reasons. As a result of concerted efforts, fortification of communities has ended, major crimes like ransom, kidnapping, targeted killing, and possessing illegal weapons have gone down exponentially.

Efforts to bring normalcy bore fruit and individuals and business' confidence was restored, leading to improved business, investment, and economic activities. This is obvious from of Sindh government's collaboration with the World Bank for the Karachi Transformation Strategy and subsequent investment of around $2.5 billion in various sectors.

The process of improving law and order from meltdown to restoration would not have happened without a substantial investment in equipment, logistics, surveillance, and human resources. Law and order and safety (including home, police, prisons, rangers, and other security agencies) is the second largest function in terms of resource allocation with a share of 15 per cent in total current revenue expenditure in recent budgets. In addition to this, a forensic lab is being constructed to provide a state-of-the-art centre for Sindh Police to investigate and solve complex crimes, along with intelligence school and data centre for the Sindh Police and anti-terrorism courts have also been modernised.

* * *

The overall economic thought on the development in Sindh owes a lot to Dr Ishrat Husain. He remains a key advocate for devolution of power which in turn provided legal, fiscal, policy, and strategic space for sustainable development and shared prosperity for the province. These ideas have been well articulated in his book, *The Economy of Modern Sindh* published by the Oxford University Press. The Government of Sindh has embarked on a journey to achieve these goals but there is a long way to go. The aforementioned sections sketch a comprehensive approach, but transformation requires strong institutions, transparent operations, and accountability. In this context, a lot more needs to be achieved. Strategic clarity must be complemented with strong institutions if dreams of shared growth are to be realised.

Notes

1. This chapter has benefited from the unpublished research and data by Naheed Durrani, former chairperson, Planning & Development Board, Sindh.
2. Hafiz A. Pasha, 'Growth of the Provincial Economies,' Institute for Policy Reforms, IPR Brief (December 2015).
3. To improve attractiveness of Karachi, there is a requirement to investment in the municipal infrastructure, both in trunk and distribution, solid waste management, urban transport. Besides, there is a need for major regulatory reforms to improve Pakistan's ranking on Ease of Doing Business.
4. 'Report and Recommendation of the President to the Board of Directors,' Asian Development Bank, Project Number: 37220 (November 2008).
5. 'Transforming Karachi into a Livable and Competitive Megacity A City Diagnostic and Transformation Strategy,' World Bank (2018).
6. 'The Study for Karachi Transportation Improvement Project in the Islamic Republic of Pakistan: Final Report Volume-1 (Master Plan)' Karachi Metropolitan Corporation, Japan International Cooperation Agency (December 2021).

CHAPTER 9

Envisioning Inclusive Growth in Balochistan

ABDUL SALAM LODHI

ECONOMIC GROWTH IN BALOCHISTAN

Balochistan, the largest in terms of area, to date remains the least populated and least economically developed province of Pakistan. It covers about 44 per cent of the country with an area of 347, 200 square km, occupying an important geo-strategic location in the context of resource-rich Central Asia.[1] The province has land access from Europe to South Asia and a vital link in the road corridor from Central Asian countries to the Arabian Sea.

The economy of Balochistan is mainly dependent on natural resources, agriculture, and livestock. Natural gas, barytes, coal, marble, chromite, iron ore, quartzite, limestone, and sulphur are the main minerals of the province. However, it is underdeveloped by many standards. In different eras, the province has faced insurgencies that affected the education system and the overall development process gravely. Currently, the insurgencies have been curtailed to some extent, and it is the need of the hour to retain this peace and turn it into economic development and prosperity for the people of Balochistan in particular and for the whole nation in general. This could be achieved through an optimal use of natural resources, evidence-based policy initiatives, provision of quality education accessible to all, financial discipline, and balanced inter-sector and inter-regional development plans. On the utilisation of the natural resources of Balochistan, Dr Ishrat Husain expresses his views:

It is my contention that if the provinces are given control of their natural resources they would exploit these to the optimum level. If, for example, royalties on gas, oil and minerals are granted to the Balochistan government, the rate of exploration and development would be faster as it would be in the interest of the provincial government to remove all hurdles, open up the area and maintain law and order, because the benefits would be internalised. But if they believe that they are getting only a small fraction of the goods and the bulk of the royalties are accruing to the federal government they would not be pushed.[2]

Along with natural resources, agriculture and livestock are the second largest components the economy of Balochistan depends on. At present, only 6 per cent of the total land is under cultivation, mostly in small landholdings. Whereas, 60 per cent of the total cultivated area is under dryland farming and hence in such type of farming most crops give marginal yields.[3] At the same time these crops are important in the subsistence economy of the province. On the other hand, orchards in the upland valleys of the province produce high returns. There are many problems in the agricultural sector of Balochistan that need to be addressed. The most important ones are related to the extensive and inefficient use of pesticides and excessive, often indiscriminate, use of underground water that may be the result of the existing unfair subsidy of electricity for extraction of underground water. However, now farmers are facing problems due to long hours of load-shedding of electricity.

In livestock, people mostly keep small animals and use the vast rangelands for their survival. Rangelands constitute a major area of the province. A majority of the country's livestock can be found in Balochistan, most of which are low in productivity and prone to a variety of diseases and pests. According to the Livestock Census of Pakistan 2006, the percentage share of sheep, camels, goats, cattle, buffalo, and pack animals of the province in the national livestock population was 48.3 per cent, 41.2 per cent, 21.9 per cent, 7.6 per cent, 1.2 per cent, and 11.3 per cent, respectively.[4] Approximately 93 per cent of the total area in the province (34 million hectare) is covered by rangelands and, of that, 21 million hectare is considered medium-to-good grazing land.[5] These rangelands provide the bulk of feed requirements of the animals.

The livestock sector of Balochistan has immense potential to earn foreign exchange through the export of livestock and its products. However, upgradation and innovation are needed in this sector through breed improvement plans and herd farming. Improving goat, sheep, and cattle breeding through artificial insemination can increase livestock production.

There is a need for creating awareness for keeping disease-free herds, germ-plasma improvement, and scientific packaging of dairy products, such as meat, milk, hide, etc. The local nomadic and sedentary community should opt for pasture management through control and rotational grazing and seeding of rangelands with suitable grass species. Trainings and short courses may be organised for livestock-specific small-scale enterprises, such as value chain development of meat, milk, wool, and hides.

On the basis of agro-ecology, the province can be divided into five agro-ecological zones: the upper highlands, lower highlands, plane area, deserts, and costal area. The highlands of the province are characterised by herds of goats and sheep and the periodic movements of nomads and transhumant pastoralists. It is a traditional way of life, full of social, cultural traditions, and characterised by well-known seasonal migratory arrangements among the different agro-ecological zones of Balochistan.

In agriculture, focus should be on the cultivation of high value and low delta crops, such as cotton, *sorghum, jowar,* millet, maize, pulses, and legumes should be promoted. In case of fruit in the highland and northern areas of the province, plantation of almond, grapes, peach, pomegranate, dates, olive, and pistachio should be given priority. Trickle and drip irrigation system should be promoted in these areas. In the southern and coastal areas of Balochistan, palm oil and dates can be produced on a large scale to accomplish the needs of the country and for exporting to other countries. Furthermore, to make agriculture more profitable, the private sector should encourage the installation of fruit-processing plants, such as apple treatment, date-processing, tomato paste manufacturing, fried/dried onion plants, cut-flower and floriculture business, and palm processing. At the same time, several spells of drought make it necessary to repair water resources, such as tube wells, water courses, karees, etc., for agriculture and livestock.

When one talks about the development of the province, with a huge geographic area and spread of population, it is very difficult to develop all areas of the province. In terms of population density, the highest density of population is in Quetta (286/square km), followed by Jaffarabad (177/square km), and Killa Abdullah (112/square km). The social and geographical condition of the province suggests that it would be better to develop growth canters, which can serve as growth stimulus and stimulate growth in the surrounding areas. In this way, the benefits could reach the scattered population. Relatively large urban settlements are rare in the history of Balochistan, particularly in the colonial era, except Quetta, which resulted in low economic activities in the southern part of the country.

The province has two-thirds area of the country's coastline which can be used to promote blue economy. Despite these endowments, Balochistan has the second highest incidence of multidimensional poverty in Pakistan—overall, 71 per cent of the population is multi-dimensionally poor, rural population is 85 per cent and urban population is 38 per cent multidimensionally poor.[6] Furthermore, 45 per cent of the population is illiterate, which include 30 per cent males and 63 per cent females. The literacy rate is low in the rural areas (50 per cent), compared to the urban areas, where it is 68 per cent.[7] Literacy and poverty are interlinked with each other and have positive implications on health preventive measures. The result of a study conducted by Gounder and Zhongwei shows that education has a progressive and significant influence on the tendency of the people to engage in preventive healthcare.[8] Therefore, improvement in literacy indicators will lead to sustainable development of the province. Sectors such as education and health also need special attention in the forthcoming development plans and provincial budgets.

POVERTY ALLEVIATION STRATEGIES

Sustainable industrial development can be used as a key pillar for poverty alleviation in Balochistan. Industrial development could result in the eradication of poverty if the natural resources of the province are used efficiently and effectively to generate income and provide jobs to the rural masses. The efficiency in production, processing, and marketing of mineral products will not only cater to local needs but is likely to increase exports of the country. Poverty alleviation can only be achieved if it focused on sectors where the province has a comparative advantage. Balochistan has a huge potential in mineral mining. At present, there are numerous factors such as outdated mining methods, practices and techniques, and inefficiency that are adversely affecting mineral exploration and development.

The primary aim should be to launch industrial parks and skill development centres where these industrial parks strongly link with the natural resources and raw materials of the area and indigenous entrepreneurial skills. The production hubs should be connected with the local, provincial, national, and export markets. In the past, we had the Harnai Wool Centre, Mustung Wool Centre, Seriab Mill, Lasbela Textile Mill (LTM), Baleli Textile Mill, etc. Now, none of them exists in its original shape.

Balochistan has a lot of potential for the installation of small- and large-scale manufacturing units. Large-scale manufacturing units have become profitable and feasible at the adjoining districts of Khyber Pakhtunkhwa, Punjab, and Sindh. If we analyse the insurgency in Balochistan, one of the main reasons is the dearth of economic activities. It is time to increase the pace of development in Balochistan by starting economic activities along with the provision of quality education. In the absence of industry in the province, the youth is mostly unemployed. For a few public jobs, thousands of applications are submitted which, instead of solving the problem of unemployment, further aggravates it.

Mineral processing plants are needed in the areas where big reservoirs of mineral are present. This will not only increase the tax revenue of the provincial government but also overcome the unemployment problem of the province. These processing units may ensure efficiency and minimise the waste of the mineral resources during mining and/or extraction.

It is a fact that the fisheries and resources of the coastal areas are an important natural resource for food security, growth, and economic development and also a critical capital asset which can help reduce poverty of the coastal communities both through generating income for them and providing food security. The international experience, however, shows that this sector's performance ultimately hinges on better policy frameworks and efficient management systems for sustainable benefits for the fishermen and the fisheries industry and trade as a whole.

Balochistan, has a huge expanse of over 750 km of coastline, having about 8 large landing sites and 30 smaller sites. Furthermore, the province is endowed with enormous opportunities in marine and fisheries which, if explored adequately, can create great benefits for the fishermen communities, besides creating related industry and associated jobs. The bigger landing sites on the coast are at Jiwani, Pishukan, Gwadar, Sur Bandar, Pasni, Ormara, Damb, Kund Malir, and Gaddani. These coastal belts provide ample livelihood opportunities for trade and fisheries. The establishment of tourist points on the vast costal belts of Balochistan can generate revenue for the state. The establishment of research and processing units of aquaculture and fisheries and dates is the need of the hour. The establishment of vocational training centres could help local households in this area to better contribute to productivity activities.

EDUCATION AND LITERACY ENHANCEMENT STRATEGIES

Education is essential for the socioeconomic development of a nation. It plays an important role in human capital formation and accelerates economic growth through knowledge, skills, and creative strength of a society. The positive outcomes of education include reduction in poverty and inequality, improvement in health status, and good governance in the implementation of socioeconomic policies. The multifaceted impact of education makes it an essential element for policy framework, particularly in the countries and regions where literacy rate is low or stagnant.[9] The case of Balochistan province is quite relevant in this regard.

When we talk about access and quality of education the province faces serious challenges. As the province is least developed which is an obstacle in the progress of education and literacy. According to an estimate, out of the 22,000 settlements, only for 10,000 settlements schools are available. A slow growth in enrolments, low survival and transition rates, and wide gender gaps in the attainment of education mean a large number of children remain out of school.[10]

Hence, school participation rates at all levels of schooling are low, especially for girls. Only 20 per cent of women in the province have ever joined school and only 13 per cent have finished primary level or above successfully. The primary net enrolment rate for the province is only 47 per cent compared to the national rate, which is 57 per cent. The participation rate at the middle and secondary level is worse. The net enrolment rates at the middle level for the age groups of 11- and 13-year-old reduces to 23.5 per cent and at secondary level this rate reduces to 12.5 per cent for the age groups of 14 to 15 years. The net enrolment rates for girls at the middle and secondary level are only 13 per cent and 4 per cent, respectively.[11]

Female participation under all educational programmes is very low. Under all literacy strengthening programmes, women's participation should be ensured on a priority basis. Furthermore, a large number of madrasas are operating in Balochistan. The government should subsequently engage with the madrasas for considering the adoption of the national curriculum in their studies.

Public-private partnerships certainly provide a long-term opportunity. However, it should be discouraged for goods and services, the demand for which is highly inelastic, such as education and health. It is unfortunate, particularly in the health and education sector that instead of competition and improvement in the services, there is a gradual deterioration in the public sector service delivery after the induction of the private sector. The public sector schools and colleges are mostly performing less efficiently because of abuse of authority, poor provision of service, and absence of a clear monitoring and evaluation framework.

An intensive analysis of the education system of Balochistan for the last 40 years suggests that inequalities have expanded and created different social classes. The educational system of the country, broadly, can be categorised into religious, Urdu- and English-medium schools. Hence, instead of individual merit, social and economic status is the main criteria for a child to gain admission in these private educational institutions. Therefore, each type of school can be sub-divided into several types based on the quality, teaching materials, and the environment in which they accommodate children of higher, middle, and lower classes.

The religious schools can be sub-divided on the basis of sub-sect, such as Deobandi, Barelvi, Shia, etc. The alarming thing is that these educational institutions (religious and non-religious) are creating different classes in society. This unethical way of progress not only creates obstacles in the way of development but also results in violence and social conflicts among these classes.

Free education for the children of up to 5–14 years of age has been regarded as a basic right given by the state without any discrimination of gender, social, and economic status and with a complete ban on any type of work by children till the age of 14 years. However, efforts are needed to address educational inequalities.

The attainment of education is an important determinant of future educational outcomes for future generations. Hence, it shows that policies concerned with reducing present dropout rates and increasing educational timeframe of children will have positive effects on the overall educational development. The demand for education can also be enhanced through programmes that teach parents the value of schooling. Adult literacy programmes for the uneducated for 30 years of age and above can also help in enhancing school enrolments of children.

If a country is poor due of the lack of skills, then those few who are skilled will manage to earn higher incomes. If such a scenario prolongs, the skilled individuals are likely to become influential and would support policies that would benefit them. In the long run, such a situation can cause inequality in society. This could lead to the loss important human resources in the country. All this can be avoided by a strong intervention of government in the provision of basic education for the masses without any discrimination.

Underprivileged masses in a developed society invest in their future since the direct and indirect costs of education are less than the returns in future. The cost of education is higher for poorer people and there are lesser chances of a prosperous future. Therefore, they are reluctant in sending their children to school. Hence, along with the enforcement of the laws of sending children to school, the underprivileged require subsidies to their income in order to grow.[12]

The solutions are a lot more difficult to describe than the problems. As the numbers for education show that the province is lagging in education and literacy. This situation requires major steps to bring the province at par with other regions of the country. At present, there is one secondary and intermediate board in Balochistan responsible for conducting of secondary and intermediate examinations and announcing of the results, respectively. The board is ensuring a standard examination for both the secondary and intermediate level without any monitoring system of the quality during learning and teaching processes.

There is an absence of a mechanism to check the quality of education in schools below the secondary level. It is suggested that boards should be established at the divisional level for checking the quality of education and ensuring standard examination and monitoring system till the middle levels. Along with the quality of education, these boards should be responsible for the enrolment of children of the area. If these boards could have access to the data of children under five years of age, they would be able to suggest on the required number of schools in each area in the coming years. The data could be easily obtained from the National Database and Registration Authority (NADRA). Hence, these boards, along with the divisional education office, should be responsible for not only ensuring quality of education but also for implementing the Balochistan Compulsory Act 2014. At each divisional level, there should be a competition regarding the quality of education and best schools should be given some benefits and there should be a completion of 100 per cent enrolment target in the districts.

HEALTHCARE FACILITIES

Because of poverty in most rural areas of Balochistan, the majority of people rely on public health facilities. These facilities are very poorly managed. There is evidence that in few district headquarters public hospitals, male doctors are handling gynaecology cases because of the absence of female doctors.[13] The provincial health spending has remained static at around 6 per cent of the total provincial expenditure from 2006 to 2012.[14]

If we look at the health budget, it shows that salaries constitute 75 per cent of the total spending, which leaves little space for other non-salary expenditures. On the other hand, absenteeism is a big issue in the hospitals in rural areas. The doctors who are selected on the seats of the districts after completing their degrees are not willing to serve in their district hospitals. A strong policy intervention is needed in this regard and the composition of health budget needs to be corrected as a large part of this goes to aspects which do not cater to quality in healthcare.

GOVERNANCE ISSUES

The quality of governance plays an important role in enabling an environment for poverty alleviation, growth, and sustainable development. While lack of good governance and public accountability are major issues of the Pakistani economy, however, these problems are more serious in the context of Balochistan's economy. Lack of capacity, combined with the lack of will towards an urgent change, are the most important impediments to sustainable growth and development. In most cases, there is dearth of technical skills and expertise combined with the lack of knowledge at all levels of government and in civil society organisations. Our education systems have failed to develop minds and prepare responsible citizens.

Governance and accountability issues become sever in the areas where a majority of the masses are unaware about their rights. Because of low literacy and awareness, they think abiding by government's laws is not beneficial for them and, at the same time, they are oblivious to the concepts of social accountability.

For a smooth performance of the public sector, all provincial government departments require (provincial) secretaries to head these organisations, having relevant training in the technical portfolio. The problem of frequent transfers and postings of civil servants should also be avoided.

PROMOTING TOURISM

There are a significant number of initiatives that can be taken to create a basic infrastructure for promoting tourism in the province. In the northern areas and the coastal belt of the province, there is potential to attract a significant number of tourists every year. After the 18th Amendment, there are several issues which are undecided at the level of the federal government, such as transfer of tourist information centres in different cities, e.g., Ziarat, Chaman, Khuzdar, and Gwadar. Since the Amendment, the role and responsibilities of the provincial government has increased and it requires more financial and technical support for this sector.

The archaeological sites also need immediate attention from the government. Conservation and gradually rebuilding the historical monuments require relevant skills. These could be a source of revenue generation.

DEVELOPMENT OF INFRASTRUCTURE

Poor infrastructure is perhaps the most severe constraint on growth and economic development—especially for regions like Balochistan where distances have largely determined the history of its development. The government should assign high priority to essential infrastructure that can improve liveability and support businesses. Special focus is required on the condition of road network, housing, energy, water conservation, harnessing flash floods water, water supply, and waste water management.

Under CPEC, the projects of infrastructure, particularly the development of the western route of CPEC, will enhance connectivity and help in developing the deprived and marginalised areas of Balochistan. Under the western route, the projects that are completed, such as the routes of Surab-Hoshab (N-85) and Gwadar-Turbat-Hoshab (M-8), have reduced the travelling time of Quetta to Turbat and Gwadar from 30–36 hours to 10 hours. The parts of the western route—where work is under progress, such as the D. I. Khan to Zhob, Khuzdar to Basima, and dualisation of Quetta to Zhob and Khuzdar-Quetta-Chaman Section (N-25)—will not only play an important role in the connectivity of the marginalised areas of the province with the main cities but also reduce the travelling time.

PARALLEL ECONOMY

Smuggling and informal trade is another big issue of the Balochistan's economy. The province has vast and porous borders with Iran and Afghanistan. At present, this geographical location became a threat to the local industry instead of becoming an opportunity for accelerating trade and generating revenue for the country. Unfortunately, provincial or federal governments do not have any concreate plan of legalising these cross-border trades and generating revenue out of it.

Similarly, according to Sharif, Farooq, and Bashir, a large number of commodities are traded illegally at the Afghanistan-Pakistan and Iran-Pakistan borders.[15] They also found that, in the past, this trade balance was found in favour of Pakistan at the Afghanistan-Pakistan border, whereas there were times when this trade balance was found in favour of Iran at the Pakistan-Iran border. Illegal trade results in a large pecuniary loss to our country in terms of public revenues that could be collected in the form of duties and taxes if these commodities were legally traded at these borders of our country. They also found that a substantial amount is also paid as bribery for keeping such informal trade flows going.

According to a *Business Recorder* report in 2019 by Wasim Iqbal, the government has been facing a revenue leakage of around Rs 60 billion annually only from illegal cross-border trade of petroleum products at the Iran-Pakistan border, which is increasing due to the US sanctions on Iran. Hence, few merchants and officials are getting a lot out of it and these activities are creating governance issues in the province. From the borders on entry points of each district and sub-district, these officials have their check posts to collect fee from the smugglers. At present, it seems that the government, willingly or unwillingly, has failed to control this smuggling. By legalising these trade activities by imposing some laws, tariff, and fees, the government could be able to protect the producers, consumers, wherever needed and also generate revenue.

REVIVAL OF LOCAL GOVERNMENT SYSTEM

The local government provides basic public goods and services at the grassroots level, it is more accessible to the people, and is also responsible for providing physical infrastructure—roads, water supply, waste management—and promotion of public health, education, and environmental sustainability. The local government should ideally ensure a secure and stable environment in which economic development can take place.

There is a strong need for the revival of a local government system that could ensure the availability of basic necessities which are desperately needed not only in the remote cities but also in most district headquarters. According to Gruber, the local spending should be focused on the programmes that have few externalities and relatively low economies of scale, such as local road repair, provision of street lights, garbage collection, and street cleaning.[16] This system can also monitor schools and hospitals at district level very effectively compared to the provincial and federal governments. The local governments could generate revenue on their own if trained properly. On delegation of power at the lower tiers, Dr Ishrat Husain states:

> The country would gain enormously as more and more gas, oil and coal fields, dormant at present, become operational and energy shortages are eased as the national revenue collection increases. The delegation of financial powers to the lower tiers of government, where most services essential to the welfare of the people are offered, would remove the present vertical imbalances and inefficiencies. To sum up, the economic health and vitality of Pakistan and the delivery of services to the citizens are likely to improve if the provinces and districts are given a larger share of the financial and human resources, over-centralisation and personalised decision-making are substituted by institutionalised and delegated processes and a balance is struck between the powers and authority of the federal government, provinces and districts.[17]

ENERGY AND POWER

Balochistan is facing a serious energy crisis even though the province has large reserves of natural gas, coal, and a huge potential for alternative energy production. At present, about 80 per cent of its energy needs are fulfilled through the use of biomass energy—firewood and dung cakes. According to an estimate, every year about two million tonnes of wood are burned to satisfy the energy requirements. That is a serious threat to the environment and scarce forest resources. Supply of piped natural gas is limited to few areas. Whereas, about half of the communities in the province are connected with the national grid for electricity. However, they are suffering from frequent interruptions in service delivery. The provision of infrastructure for the supply of gas and electricity is not economical in far-flung rural areas, therefore, alternative approaches and energy sources need to be sought.

Balochistan is rich in energy resources including oil, gas, renewable energy (solar and wind), and coal, etc. However, the province presents a very unfortunate situation of energy. Solar and wind energy have a lot of potential. According to a study conducted by Nasir, Raza, and Abidi on the potential of wind energy in Balochistan, there are some high potential areas more useful and suitable for the use of wind energy for running windmills and meeting electricity requirements for the scattered population of the province.[18] Projects are needed to utilise these idle resources of the province and to provide benefit in the remote areas. The province has a lot of capability for hydroelectricity generation as well. There are natural places where dams could be built for power generation. The existing Sabakazi Dam and Mirani Dam could also be used to generate power.

Notes

1. 'The Balochistan Conservation Strategy,' IUCN Pakistan and Government of Balochistan (2000).
2. Ishrat Husain, 'A confused federalism,' Dawn, June 21, 2009.
3. 'The Balochistan Conservation Strategy.'
4. 'Pakistan Livestock Census 2006,' Pakistan Bureau of Statistics (2006).
5. Saniya Tahir, 'Degradation of rangeland resources in Balochistan,' Envirocivil, April 26, 2014.
6. 'Balochistan Drought Needs Assessment (BDNA) Report February 2019,' Government of Balochistan (February 2019).
7. 'Labour Force Survey 2017-18 (Annual Report),' Pakistan Bureau of Statistics (2018).

8. Rukmani Gounder and Zhongwei Xing, 'Impact of education and health on poverty reduction: Monetary and non-monetary evidence from Fiji,' *Economic Modelling* 29, no. 3 (2012): 787–794.

9. Abdul Salam Lodhi, *Education, Child Labor and Human Capital Formation in Selected Urban and Rural Settings of Pakistan* (Bern: Peter Lang Publishing, 2013).

10. Abdus Sami Khan, 'Policy Analysis of Education in Balochistan,' UNESCO (2001).

11. 'Balochistan Comprehensive Development Strategy 2013–2020,' Government of Balochistan (2013).

12. William R. Easterly, *The Elusive Quest for Growth: Economists' Adventures and Misadventures in the Tropics Development Research Institute* (MIT Press, 2001).

13. Chief Justice Balochistan High Court's statement published in Urdu daily, *Jang,* December 8, 2019.

14. 'Balochistan Comprehensive Development Strategy 2013–2020.'

15. Muhammad Sharif, Umar Farooq, and Arshed Bashir, 'Illegal Trade of Pakistan with Afghanistan and Iran through Balochistan: Size, Balance and loss to the Public Exchequer,' *International Journal of Agriculture and Biology* 2, no. 3 (2000): 199–203.

16. Jonathan Gruber, *Public Finance and Public Policy*, 3rd ed. (New York: Worth Publishers, 2011).

17. Husain, 'A confused federalism.'

18. S. M. Nasir, S. M. Raza, and S. B. H. Abidi, 'Wind Energy in Balochistan (Pakistan),' *Renewable Energy* 1, no. 3–4 (1991): 523–526.

CHAPTER 10

Envisioning Development in Gilgit-Baltistan

SARANJAM BAIG

INTRODUCTION

> It is the quality, robustness, and responsiveness of social and economic institutions through which the implementation of social and economic policies take place.[1]

Gilgit-Baltistan is, on one hand, rich in natural and mineral resources. It has plentiful freshwater from the glaciers of Himalaya and Karakoram and potential for hydroelectric power generation. A large number of tourists visit the area each year.[2] Expeditions for mountaineering and trophy hunting are on the rise. Yet, on the other hand, Gilgit-Baltistan is behind in most of the social and economic indicators. In this backdrop, it seems imperative to examine the factors that explain the inability of governments to translate and channel the benefits of these reservoirs into economic growth and development. While Dr Ishrat Husain, in his many studies,[3] considers poor quality of institutions and bad governance responsible for low levels of economic growth and development in Pakistan. This chapter is an attempt to relate his work to the fragility of institutions in Gilgit-Baltistan.

Gilgit-Baltistan is a quasi-province in the north of Pakistan. It is endowed with natural beauty, highest peaks, glaciers, freshwater, lakes, and valleys. The region is also home to several cultures and ethnicities. It has been a centre of attention for tourists from around the globe. Moreover, Gilgit-Baltistan is located at a junction of neighbouring countries, including Central Asian countries and China. However, institutional weaknesses and fragility, deteriorating security conditions as well as inadequate infrastructure have been the major constraints in fully tapping its economic potential.[4] Besides its natural attractions, historically, the region has been strategically important, known to be the gateway to Central Asia. Today, being the gateway to CPEC, the region is witnessing improved road infrastructure and better communication systems. Likewise, the revival of peace and stability is yet another by-product of CPEC. All these factors are promoting the economic growth and development in Gilgit-Baltistan. Although, a 'policy window' in the shape of CPEC is open, taking the maximum out of it depends on the institutional capacity in the region. Improvements in infrastructure and communications, revival of peace and stability in the region in particular and in the country in general are fostering tourism in Gilgit-Baltistan. However, sustaining and translating the positive effects of tourism into development, efforts to mitigate the negative effects, and crafting a roadmap to adopt it as a strategy for improving livelihoods crucially depends on the quality of governance and institutions. The slow pace of economic development in the region shows government failures to transform increasing economic opportunities into development. It has been argued that failed institutions lead to various problems faced by the society and economic failures are the ultimate outcome.[5] For instance, Dr Ishrat Husain, in his path-breaking work on governance and institutions,[6] considers good governance a prerequisite for achieving and sustaining economic growth and development in an economy.

Keeping the aforementioned factors in mind, the purpose of the chapter is to explore the effects of institutional fragility on growth and development in the region and to garner some wisdom from Dr Husain's work on governance and institutions and to purpose institutional reforms in Gilgit-Baltistan. At the very outset, it must be noted that no time series data exists for any social and economic indicator in Gilgit-Baltistan. The region has never been included in any national, economic, and social surveys. This data constraint makes comparison of growth and development over time impossible. The discussion in this chapter is based on anecdotes, cross-sectional studies by international organisations, such as the World Bank (WB), the Asian Development Bank (ADB), and observations.

GEO-STRATEGIC AND GEO-ECONOMIC IMPORTANCE: OPPORTUNITIES AND CHALLENGES

At the tri-junction of the Hindukush, Karakoram, and Pamir mountains, Gilgit-Baltistan is situated between the frontiers of India, China, Pakistan, Afghanistan, and Central Asia. Being the gateway to Asia, Gilgit-Baltistan has been the centre of strategic interactions between the British India and Russia. These strategic interactions have been coined as the 'great game' or 'tournament of shadows'. The strategic importance of Gilgit is further evident by the fact that it remained the centre of politico-strategic activities for the British. The British were so concerned about the strategic importance of the region that their army generals did not want it to be a part of India after Partition.[7] History unfolds that even in the nineteenth century, the British and Russia knew the pivotal importance of the region very well.

Historically, the region connected China to the countries in Central Asia and Europe via the ancient Silk Route. With the initiation of the multi-billion investment agreements between China and Pakistan under China's Belt and Road Initiative (BRI), Gilgit-Baltistan is once again in the limelight. Being the gateway to CPEC—a flagship project of the BRI—the geo-strategic and geo-economic importance of the region has increased manifold. According to Ahmed, benefits of investments under CPEC would remain unrealised unless Pakistan moves towards accelerating macro-level reforms to support private enterprise competitiveness.[8] Ahmed further suggests that institutional reforms are crucial to the development and survival of Pakistan's large, small, and medium-sized enterprises.[9] This applies to Gilgit-Baltistan as well. CPEC is a harbinger of opportunities. However, making the opportunities work crucially depends on the institutional reforms.

Yet again, despite being rich in gems and mineral deposits, the lack of a comprehensive and local-friendly minerals policy has been the hiccup in converting economic gains from the minerals into economic development. According to the Government of Gilgit-Baltistan,

the minerals include metallic, non-metallic, energy minerals, precious stones and different rocks of industrial use. The southern areas of this region have substantial deposits of nickel, lead, copper and zircon. In its northern regions, it contains deposits of iron, silver, gold, garnet and topaz. Mining for these minerals is carried out in valleys and along the Indus River. Skardu and Shiger valleys are said to be rich in gold and copper deposits.[10]

Lying at the confluence of the Karakoram, the Hindukush, and the Himalaya Mountain ranges, the region has 27 per cent of the world's glaciers and snow deposits. On one hand, it has been argued that the capacity for hydroelectric generation on the Indus and its tributaries is over 40,000 MW. On the other hand, Gilgit-Baltistan has one of the worst load-shedding in the country. For instance, the Hunza Valley remains in the dark for more than 20 hours a day. It has been further argued that proper management and harnessing of the above potential can generate revenue worth $21 billion (Rs 2,163 billion) per annum. These facts are mentioned in the government documents.[11] If hydropower generation has the capacity to create economic opportunities, the question that remains unanswered is that why is the government not utilising it as a strategy for poverty alleviation and reducing inequality. The answer perhaps lies in Dr Ishrat Husain's argument that:

> The link between institutions and economic and social development is through investment in physical and human capital. Both the efficiency and the volume of investment could depend upon the quality of institutions. The writ of the state, delivery of services, macroeconomic stability, and equitable distribution of benefits can be effectively achieved only if these institutions are functioning effectively.[12]

The economy of Gilgit-Baltistan was dependent on tourism, especially foreign tourism, before the events of 9/11. The tourism industry collapsed after 9/11 and resulted in unemployment that eventually turned the economy into recession. The official figures show that the number of tourists visiting Gilgit-Baltistan has steadily increased over the years, notwithstanding the dip in figures immediately following 9/11.[13] The exponential growth in domestic tourism after 2015 as presented in Table 1 was a manifestation of economic gains in the region. However, Baig, Ahmed Khan, Ali Khan, and Bano suggest the exponential increase in tourism has led to rapid urbanisation that is happening without any planning and approvals.[14] According to their study, unplanned urbanisation has the potential to create risks of social sustainability, economic sustainability, and environmental sustainability as well as political instability. Making economic gains from the recent phenomenon inclusive and sustainable in the region requires planning, which seems to be missing at the moment. Unfortunately, the dysfunctionality of institutions, both at micro and macro level, is the biggest hindrance in making the economic benefits translate into development. Dr Ishrat Husain has very succinctly narrated the impact of dysfunctional institutions, 'It is not a worsening security situation, patterns of foreign assistance, disproportionate defence expenditures, or external economic factors, among other frequently cited explanations, but rather the decay of institutions of governance' that impedes economic growth.[15]

Table 1: Tourist inflow

Total number of tourist inflow (2015-17)			
Year	Domestic	Foreign	Total
2015	200,651	4,082	204,733
2016	439,685	8,813	448,498
2017	781,224	6,112	787,336

Source: Department of Tourism, Government of Gilgit-Baltistan

ECONOMIC GROWTH AND DEVELOPMENT IN GILGIT-BALTISTAN: AN OVERVIEW

It has already been noted that little data on economic and social indicators exists for Gilgit-Baltistan. Most reports on the socioeconomic status of Gilgit-Baltistan are based on data collected by INGOs and is cross-sectional in nature. Major data sources include: Gilgit-Baltistan Economic Report[16] and Multiple Indicator Cluster Survey.[17] The Pakistan Bureau of Statistics (PBS) does not include Gilgit-Baltistan in its national surveys. This leads to an understanding that most of the policymaking in Gilgit-Baltistan is not evidence-based. In an era where evidence-based policymaking is the hallmark of successful governments, lack of mechanisms to collect data and base decisions on it is a manifestation of fragility of institutions.

However, according to the Gilgit-Baltistan Economic Report,[18] there are improvements in various socioeconomic indicators in the decade between 1995 to 2005. The analysis is based on the periodic household economic surveys carried out by the Aga Khan Rural Support Programme (AKRSP). The World Bank reports that the GDP for Gilgit-Baltistan for the fiscal year 2004–2005 was Rs 37 billion in and the per capita income was $600. In contrast, national reports and surveys as presented in Table 2 suggest that the per capita income for Gilgit-Baltistan in 2015–2016 was $350 compared to the national per capital of $1,046. The purchasing power has declined over the last decade for whatsoever reasons, contradicting the expectations shown by the Gilgit-Baltistan Economic Report:

GB accounts for less than 1 per cent of Pakistan's economy, but appears to be growing strongly, with annual per capita income growth of 6.5 per cent between 2001 and 2005, somewhat faster than the national average of approximately 5.3 per cent. This is helping to narrow the gap in its per capita income compared with the rest of Pakistan but it should be noted that there are major variations across GB's districts.[19]

Table 2: Socioeconomic Indicators (2015–2016)

Indicators	GB	National
Population (Millions)	1.8	197
Per capita Income ($)	350	1,046
Literacy Rate (%)	36	56
Poverty rate Headcount ratio	29	21
Multidimensional Poverty Incidence	43	39
Migration Rate (%)	43	25

Source: Economic Survey 2015–2016, Assessment of Socioeconomic indicators in GB, 2005, Population Census 1998 (Annual Plan, Planning Commission and GB Government)

According to the Gilgit-Baltistan Economic Report, growth was driven by the incremental commercialisation of agriculture and economic diversification outside the agricultural sector.[20] The construction of the Karakoram Highway (KKH) played a pivotal role in promoting agri-business in the region. In a similar vein, it is anticipated that the initiation of CPEC will be a harbinger of economic transformation in the region. However, CPEC is not an Aladdin's Lamp. Getting maximum out of CPEC is conditional upon timely planning and preparation, which is lacking on behalf of the decision-makers in the region. Non-farm contribution to the livelihoods is also quite visible.

According to Ismail and Husain,[21] the small and medium enterprises in the region comprise 'flour mills, sawmills, furniture and wood workshops, hydro-power stations, and hotels. The production by these industries is just enough for local needs. The transport sector, having assets worth of Rs 316 million, is the largest sector in trade and commerce in the region. With 34 per cent of the total private sector assets, 'businesses such as automobile workshops, spare-parts shops, service stations, etc.'[22] are part of the transport sector. Similarly, with Rs 144 million worth of assets, general trade is identified as the second largest sector. The trade of goods and services for the consumption of the local economy constitutes the 'general trade sector' in Gilgit-Baltistan. The local populace is entitled a visa-free entry and trade with the autonomous region of Xinjiang. The implications of this policy on the livelihoods in Gilgit-Baltistan are yet to be examined. However, the data available with the customs department reveals low exports to China as compared to imports via the Sost dry port. On one hand, trade with China via Sost dry port has provided employment and income opportunities for hundreds of people. On the other hand, it is creating a competition for the local producers. For instance, the import of fruits and dry-fruits from China is crowding out local producers since Chinese products are cheaper due to the economies of scale. The trade will increase manifold once CPEC is completely operational. However, there's a threat that the local market will be captured by the Chinese imports and, since the economy of Gilgit-Baltistan comprises of micro and small enterprise, uncertainty persists that Multinational Corporations (MNCs) will capture the market, driving micro and small enterprise out of business. At this stage, protecting the rights of the local businesses requires negotiations between the Government of Gilgit-Baltistan and the Government of Xinjiang.

According to a NASSD Background paper,[23] import and export-related trade has the largest share (95 per cent) of private asset holdings within the general trade sector. Whereas trading services and retail trade make 5 per cent and 2 per cent of the general trade sector, respectively.

The agriculture sector is the third largest sector. Despite that, 90 per cent of the population is associated with agriculture and agriculture-related businesses, this sector holds only 13 per cent of the total private assets. No current data is available on the supply and demand of fruits and dried fruits in the region. However, it seems quite obvious that the wastage of fruit is visibly high. As many valleys are still far from the main cities, access to markets is the major determinant of agro-products wastage.

The infrastructure sector is the fourth largest sector that includes 'businesses related to the construction of roads, buildings, and power generation'.[24] Despite having the potential for boosting tourism and using it as a tool for local development and economic growth, this sector holds a meagre 8 per cent of the total private assets. However, being the gateway to CPEC, it is predicted that tourism will improve in the years to come. In 2016, the estimated tourist inflow was around 1 million, according to the government officials. Likewise, the region has a high potential for producing local products, such as 'handicrafts, stone carving, woodcarving, traditional jewellery, traditional textile (wool spinning and weaving), fruit processing (dry fruit products) etc.'[25] Ironically, businesses under this category constitute only 1 per cent of the total private sector asset holdings. Despite having the potential, the mining sector remained unexplored with holdings of a meagre 3 per cent of the total private assets in Gilgit-Baltistan. The opening of CPEC heralds an era of new investments in the mining sector.

Although data for economic indicators is rarely available for Gilgit-Baltistan, cross-sectional survey data on social indicators for recent years is made available by UNICEF. According to the Gilgit-Baltistan Economic Report,[26] the incidence of poverty[27] for the year 2004–2005 was 29 per cent vis-à-vis 24 per cent on the national level. Multidimensional poverty and Human Development Index for various years is reported in Tables 3 and 4, respectively.

Table 3: Multidimensional Poverty in Gilgit-Baltistan (2015)

MPI	Headcount (H)	Intensity (A)	Education	Health	Living Standards
0.209	43.4	48.3	47.7	17.7	35.6

Source: Pakistan Human Development Index Report 2017

However, the latest data released by Multiple Indicator Cluster Survey shows that the headcount ratio (the percentage of poor people) in Gilgit-Baltistan is 34.8 per cent as presented in Table 5.[28] In 2005, poverty in district Gilgit and district Ghanche was 14 per cent and 33 per cent, respectively. However, the incidence of poverty in 2017[29] measured by the headcount method in Gilgit and Ghanche was 17.1 per cent and 24 per cent, respectively. Diamer was reported to have the highest incidence of poverty, while district Hunza has the lowest incidence of poverty.

Table 4: Human Development Index for Gilgit-Baltistan

Year	2007	2011	2013
HDI	0.406	0.426	0.523

Source: Pakistan HDI Report 2017

Table 5 reveals that headcount ratio (H) in GB is 34.8 per cent. The average poverty level among the poor (A), which represents the average share of deprivations faced by every poor person is 51.5 per cent. It yields a value of 0.179 because the Multidimensional Poverty Index (MPI) is the combination of H and A. This means that people in Gilgit-Baltistan who are multidimensionally disadvantaged face 17.9 per cent of the overall deprivations that would be faced if all residents were deprived in all metrics. In urban regions, the percentage of multidimensional poverty is slightly smaller than in rural areas—16.9 per cent and 36.5 per cent, respectively. Between districts, Diamer continues to face the highest rate of multidimensional deprivation led by Shigar (44.8 per cent), and the lowest in Hunza district.

Delving deep into the social indicators reveal that '91.1 per cent children of primary school age are currently enrolled for primary education and 89.3 per cent of all children have completed primary education'.[30] The Gilgit-Baltistan Economic Report claims that literacy rate was 51 per cent for the year 2005.[31] Unavailability and discrepancies in the existing data poses a serious challenge in designing policies based on evidence.

Table 5: Multidimensional Poverty

District	Headcount (H)	Intensity (A)	MPI (H*A)
Astore	34.9	48	0.167
Diamer	74.2	57.8	0.429
Ghanche	24	44.4	0.106
Ghizer	14.3	46.2	0.066
Gilgit	17.1	47.5	0.081
Hunza	2	38	0.008
Kharmang	34	46.1	0.157
Nagar	15.2	42.9	0.065
Shigar	44.8	47.1	0.211
Skardu	36.1	47.7	0.172
Gilgit-Baltistan	34.8	51.5	0.179

Source: Gilgit-Baltistan Multiple Indicator Cluster Survey 2017

Likewise, the infant mortality rate was 122 per thousand live births for 1998–1999, 78 in 2006–2007, 71 in 2012, and 73.5 in 2016–2017.[32] Also, at nearly 3 percentage points, under-five mortality increased from 89 per 1,000 live births to 91.8 per 1,000 live births; the maximum incidence among the 20 to 24-month age group.

PRE- AND POST-PARTITION POLITICAL AND GOVERNANCE STRUCTURE

The modern history of Gilgit-Baltistan starts from 1842 when troops from Kashmir took control of the Gilgit Agency. However, it was Raja Gohar Aman who conquered Gilgit in 1946 and ruled it till his death in 1960. The same year Kashmir restored its rule. From 1879 to 1935, except the years from 1881–1888, Gilgit remained under the dual administration of Kashmir and British India until 1935 when Gilgit

Agency was leased by the British that also brought an end to dual control. However, the British transferred the rule of Gilgit Agency to Dogra Raj in July 1947. Soon after the Indo-Pak Partition, a liberation war was fought by the people of the region that led them to liberation on November 1, 1947. After 15 days of its liberation, the Gilgit Agency announced accession to Pakistan on November 16, 1947.

After 1947, the federal government kept on experimenting with various political and governance packages in Gilgit-Baltistan. Initially, the region was ruled through a junior bureaucrat that Pakistan sent as its representative to Gilgit and remained under the administrative control of the Azad Kashmir government until 1949 when the Karachi Agreement was signed and the administrative control of Gilgit-Baltistan was handed over to Pakistan. The Frontier Tribal Regulation (FTR) was imposed in the region to run the political and administrative affairs. Later in 1969, without giving any legislation and decision-making powers, the NA Advisory Council (NAAC) was established. Likewise, all the princely states in Gilgit-Baltistan as well as the FTR were abolished in the 1970s. The then federal government replaced the FTR with Northern Areas Council Legal Framework Order in 1974–1975. However, this 'Order' also failed to empower the local populace. In 1994, the Pakistan Peoples Party (PPP) government introduced the Northern Areas Legal Framework Order (LFO). This order gave most powers to the federal minister for Kashmir Affairs and the Northern Areas, thus making the de facto ruler of the region. In response to the 1999 decision of the Pakistan Supreme Court to extend fundamental freedom to the region, Pakistan's government delegated additional administrative and financial powers to the Northern Areas Legislative Council (NALC), following minor amendments to the 1994 Legal Framework Order. To appease the local populace, the federal government once again made an incremental change in the LFO in 2007. This time the NALC was graduated into a legislative assembly. The undemocratic nature of this incremental change can be gauged by the fact that the federal minister of Kashmir Affairs was made the de factor ruler as ex-officio Chairman of the Legislative Assembly.

The PPP-led federal government in August 2009 initiated the Gilgit-Baltistan Self-Governance Order Empowerment. Among many features, the Self-Governance Order included the change of the name of the region from Northern Areas to Gilgit-Baltistan, creation of the new offices of the Governor and the Chief Minister, authority to establish Public Service Commission, Election Commission, and the office of the provincial Auditor General. With the Prime Minister of Pakistan as its ex-officio Chairperson, an Upper House as the Gilgit-Baltistan Council was also established comprising 15 members. However, the Governance Order 2009 has not altered the undemocratic nature of the previous orders in any significant manner given the fact that it lacks constitutional integrity.

Many critics have criticised the Order calling it 'political uplifting';[33] 'quasi-formal' Pakistani province,[34] and for the concentration of powers in the Gilgit-Baltistan (GB) Council. In 2018, an attempt was made for the federal government to replace the Governance Order 2009 with another reform package that promised abolishment of the GB Council and transferring of more legislation powers to the provincial assembly. However, it could not be implemented in its true spirit. The federal government of the PTI came up with its own version of the reforms package in 2019. On the intervention of the Supreme Court of Pakistan (SCP), the Order 2019 was retracted for another review.

The SCP observed that: 'Under these circumstances, it is surely a denial of fundamental rights to have the people of GB linger on in legal limbo—deprived of rights simply because they await a future event that may not practically occur within their individual lifetimes.'[35]

In response, in 2020, the federal government came up with a revised version of Governance Order 2009. However, its implementation is still pending while the constitutional limbo continues. The rhetoric by the incumbent governments has been that the provincial government of Gilgit-Baltistan has the authority of legislation on all matters referred to the provinces under the 18th Amendment in the Constitution of Pakistan. The reality seems contradicting. All the revenue-generating subjects are left with the Gilgit-Baltistan Council which is headed by the Prime Minister and almost half of its members are appointed by him. This mechanism leaves the provincial government at the mercy of the federal government for grants—both development and non-development. And since no constituencies exist for members of the parliament, the Gilgit-Baltistan region remains neglected in general.

INSTITUTIONAL FRAGILITY IN GILGIT-BALTISTAN

Dr Ishrat Husain's argument that institutional failures are responsible for failures of the state organs to deliver is in line with the earlier arguments presented by Olson and Onuf[36] and Acemoglu and Robinson.[37] Some of the institutional failures in Gilgit-Baltistan are discussed below.

Constitutional Limbo

On one hand, it has been argued that Gilgit-Baltistan is rich in minerals and natural resources and economically important for both China and Pakistan. On the other hand, per capita income of Gilgit-Baltistan is almost 30 per cent of the national level. What explains this difference? The constitutional limbo that the region is experiencing for the last seven decades has created both opportunities and ambiguities. Opportunities for those who favour the status quo because the status quo has provided opportunities for extraction and rent-seeking. As discussed earlier, Gilgit-Baltistan has been a laboratory of political reform packages. One feature that remained common in all the reform packages is keeping the actual power with the omnipotent bureaucracy by limiting powers of the elected officials.

The absence of democracy and lack of a mechanism for accountability of public officials has created an environment of ineptitude, negligence, and corruption. Due to the constitutional limbo, the region neither gets a share in the National Financial Commission (NFC) Award nor any royalty for the Indus River. Likewise, the lack of clarity on the constitutional status has discouraged foreign investments in the region under the multi-billion CPEC. Taking advantage of Pakistan's stance on Gilgit-Baltistan's political status, India has continuously been opposing funding by international organisations for megaprojects, such as the Diamer-Basha Dam. Dr Husain considers political legitimacy a necessary condition for sustaining economic growth. For instance, he suggests, '[...] economic progress, devoid of political legitimacy—however impressive—may prove to be elusive and transient, and leave no lasting footprints.'[38] Social and economic costs of keeping the region in constitutional limbo for the local populace seem to be quite high. As it is also argued by Acemoglu and

Robinson[39] and echoed in *Governing the Ungovernable* by Husain, 'Nations fail when institutions are "extractive"', protecting the political and economic power of only a small elite that extracts income from everyone else.'[40] The constitutional limbo is benefitting small elite at the cost of the masses.

Institutional Dysfunctionality

As the Gilgit-Baltistan Governance Order 2009 is mum on accountability and transparency procedures, it has created an environment of dysfunctionality and ineptitude in public offices. Dr Husain argues, 'If the access to the institutions of governance for common citizens is difficult, time-consuming, and expensive, the benefits from growth get distributed unevenly, for the gainers are only those who enjoy preferential access to these institutions.'[41] The same seems to be the case with Gilgit-Baltistan where institutions responsible for stimulating economic development are dysfunctional. Take the instance of the CPEC Support Unit (CSU) at the Planning & Development Department, Government of Gilgit-Baltistan. Rather than playing a proactive role in guiding aspirants of start-ups and supporting the investors, CSU is dormant since its inception and even surrenders its budgetary allocation each year. Yet another example is that of the provincial Board of Investment (BOI), which is so ineffective that it could not hire its professional staff since its inception in 2017. As has been argued by many studies, investment is positively correlated with economic growth, the ineffectiveness of the BOI endorses the arguments of Husain, Acemoglu and Robinson, and Olson that bad institutions impede economic growth. Likewise, the dysfunctionality of the GB Council, which has the Prime Minister of Pakistan as its Chairman, is evident by the fact that it could not hold a single meeting since the PTI government came to power. Although, the GB Governance Order 2009 authorises the provincial government to establish provincial public service commission, the failure to do so by the provincial governments in the last 10 years is itself a manifestation of institutional weaknesses.

While dysfunctionality prevails at all the layers of the provincial government, these are just a few examples. When inclusive institutions remain fragile and dysfunctional, it hinders growth and development and the losers are the masses. According to Human Development in South Asia Report (2005) as quoted by Dr Husain:

> Governance constitutes for [ordinary people] a daily struggle for survival and dignity. Ordinary people are too often humiliated at the hands of public institutions. For them, lack of good governance means police brutality, corruption in accessing basic public services, ghost schools, teachers' absenteeism, missing medicines, high cost of and low access to justice, criminalization of politics, and lack of social justice. These are just a few manifestations of the crisis of governance.[42]

MAKING GROWTH INCLUSIVE: WAYS AHEAD

Making growth inclusive for all the segments of society in Gilgit-Baltistan hinges on the government's ability in making institutions of governance inclusive. Wisdom could be garnered by Dr Ishrat Husain's various studies on making institutions work.

Empowering Political Institutions

The unstable political and constitutional status in Gilgit-Baltistan has created confusions and ambiguities. As discussed earlier, a tiny elite is the beneficiary of the status quo, which has promoted self-serving extractive institutions rather than inclusive ones. Acemoglu and Robinson suggest that the differences in the quality of life and prosperity across societies crucially depend on the quality of economic institutions.[43] However, they argue that the economic institutions are the choices made by political institutions. With this in the backdrop, prosperity in Gilgit-Baltistan is subject to making the political institutions inclusive. According to the Human Rights Commission for Pakistan's (HRCP) report, 'the people of GB are nearly unanimous in seeking their territory's recognition as a part of Pakistan, by virtue of their accession to the state in November 1947 and allowed status of a full unit of the federation.'[44] Many existing studies have suggested different political models for solving the constitutional limbo in Gilgit-Baltistan.[45]

The HRCP mission in Gilgit-Baltistan further recommends: 'the dominance of bureaucracy in all the administrative and political affairs of Gilgit-Baltistan needs to be ended. The political representatives of the people of the region need to be empowered so that they deal with the issues that might not otherwise fall under the direct purview of bureaucracy.[46] In other words, the HRCP is, in fact, recommending replacing the extractive institutions with more inclusive ones.

However, past trends imply that the constitutional status quo in the region may not change at least in the foreseeable future. In these circumstances, a more practical solution to political empowerment would be the establishment of a strong local government system and devolution of power at the grassroots level. Dr Husain has also advocated devolution and suggests:

> Devolve powers, responsibilities, and resources for basic public services from the provincial governments to the district governments. A new cadre, a district civil service, should be established on the lines of the provincial and federal civil services.[47]

Promoting Small and Micro Entrepreneurship

The region owns no industries and factories to generate employment for the potential labour force. Given the geography, population, distance from huge markets, and supply of skilled labour, chances are slim that large-scale firms could establish their business in the region. However, in recent years, due to the expansion of the Karakoram Highway under CPEC, there have been increasing opportunities for small and micro entrepreneurship, which should be used to create jobs for the unemployed youth in the region. In this regard, access to finance and borrowings has to be inclusive.

Tourism for Growth and Development

CPEC has been instrumental in attracting domestic tourism. Improvements in communication networks and restoration of peace and stability, as the by-products, have been the major factors behind the record inflow of tourists to the region. CPEC's Long-Term Plan (LTP) outlines that: 'China and Pakistan should further exploit the potential advantages of the tourism resources in the regions along the

CPEC, especially the China-Pakistan border areas.[48] Gilgit-Baltistan is not only the gateway to CPEC but a good chunk of the region lies along territorial alignment of CPEC route from Khunjerab to Chilas. 'CPEC-Tourism' can be leveraged for improving the quality of life in the region. However, the challenge ahead is not merely to increase the number of tourists visiting Gilgit-Baltistan but also to consider how tourism can be better promoted without affecting the natural and cultural heritage of the area, while also improving the quality of life of people to the desired levels.

However, not all the districts in Gilgit-Baltistan are getting similar benefits. Inequality among districts regarding tourist inflow needs to be addressed on a priority basis. Tourists prefer visiting areas with better infrastructure and living facilities. Making the tourists visit neglected districts, which are equally rich in natural attractions, is conditional upon the government's planning. A nuanced tourism policy that provides incentives to tourists to visit under-visited areas and encouraging the investors to invest in hotel/hospitality industry in these areas seems imperative at this stage.

The attention by the government so far has been on holding one-time mega events, such as jeep and bicycle rallies, given the opportunities it provides for enormous rent-seeking. In order to make tourism a tool for inclusive growth and development, Gilgit-Baltistan needs a master plan for the development of its tourism sector. Introducing CPEC-tourism, eco-tourism, tourism for neglected areas, and cultural/heritage tourism can help harness economic growth in the region. Tourist numbers themselves do not reflect improvement in the quality of life in the destination places. Making the numbers translate into prosperity and making them inclusive for segments of society and areas is conditional upon the will and planning. CPEC provides this opportunity.

ICT and Skills for Income Generation

In the fast-digitising world, economies in the underdeveloped region have the opportunity to use ICT as a strategy for employment of the educated youth. Technology will help create self-employment opportunities for the educated youth. It would further let the businesses take advantage of e-commerce and e-business tools. Dr Husain has very succinctly highlighted the importance of acquiring skills and training for income and employment generation.[49] For instance, he argues that:

> We have also remained slack in skills and knowledge development. There is a mismatch between the skills required by the economy and the skills produced by our educational institutions. We are way behind other developing countries in these two aspects.[50]

It is expected that demand for skilled human resource will increase due to the installation of fibre optic under CPEC in the years to come. According to TVET,[51] the region is in short supply of skilled labour. The government has to provide opportunities for technical education on a war footing. Dr Husain has further elaborated that:

> One of the prospective benefits for CPEC projects for Pakistan would be the training and development of skilled manpower. Plans have to be made to assess the long term [sic] manpower requirements, both for construction as well as operational phases of CPEC projects. In light of this assessment, different categories and different levels of training programs have to be designed and then assigned to credible pre-qualified providers. Particular attention should be given to train the youth from the backward districts of the country, starting with Gwadar all the way to the Karakoram Highway.[52]

Hydroelectric Power Generation

Gilgit-Baltistan is endowed with rich natural resources and freshwater which provide vast prospects of hydroelectric power generation. The government of Gilgit-Baltistan must bank on CPEC to produce hydro-electricity. According to one estimate, the region has the capacity to produce 40,000 MWs of hydroelectricity which can generate revenue of $21 billion according to the Government of Gilgit-Baltistan.[53] No investor would be willing to invest in the power industry unless the regional grid is connected to the national grid.

CONCLUSION

Gilgit-Baltistan is rich in natural and mineral resources. It has reservoirs of freshwater from the glaciers. Likewise, it attracts a huge number of visitors each year. Yet, the governments have not shown the resolve to convert these assets into economic growth and development. As a result, the region lags behind the national level in most of the social and economic indicators. The unavailability of authentic data on almost all the socioeconomic indicators is itself a manifestation of fragility of institutions. Discrepancies between different sources exist for the available data even for the same indicators. For instance, one source reports 51 per cent literacy rate for Gilgit-Baltistan for the year 2005 while the other source reports 36 per cent for the year 2015–2016. Likewise, Gilgit-Baltistan has been a laboratory of 'cosmetic' political packages since its independence in 1947 that give rise to extractive institutions. CPEC presents enormous prospects for its inhabitants. However, taking advantage from the opportunities requires institutional reforms. Dr Ishrat Husain has, in his various studies, presented nuanced policy alternatives for making institutions inclusive. Garnering wisdom from his work, this chapter has attempted to explore various opportunities and challenges in harnessing growth and development in Gilgit-Baltistan.

It is suggested that keeping the region in constitutional limbo will strengthen the extractive institutions while benefiting only a small elite. A strong local government system could be an interim solution for empowering the local populace. It will encourage the birth of inclusive institutions. Banking on tourism, efforts to generate hydroelectric power, and enabling the youth to acquire skills will enormously help the region on its path to economic growth and development.

Notes

1. Ishrat Husain, *Governing the Ungovernable: Institutional Reforms for Democratic Governance* (Karachi: Oxford University Press, 2018c), 9.
2. Saranjam Baig, M. Qasim, L. Xuemei, and Khalid Mehmood Alam, 'Is the China-Pakistan Economic Corridor an Opportunity or a Threat for Small and Micro-Entrepreneurs? Empirical Evidence from Northern Pakistan,' *Sustainability* 12, no. 5 (2020): 1727–1746.

3. Ishrat Husain, 'Economic policymaking,' *Dawn*, July 30, 2018a; Ishrat Husain, 'Capacity to reform,' *Dawn*, August 13, 2018b; Ishrat Husain, *Governing the Ungovernable*; Ishrat Husain, 'Policy imperatives for CPEC,' *Dawn*, April 10, 2017; Ishrat Husain, 'Bureaucracy needs reforms,' *Dawn*, January 25, 2014; Ishrat Husain, 'Pakistan's economic turnaround - an untold story,' Pakistan Supplement Global Agenda (Davos: World Economic Forum Annual Meeting, 2005); Ishrat Husain, 'Unleashing entrepreneurship,' UN Secretary General's Report on Unleashing entrepreneurship (Karachi, 2004a); and Ishrat Husain, 'Key Issues in Managing Pakistan's Economy Inaugural Address,' The Lahore Journal of Economics (2004b).
4. Saranjam Baig, 'Policy Considerations for Designing Effective Anti-Corruption Strategies in Pakistan,' *Global Social Sciences Review* 4, no. 2 (2019b): 291–297.
5. Ibid.
6. Husain, *Governing the Ungovernable*.
7. Ehsan Mehmood Khan, 'Constitutional Status of Gilgit Baltistan: An Issue of Human Security,' Margalla Papers (2017); and M. A. Mir, 'Emphatic "No" by AJK for G-B's provincial status,' *The Express Tribune*, January 14, 2016.
8. Vaqar Ahmed, *Pakistan's Agenda for Economic Reforms* (Karachi: Oxford University Press, 2017).
9. Ibid.
10. 'Mineral Sector of Gilgit-Baltistan Region,' Gateway to Gilgit Baltistan.
11. Ibid.
12. Husain, *Governing the Ungovernable*, 10.
13. Department of Tourism, Government of Gilgit-Baltistan.
14. Saranjam Baig, Aftab Ahmed Khan, Amjad Ali Khan, and Salma Bano, 'Rural Tourism, Income, and Rapid Urbanization: Exploring the Nexus using a Multidisciplinary Approach,' *International Journal of Economic and Environmental Geology* 10, no. 4 (2019a): 01–06.
15. Michael Kugelman and Ishrat Husain, 'Pakistan's Institutions: We Know They Matter, But How Can They Work Better?' The Wilson Center (2018).
16. 'Pakistan - Gilgit-Baltistan Economic Report: Broadening the Transformation,' World Bank (2010).
17. 'Gilgit-Baltistan Multiple Indicator Cluster Survey,' GB-MICS, Planning & Development Department Government of Gilgit-Baltistan (2017).
18. 'Pakistan - Gilgit-Baltistan Economic Report.'
19. Ibid.
20. Ibid.
21. Muhammad Ismail and Fazal Husain, 'Fiscal Discretion and its Impact on Pakistan Economy,' *The Pakistan Development Review* 51, no.4 Part II (2003).
22. Ibid.
23. 'Northern Areas Strategy for Sustainable Development,' International Union for Conservation of Nature, NASSD Background paper (2003).
24. Muhammad Ismail and Fazal Husain, 'Fiscal Discretion and its Impact on Pakistan Economy,' *The Pakistan Development Review* 51, no.4 Part II (2003).
25. Ibid.
26. 'Pakistan - Gilgit-Baltistan Economic Report.'

27. It determines what percentage of the population (or households) lives below the poverty line.

28. 'Gilgit-Baltistan Multiple Indicator Cluster Survey.'

29. Ibid.

30. Ibid.

31. 'Pakistan - Gilgit-Baltistan Economic Report.'

32. Ibid.; 'Gilgit-Baltistan Multiple Indicator Cluster Survey'; and Pakistan Demographic and Health Survey (PDHS) (2012–2013).

33. Hermann Kreutzmann, 'Boundaries and space in Gilgit-Baltistan,' *Contemporary South Asia* 23, no. 3 (2015): 276–291.

34. Luv Puri, 'Pakistan's Northern Areas: Time for a Reality Check,' *Economic and Political Weekly* 44, no. 39 (2009): 13–15.

35. Farman Ali, 'Gilgit-Baltistan is a disputed region, declares SC,' *The High Asia Herald*, January 18, 2019.

36. William C. Olson and Nicholas Onuf, *The Growth of a Discipline: Reviewed*, in *International Relations: British and American Perspectives*, ed., Steve Smith (Oxford: Basil Blackwell, 1985), 1–28.

37. Daron Acemoglu and James Robinson, *Why Nations Fail: The Origins of Power, Prosperity, and Poverty* (London: Profile Books, 2012).

38. Husain, *Governing the Ungovernable*, 96.

39. Acemoglu and Robinson, *Why Nations Fail*.

40. Husain, *Governing the Ungovernable*, 15.

41. Ibid., 9.

42. Ibid., 10.

43. Daron Acemoglu and James Robinson, 'The Role of Institutions in Growth and Development,' Commission on Growth and Development, Working Paper No. 10 (World Bank, 2008).

44. 'Gilgit-Baltistan: Aspirations for Identity, Integration & Autonomy,' HRCP (2018).

45. For example, see Khan, 'Constitutional Status of Gilgit Baltistan'; Mir, 'Emphatic "No" by AJK for G-B's provincial status'; and Omar Farooq Zain, 'A Socio-Political Study of Gilgit Baltistan Province,' *Pakistan Journal of Social Sciences (PJSS)* 30, no. 1 (September 2010): 181–190.

46. 'Gilgit-Baltistan: Aspirations for Identity, Integration & Autonomy.'

47. Husain, *Governing the Ungovernable*, 179.

48. 'CPEC To Turn Pak-China Ties Into Long Term Strategic Economic Partnership: Ahsan,' China Pakistan Economic Corridor (CPEC) M/o Planning, Development & Special Initiatives.

49. Husain, 'Unleashing entrepreneurship'; and Husain, 'Economic policymaking.'

50. Husain, 'Unleashing entrepreneurship.'

51. 'Study on Producing Skilled Workforce for Potential Economic Sectors in Gilgit Baltistan,' Deutsche Gesellschaft für. Internationale Zusammenarbeit (GIZ) GmbH, TVET Report (2017).

52. Ishrat Husain, *CPEC & Pakistan Economy: An Appraisal* (Islamabad: Centre of Excellence For CPEC).

53. Investment Potential, Hydro Energy, Gateway to Gilgit Baltistan.

Part

3

FINANCIAL MARKET:
PROSPECTS AND CHALLENGES

CHAPTER 11

The Capital Markets of Pakistan

FAHEEM SARDAR

apital markets have and always will have great significance in the economy of a country. Capital markets will continue to play an important role in development, provided they are used to that effect and are facilitated in that direction. The present-day capital markets in practically every country are very different from their common origins from the 1500s, which are believed to have been in present-day Holland when 'brokers' used to trade government-issued bonds in a presumably abandoned warehouse. Although the capital market of today can only be linked to its history for perhaps nostalgic purposes, the current capital markets still serve the same critical functionalities of providing funding (to the economy, businesses, and government) and liquidity (to the holders of financial assets traded on the capital market). Fast forward to recent times—where capital markets are depicted by fast-moving numbers, media images, graphs, glitzy movies from Hollywood and news of markets going up and down, and much more—the original functionalities still remain at the core.

It is a long debate as to what the main functionalities of a strong capital market actually are, given the large menu of financial products, changing market scenarios, and changing sentiments, but when all is distilled for practical application, the following arise. Stable systemics, ease of asset trade, ease of asset (i.e., scrip/share/product) settlement, ease of financial settlement, and linkage with the banking framework come up as essential components for a strong capital market. The successful interplay of these components brings with it many bounties for the economy, the public, and the government—much of which is in the form of a bustling economy, many new companies coming up and in the lives of the public, heavy but managed traffic, lots of interaction and, needless to say, a large amount of money being made in all quarters and segments of life. The failure of any of these components spells disaster for the market and the public, the opposite of what has just been described, another financial headache for the government.

Pakistan has come a long way in its capital market journey and still has a long way to go in its pursuit of enabling this market to become integrated with other leading markets. Many aspects of what is called a strong capital market have been effectively delved into by Pakistan with a clear focus on best practices and what International Organization of Securities Commissions (IOSCO) advocates as best for the global capital market family but there are aspects that need to be looked at more deeply.

A deeper focus has been applied since 1990s towards international best practices based on what other countries are doing and what international economic and regulatory bodies are advocating. That has led to a better functionality of the capital market in Pakistan with the verticals mentioned above, having been strengthened. Along the way, despite being one of the best markets, not once but a few times, Pakistan has not fully encashed these developments and achievements for reasons that fall in the realm of policy certainty and market transparency. Now, for the capital market, there should be a clear focus on the: (i) simplicity in compliance and (ii) seamless link with banking as essential targets of the future, which have not been efficaciously achieved until now, especially since the global environment has changed and the efficiency and commercial activity of other capital markets have reached stratospheric proportions. In this discussion, there is a specific focus on what role banking has played in the developments so far and what role banking will play in the future, in the strength of Pakistan's capital market.

Banking in Pakistan has had an interesting and long journey. From 1947 to the present, there has been a path that requires a series of conferences to describe it, which cannot be done justice to within a short essay. Nonetheless, as our focus is on the banking developments of the recent past with a specific interest in the effect these developments have had on the capital market, it is important to bring the period from mid/late 1990s to the present into study. There has been evolution in banking in this period, especially the early part, however, from 2000 onwards there has been a sea change. From a banking system that was then relatively primitive, with the clinking of metal tokens, to credit cards that were very difficult to get; to limited consumer finance; to marginal, if any, permeation of financial services in the public to credit methods that were based on static collateral methodology; to the general sluggishness of the banking industry, to all of this linked to the capital market; changes were made at all levels and in all of the mentioned, and more.[1]

These changes brought in better management, a modern system; plastic money being readily available to the public rather than to an esoteric few; to consumer finance being available for the public; to financial products and services becoming part of our daily lives, to the start of fintech; to the possibility of financial inclusion across the country; to the intensification of financial inclusion across the country; to faster settlements, to credit now being based on dynamic collateral assessment bases; to a capital market that is better integrated with all of these. However, we have to pause here for a moment. It is not complete or fulfilling to say that such and such changes were brought in the early 2000s, but it is better to say that the much-needed element of evolution was brought into the banking system of Pakistan, which has now made banking into a solid and exemplary industry in the country, which is evolving on a continuous basis rather than forced spurts.

Dr Ishrat Husain, who was the Governor of the State Bank of Pakistan from December 1999 to December 2005, has greatly contributed to the changes mentioned above, and more importantly, the inclusion or rather splicing of evolution into the banking DNA of Pakistan. His contributions are not limited to the banking industry, which he was focusing on but also the capital market, which is the focus of this chapter, as banking and the capital market had to have, and will always have to have a seamless relation, or rather bond.

Dr Husain helped put this system on the path of the much-needed evolution, streamlined banking, automated processes, improved settlement systems, brought private forces into banking, brought private sector mindedness into banking, brought competitiveness into banking, helped deal with the stock market problems of 2004–2005, among other things. With these changes the capital market experienced some of the highest volumes, highest levels and accolades that it still quotes simply because there was a more efficient banking system supporting it. In the converse flow, banks gained tremendously from the growth in the capital market in the form of higher deposits, higher transactions, service revenue, credit revenue, higher stock market value (of banks), and much more.

In July 2004, Dr Husain explained during one of his speeches:

> [...] it is my endeavour that Pakistan becomes an exporter of financial services first to the Middle East, Central Asia and North Africa and then to the rest of the world. [...] there are a number of steps we have to take. These are:

(a) Develop, attract, retain and motivate high quality skills who can carry out world-class professional work relating to technical, marketing and management of these institutions in third countries.

(b) Acquire core competencies which are needed to compete in an integrated and globalized financial market.

(c) Focus on business areas and niches which allow a competitive edge to our exporters of financial services.

(d) Concentrate on innovation, speed, responsiveness and tailoring to meet the specific customer needs in credit delivery.

(e) Use technology as an enabler to digitally secure product access and service delivery, reduce transaction costs and provide convenience to customers.

(f) Introduce control mechanism for cost structure and operational efficiency.

(g) Build high quality research, market information gathering and analysis capacity to keep in continuous touch with the changing trends and demand patterns.[2]

* * *

The quintessential question here is: where is Pakistan's capital market supposed to be in the next five, ten, thirty, and more years? The author of this chapter, who directly saw and participated in the changes in the capital market in the period mentioned and who used to watch changes happening in the banking industry believes, like many, that the true potential of Pakistan's capital market remains untapped. In the coming years, the capital market should be funding the economy, it should be funding large, medium and small-sized companies, it should be catering to the five million SME's in Pakistan, it should be supporting venture capital functionality, it should be a hub for regional capital concentration and deployment, it should have multiple forms, i.e., many stock exchanges, catering to specific requirements, and above all it should have a very close and seamless relation with its local and international banking networks. The evolution mentioned above is and will remain necessary. The day the capital market and the banking industry move together, true value will be unlocked, for all.

Notes

1. More recently the State Bank has also embarked on reforms which ease injection of foreign capital in the economy. As Vaqar Ahmed ['Who is failing Pakistani startups?' *Arab News*, February 22, 2021] notes, 'a recent publication widely cited in media now recognises how the foreign exchange manual at State Bank of Pakistan (SBP) continued to pose constraints on raising capital for new private enterprises. For decades this has discouraged venture capital, private equity funds, and angels to invest. The collateral issues were never resolved through creative solutions seen in peer economies. Potential investors willing to support startups through a loan with the possibility of later converting this into equity could not be facilitated.'

2. 'Ishrat Husain: Vision for Pakistan's financial service industry,' address by Dr Ishrat Husain, as the chief guest at the ceremony hosted by the BMA Capital and Abraaj Capita, Karachi, July 29, 2004.

CHAPTER 12

Islamic Banking and Finance in Pakistan

AHMED ALI SIDDIQUI

G rowth of Islamic banking and finance has generated considerable interest in the financial world in the last four decades, especially in the last twenty-five years. The concept of Islamic banking has received encouraging response from different corners of the globe as one discovers its ideological dimensions and practical significance. Given its ability to offer diverse and innovative financial solutions—ranging from basic financial needs in under-served markets, especially in the Muslim world, to complex financial requirement of the modern times—it is seen as a socially responsible and ethical financial model with considerable growth potential.

In the Muslim world and increasingly in the Western markets, significant segments of the institutional and retail markets are choosing Islamic finance for their financing and investment needs. The Islamic financial system also draws its strength not only from its asset-based nature and direct linkage to the real economic transactions but also due to avoidance of any element of interest, artificial financial deals, and speculative activity.

Built on the basis of Islamic teachings and philosophy, Islamic economic thoughts accept that every human being needs involvement in some kind of economic activity for survival and it is a legitimate right for individuals to strive and participate in the economy to earn their due share but only by using ways and methods declared permissible in the Islamic commercial law. Driving its fundamental principles from the Divine guidelines, Islamic finance, as an integral component of overall Islamic economic system, aims to provide an ideologically superior model to the modern-day economic problems and aims for the establishment of a just and fair society. The focus of Islamic finance is the well-being of the common people by avoiding exploitation and promoting fair distribution of wealth in society. The central philosophy emerges from the Divine guidelines allowing trade as an alternative of interest or usury.[1]

Thus, at the very onset, Islamic finance tries to promote the idea of real trade, risk-sharing, profit-sharing partnership, and business enterprise. Similarly, Islamic financial institutions are expected to participate in the real economic activities rather than just lending money against interest or usury.

OBJECTIVES OF ISLAMIC BANKING AND FINANCE

The Islamic banking and financial system aim to:

- Establish a fair and equitable financial system based on the principles of Islam that aim to help in the eradication of poverty, hunger, and exploitation, and lead to the establishment of a welfare state for the prosperity of the common people.
- Avoid all transactions that are impermissible as per the teachings of the Holy Quran and Sunnah, including:

  o All types of Riba[2] (including interest, usury)
  o Maysir or gambling-based transaction
  o Transaction involving Gharar or high level of uncertainty[3]
  o Uqood-e-Fasida or legal contracts that are not in line with Islamic law

- Promote genuine economic transaction by participation in real trade and business activities and encourage real asset-based financing.
- Address socially acceptable and ethical (halal) customer needs and promote projects that bring socioeconomic impact and benefit to society in-line with the Maqasid-e-Shariah.
- Provide halal returns to the investors based on the principles of partnership and risk and reward-sharing.
- Encourage financial inclusion and promote access to finance for all segments of society fairly.

- Ensure adherence to Islamic Shariah in all its transactions, dealings, and operations.

Prohibition of Interest in Islam

The main guiding rule for Islamic finance is the prohibition of interest or Riba which is clearly mentioned in the Holy Quran and in several hadiths of the Prophet (PBUH). On several occasions, the Holy Quran has directed the believer about the harms of interest and advised them to avoid it.[4]

Definition and types of Riba[5]

As per Islamic jurisprudence, there are two types of Riba:

1. Riba An Nasiyah is the most common and prevalent form of Riba and it is normally referred as interest or usury. It refers to the excess amount or compensation over the principle in a contract of loan. Most of the modern-day conventional banking and financial transaction involves this type of Riba, thus, considered against the rules of Islamic Shariah.
2. Riba Al Fadl is the second type of Riba and it is that excess which results in exchange of specific homogenous commodities and is encountered in their hand-to-hand purchase and sale. This type of Riba is normally involved in barter transactions and commodity exchange transactions and it is prohibited by the Prophet (PBUH).

UNDERSTANDING THE DIFFERENCE

Islamic banking is a type of financial intermediation based on the principles of trade, investment, and partnership, thus these institutions use different Islamic modes of financing, including partnership, different type of sale, rental, and agency contract. This model of Islamic banks is quite different from the conventional banking model that works as a lending and borrowing institute with interest involved on both sides of the balance sheet. To understand the differences between Islamic financial institutes and the interest-based conventional financial institutes, we find that the differences are at three levels:

1. Conceptual and socio-religious level
2. Business model and governing framework
3. Product-level implementation

Without a clear understanding of these differences, some people, even experts, tend to make a common mistake of equating Islamic banks with other conventional banks with a mere change of name.

Key differences between Islamic Banks and Conventional Interest-based Banks[6]

At Conceptual and Socio-religious Level	
• Islamic banks (IB) are not money-lending institutions but they work as a trading/investment house. • IBs work under the socio-religious guidelines that prohibit charging and paying interest and avoid all impermissible transactions like gambling, speculation, short selling and sale of debts and receivables. • Islamic banks do not permit financing to industries that can cause harm to society or unethical in nature, such as alcohol, tobacco, etc.	• Conventional interest-based banks (CB) are in the business of lending and borrowing money based on interest. • In CB, we see no such restrictions. Interest is the backbone of this system and short sale, sale of debts, and speculative transactions are common. • In CBs, all types of industries are financed, only businesses deemed illegal by the law of the land are not supported.
At Business Model and Governing Framework	
• IB's business model is based on trade, hence they need to actively participate in trade and production process and activities. • IBs have a strong Shariah governing framework in terms of Shariah Advisor and/or Shariah Supervisory Board which approves the transactions and products in light of the Shariah rulings.	• On the other hand, generally, CBs do not involve themselves in trade and business as they act only as a money lender. • In CBs, no such framework is present and it is actually a key litmus test to judge the claim of those who fail to see differences between IBs and CBs.

Product Level Implementation	
• Islamic banking products are usually asset-based and involve trading of assets, renting of fixed asset, and participation in businesses on profit and loss basis. • IBs recognise loan as non-commercial and exclude it from the domain of commercial transaction. Any loan given by IBs must be interest-free.	• CBs treat money as a commodity and lend it against interest as its compensation. • In CBs, almost all the financing and deposit side products are loan-based.

NATURE OF RELATIONSHIP WITH THE CLIENTS IN ISLAMIC BANKING INSTITUTIONS

In a conventional bank, the relationship between the bank and the customer is that of a creditor and debtor and any benefit available to either party usually falls under the ambit of interest since it is a gain on debt/loan. In Islamic banking, the relationship between the bank and the customer differs as per the modes of finance or trade adopted by the parties and the nature of the facility.

- In sale-based transaction modes, Islamic banks and the customer assume the role of 'seller' and 'buyer', respectively, and any benefit available to either party is profit on sale transaction.
- In rental-based modes, the relationship between the Islamic bank and the customer is that of 'lessor' and 'lessee', respectively, and any benefit available to the bank is in the form of rent charged for the usufruct of the underlying asset.
- In participation-based modes, the relationship between the Islamic bank and the customer is that of partnership and the gain is shared by the partners from the actual profit of the business enterprise and the losses if any are shared by the provider of capital.
- In service-based modes, the relationship between the Islamic banks and the customer is of *mustajir* (service provider) and *ajeer* (to whom service is given) respectively, and the Islamic bank gets compensation in the form of *ujrah* (fee or wage).

ISLAMIC BANKING AND FINANCE—GLOBAL GROWTH TRENDS

The global Islamic finance industry crossed the $2 trillion benchmark in 2017 by maintaining consistent growth. During the last twenty-five years, it has created high expectations in the stakeholders and has gained attention of the major players in the financial industry, regulators, and governments. Now, in a majority of jurisdictions, Islamic finance is viewed as a separate segment in the banking and finance industry.

According to the Islamic Financial Services Board Industry Stability Report 2019, and based on the industry experts' estimation, Islamic finance industry is managing assets of over $2.4 trillion as of June 2020. Keen interest in Islamic finance discipline has already extended beyond Islamic countries and, at present, over 120 countries have some type of Islamic financial institutions. Financial institutions from the Middle East, Far East, US, and Europe to Africa and South and Central Asian republics are offering Islamic banking services.

The industry now comprises of over 1,350 Islamic financial institutions, ranging from Islamic commercial banks, Islamic investment banks, Islamic windows at conventional banks, mutual funds, takaful[7] companies, housing finance provider to digital platforms for crowd-funding, and Islamic fintech start-ups.

In terms of sectorial break-up,[8] Islamic banking constitutes over 70 per cent of the Islamic finance industry followed by Islamic capital markets and Sukuk with around 27 per cent share, while takaful share is still below 2 per cent.

Global Sukuk issuance has played a significant role in the establishment of Islamic finance across different jurisdictions. According to the International Islmic Financial Market Sukuk Report 2019, the total issuance of domestic and international Sukuk till date is over $1.1 trillion, with over 7,000 Sukuk transactions being done globally.

Accounting and Auditing Organization of Islamic Financial Institutions (AAOIFI), based in Bahrain, has emerged as the leading standard setting organisation for international financial institutions (IFIs). The body has issued about 100 standards for IFIs, including

Shariah standards, accounting standards, audit standards, and governance and ethics standards. The work done by the AAOIFI is highly commendable, particularly in the domain of creating harmony among different juristic interpretations and development of internally acceptable Shariah standards for different Islamic finance-related modes, contracts, and services.

In addition to the AAOIFI, IFSB, based in Kuala Lumpur, is also playing an important role in guiding central banks and regulators of Islamic financial institutions to develop risk management, governance, and capital adequacy-related standards in their jurisdictions based on the IFSB standard guidelines.

The leading international development finance institutions (DFIs) and multilateral agencies like the World Bank, IMF, ADB, and Basel committee have not only recognised the Islamic finance industry as a separate segment of the financial sector but are now actively involved in the development of this sector, particularly due to the benefits it offers in the under-served markets.

EMERGENCE OF ISLAMIC FINANCE IN PAKISTAN

The establishment of the Islamic Republic of Pakistan in 1947 in the name of Islam is based on the ideology to have a piece of land where Muslims of the subcontinent can freely practice their faith and establish a system of governance and economy based on the teachings of Islam as guided by the Holy Quran and Sunnah of the Holy Prophet (PBUH). The ideology of Pakistan is reflected in the preamble of the 1973 Constitution of the Islamic Republic of Pakistan that states:

> [...] the Muslims shall be enabled to order their lives in the individual and collective spheres in accordance with the teachings and requirements of Islam as set out in the Holy Quran and Sunnah [...]

The desire to have a system of economy, banking, and finance in Pakistan according to the principles of Islam was expressed by Quaid-i-Azam Mohammad Ali Jinnah in his speech on the occasion of the opening ceremony of the State Bank of Pakistan on July 1, 1948:

I shall watch with keenness the work of your Research Organization in evolving banking practices compatible with Islamic ideals of social and economic life. The economic system of the West has created almost insoluble problems for humanity and to many of us it appears that only a miracle can save it from disaster that is now facing the world. It has failed to do justice between man and man and to eradicate friction from the international field. On the contrary, it was largely responsible for the two world wars in the last half century. The Western world, in spite of its advantages of mechanization and industrial efficiency is today in a worse mess than ever before in history. The adoption of Western economic theory and practice will not help us in achieving our goal of creating a happy and contented people. We must work our destiny in our own way and present to the world an economic system based on true Islamic concept of equality of manhood and social justice. We will thereby be fulfilling our mission as Muslims and giving to humanity the message of peace which alone can save it and secure the welfare, happiness and prosperity of mankind.[9]

ELIMINATION OF RIBA AS A CONSTITUTIONAL REQUIREMENT

The establishment of the injunctions of the Holy Quran and the teachings of the Holy Prophet (PBUH) are the driving force of the country's legal framework. Based on this principle, the Section 227 of the Constitution requires that all laws of the country should conform to the guidance provided by the Holy Quran and Sunnah.

All existing laws shall be brought in conformity with the Injunctions of Islam as laid down in the Holy Quran and Sunnah, in this Part referred to as the Injunctions of Islam, and no law shall be enacted which is repugnant to such injunctions.[10]

Moreover, in order to eliminate Riba and interest from the economy of Pakistan, the 1973 Constitution of Pakistan clearly assigns the responsibility on the State for the elimination of Riba at the earliest, thus leaving no ambiguity about this matter. The clause 38-f of the Constitution states: 'The State shall eliminate riba as early as possible.' However, even after the passage of over seventy years of Independence, the state has yet to complete the process of elimination of Riba and this important duty of the state is still incomplete.

EFFORTS TO ISLAMISE THE ECONOMY AND ELIMINATE RIBA IN PAKISTAN

In order to review the efforts for the establishment of Islamic financial system in Pakistan, we can divide the progress and work done into two broad phases:

Phase 1: The Foundation Phase—From Establishment of Pakistan to 2000

This phase covers the era of initial efforts and foundational work for the establishment of Islamic financial system. The efforts for Islamisation of the economy can be traced back to the opening ceremony of the SBP when Jinnah provided a clear direction to the SBP to develop a financial system based on the just and fair principles of Islam. Similarly, the passing of the Objectives Resolution by the Constituent Assembly of Pakistan on March 12, 1949 by the first Prime Minister of Pakistan, Liaquat Ali Khan, laid the foundation stone about the direction of the state in all its future matter. Important work was done by the Council of Islamic Ideology (CII) during this time. The constitutional provisions were added for the elimination of Riba.

During the 1980s, during the Ziaul Haq era, enabling regulations and legal provisions were made in the banking company ordinance (BCO). Modaraba companies were introduced to promote Islamic finance. Experiments were done by several institutions for the introduction of a Riba-free system.

On the legal front, Federal Shariat and Supreme Courts have given historic judgments providing overall guidance for the journey towards Islamic financial system. In 2000, a transformation commission was set up to expedite the efforts toward Islamic financial system with the task forces set up at the ministry of finance and the ministry of law to develop a blueprint and roadmap in this regard. Table 1 highlights the major steps taken at the government level till 2000.

Table 1: List of major steps towards Islamic financial system in Phase 1

1949	Adoption of the Objectives Resolution by the Constitutional Assembly of Pakistan.
1962	Creation of the CII in 1962.
1973	Approval of clauses in the Constitution of Pakistan demanding for elimination of Riba.
1979	Pakistan adopted a policy of gradual transformation of its banking system.
1980	A 15-member committee of the CII prepared a report on the elimination of banking and commercial interest from Pakistan, outlining the Islamic modes of financing.
1980	Modaraba Companies were introduced.
1980/83	Introduction of zakat system/introduction of Ushr system.
1985	Introduction of mark-up-based financing system in banks.
1991	Federal Shariat Court (FSC) declared mark-up procedure un-Islamic.
1999	Shariah Appellate Bench of the Supreme Court rejected all appeals against the previous and called for the establishment of an interest free financial system.
2000	A Commission for Transformation of Financial System (CTFS) was set up at the SBP. • A Task force was set up at Ministry of Finance to suggest ways to eliminate interest from government financial transactions. • Task Force was set up in the Ministry of Law to suggest amendments in the legal framework.

Source: Author's own

Phase 2: Evolution of Practical Models and Framework for Islamic Finance in Pakistan (2001 to present)

During the tenure of Dr Ishrat Husain, the thirteenth governor of the SBP, in 2001, a policy decision was taken to develop a practical and working model of Islamic finance in Pakistan. During this second phase, there was an emergence of a practical model of Islamic banking and Islamic financial institutions, development of workable, and innovative products for key market segments in Pakistan. During this time, major work was done for the development of framework and regulations in the area of banking, insurance, capital markets, mutual funds, takaful, government financing, taxation—thus providing an enabling environment for the Islamic financial sector to cater to the increasing demand of Shariah-compliant and workable financial solutions.

The SBP took the lead to develop a detailed criteria for separate licensing of Islamic banks—a separate department for Islamic banking was formed, the first ever Shariah Board was set up at the SBP, and work began on the development of regulatory framework, governance model. In 2010, the SBP also adopted the strategy for adoption of internationally recognised AAOIFI Shariah Standards in the country as part of Islamic regulations of Islamic banks and Islamic banking windows.

The Institute of Chartered Accountants of Pakistan (ICAP) started the task of developing separate Islamic accounting standards to provide a fair mechanism of recording of transaction done under interest-free modes by Islamic financial institutions.

To develop the Islamic insurance or takaful sector, in 2005, the Securities and Exchange Commission of Pakistan (SECP) allowed takaful companies to set up in Pakistan and a separate set of rules was issued for them.

In 2008, the federal government also started the Sukuk programme—a bold step was taken to convert local and foreign debt from interest-based modes to Shariah-compliant mechanism.

For the development of Islamic equity markets and supporting the operations of Islamic mutual funds, the Karachi Stock Exchange[11] partnered with the Meezan Bank and the Al-Meezan Asset Management to launch the first Shariah-compliant market index known as the KMI-30 in 2008 and later this led to the development of PSX-KMI All Shariah Islamic Index in 2016.

Table 2 highlights the key milestones for the development and transformation toward Islamic financial system done after 2001 in Pakistan by the government, regulators, and industry.

Table 2: A List of Major Steps Towards Islamic Financial System in Phase 2

2001	The SBP developed criteria for issuance of license for Islamic banks.
2002	Meezan Bank established as Pakistan's first Commercial Islamic Bank.
2003	Establishment of Islamic Banking Department at the SBP.
2003	The SBP offered first Musharakah Based Islamic Export Refinance Scheme.
2003	First Shariah Board was established at the SBP.
2005	The SECP issued the Takaful Rules 2005, allowing takaful companies for the first time to start operations in Pakistan.
2005 and 2007	Islamic Accounting standard developed by ICAP were approved by SECP for Murabaha and Ijarah.
2008	The SBP issues instruction and guidelines for Shariah compliance in Islamic banks.
2008	The Government of Pakistan Ijarah Sukuk Programme to finance its needs on Islamic basis.
2008	Pakistan's first Shariah compliant stock market index—KMI 30—was launched by the Meezan Bank and the Karachi Stock Exchange.
2010	Development of the first five-year Strategy Plan for Islamic banking.
2010	The SBP started the Adoption of AAOIFI Shariah Standard in Pakistan as part of its regulatory framework.
2014	The SBP issued Second Strategic Plan for Islamic banking (2014–2018). Formation of Steering Committee for Islamic Banking. Appointment of Deputy Governor for Islamic banking. Re-composition of Shariah Board of SBP headed by Mufti Taqi Usmani.
2015	Shariah Governance Framework for IBIs issued by the SBP. Establishment of a separate Islamic Finance Department SECP. Establishment of three Centres of Excellence in Islamic Finance at Institute of Business Administration (IBA), Karachi, Lahore University of Management Sciences (LUMS), Institute of Management Sciences (IMSciences), Peshawar
2016	All Shares Islamic Index launched at the PSX.

2018	Shariah Governance Regulations 2018, issued by SECP for companies.
2019	First Pakistan Energy Sukuk issued and listed in PSX worth Rs 200 billion.
2020	Second Pakistan Energy Sukuk issued worth Rs 200 billion. The Ministry of Finance has revived and launched an aggressive GOP Sukuk Programme targeting Sukuk issuance of Rs 1 trillion in 12 months.

Source: Author's own

ESTABLISHMENT OF LICENSED-DEDICATED ISLAMIC BANKING INSTITUTIONS IN PAKISTAN

In 2002, Islamic banking was re-launched in Pakistan with the issuance of first dedicated Islamic commercial banking license by the SBP which marked the start of the new era for Islamic finance in Pakistan. The State Bank of Pakistan granted the country's first Islamic banking license to Meezan Bank Limited.[12]

While handing over the license, Dr Ishrat Husain, then Governor of the SBP, told the founding President and CEO of Meezan Bank Limited, Irfan Siddiqui, 'the idea of Islamic banking has failed once in Pakistan; this is the second chance. If it fails this time, it will be very difficult to implement it.'

Meezan Bank Limited, which was formerly the Al Meezan Investment Bank, subsequently acquired the operations of Société Générale in Pakistan and thus, a new journey of Islamic banking started in the country.

GAUGING THE PUBLIC OPINION ON ISLAMIC FINANCE—THE KAP STUDY[13]

In order to gauge the public opinion regarding Islamic finance, the State Bank of Pakistan in collaboration with Department for International Development (DFID) (UK) conducted a large-scale survey, which was named Knowledge, Attitude and Practices (KAP) Study in 2014. According to the study, 94.5 per cent of banked respondents believed in the prohibition of interest, and 88.4 per cent considered that the contemporary practice of interest in banks is prohibited in Islam. Almost 75 per cent of the population with banking relationships expressed a desire to shift to Shariah-compliant banking on a priority basis.

Similarly, the results were not different for non-banked respondents—they are more profound than those of banked respondents. Over 98 per cent non-banked believed in the prohibition of interest while over 93 per cent considered the interest charged and given by banks as prohibited and stated as their prime reason for staying away from the financial sector.

This study not only highlighted the great potential and demand for Islamic financial services but also suggested Islamic finance as a tool for promoting financial inclusion to a large segment of the underserved population of Pakistan. The study also confirmed the previous estimates and surveys behind the growth of Islamic finance in the country. By providing the choice to conduct their financial matter free from Riba resulted in a tremendous growth for Islamic financial institutions in Pakistan and also compelled the conventional finance players to start offering Shariah-compliant financial services to their customers.

GROWTH OF THE ISLAMIC BANKING INDUSTRY— SUCCESSFUL EXPERIENCE FOR PAKISTAN

In Pakistan, Islamic banking gained momentum after its re-launch in 2002 with impressive growth and wider acceptance from the public. The re-launch was not only well received by the masses but also helped millions of people, who were wary of the financial sector due to their religious beliefs, to become part of the financial system and started availing Shariah-compliant financing.

In 2003, the State Bank of Pakistan launched the policy for establishing dedicated Islamic banking institutions as well as stand-alone Islamic banking branches of conventional banks. Very soon, a number of dedicated Islamic banks started their operations in Pakistan, including Dubai Islamic Bank (Pakistan) and Bank Islami in 2005, while Al Barakah Bank also obtained the dedicated Islamic banking license. Similarly, many conventional banks started their Islamic banking windows, including MCB, HBL, and UBL.

During the last ten years from 2010, the Islamic banking sector has recorded impressive growth despite all the challenges and lack of a level-playing field due to strong public demand. The industry was successful in establishing itself as a significant market segment with constant growth of market share and witnessed conversion of customers from conventional banking to Islamic banking.

By December 2020, the market share of Islamic banking institutions stood at 18.3 per cent in terms of deposit and it is expected to grow 30 per cent by the year 2023 with the industry comprising of 22 Islamic banking institutions, including five full-fledged Islamic banks, and 17 conventional banks having Islamic banking operations. The branch network for Islamic banks has also witnessed a sharp growth with now over 3,450 Islamic banking branches country wide serving the customers. In terms of asset, Islamic banks now control around 17 per cent of the total banking assets in Pakistan (See Table 3).

Table 3: Growth of Islamic Banking in Pakistan from 2010 to 2020[14]

Year (As of Dec 31)	Branches/ Sub Branches	Total Deposit	Deposit share in Banking Industry	Total Asset	Asset share in Banking Industry
		(PKR in billion)	(%)	(PKR in billion)	(%)
2010	751	390	7.2%	477	6.7%
2011	886	521	8.4%	641	7.8%
2012	1,097	706	9.7%	837	8.6%
2013	1,304	868	10.4%	1,014	9.6%
2014	1,574	1,070	11.6%	1,259	10.4%
2015	2,075	1,375	13.2%	1,610	11.4%
2016	2,322	1,573	13.3%	1,853	11.7%
2017	2,581	1,885	14.5%	2,272	12.4%
2018	2,851	2,203	15.5%	2,658	13.5%
2019	3,226	2,652	16.6%	3,284	14.9%
2020	3456	3389	18.3%	4269	17.0%

Source: SBP Islamic Banking Bulletins

The growth of Islamic banking, although still on the lower side being a 98 per cent Muslim country, is a great achievement in view of several challenges faced by the industry.

In the area of consumer financing, particularly housing finance and car finance, the Islamic banking sector was able to achieve greater success and now Islamic banks are market leaders for both housing and auto finance. As per the SBP's data in the housing sector, Islamic banks now command over 53 per cent market share. This performance is not surprising, keeping in view the strong public demand and inclination of the masses toward interest-free modes of finance.

ISSUANCE OF GOVERNMENT OF PAKISTAN IJARAH SUKUK

In 2008, the Government of Pakistan decided to start the Shariah-compliant Ijarah Sukuk programme in order to develop alternative to conventional T-bills and PIBs. The Sukuk programme not only helped the government move away a certain portion of Pakistan's internal debt toward Shariah-compliant mode but also helped the Islamic finance industry to have Statutory Liquidity Ratio (SLR)-eligible government instrument for managing mandatory reserve requirement and to invest their excess liquidity. However, the Sukuk programme of the government has seen different ups and downs during the last five years and thus, as a result it has also hampered the growth of Islamic finance in the country.

By June 2020, a total of 22 sovereign Government of Pakistan Ijarah Sukuks were issued with a cumulative worth of Rs 1.058 trillion against various assets, including motorways and Karachi airports. Recently, the ministry of finance has revived the Sukuk programme and has chalked out plans for the issuance of new Sukuk of approx. worth of Rs 1 trillion in the next 12 months. Table 4 summarises the issuance of the Government of Pakistan Domestic Ijarah Sukuk since 2008 to June 2020.

Table 4: Summary of Government of Pakistan Domestic Ijarah Sukuk

Sukuk Issue	Asset	Date of Issue	Date of Maturity	Size (Millions)
GIS-1	M3 Motorway	26 September 2008	26 September 2011	6,523
GIS-2	M3 Motorway	29 December 2008	29 December 2011	6,000
GIS-3	M3 Motorway	11 March 2009	11 March 2012	15,325
GIS-4	M3 Motorway	17 September 2009	17 September 2012	14,396
GIS-5	Jinnah International Airport	15 November 2010	15 November 2013	51,837
GIS-6	Jinnah International Airport	20 December 2010	20 December 2013	37,174
GIS-7	Jinnah International Airport	7 March 2011	7 March 2014	47,540
GIS-8	Jinnah International Airport	16 May 2011	16 May 2014	45,804
GIS-9	M2 Motorway	26 December 2011	21 November 2015	70,269
GIS-10	M2 Motorway	2 March 2012	21 November 2015	38,124
GIS-11	M2 Motorway	30 April 2012	21 November 2015	29,632
GIS-12	M2 Motorway	28 June 2012	21 November 2015	48,766
GIS-13	M2 Motorway	18 September 2012	21 November 2015	47,018
GIS-14	M1 Motorway	28 March 2013	28 March 2016	43,018
GIS-15	M3 Motorway	25 June 2014	25 June 2017	49,537
GIS-16	Jinnah International Airport	18 December 2015	18 December 2018	117,723
GISF-1	Jinnah International Airport	15 February 2016	15 February 2019	116,257

GISF-2	Jinnah International Airport	29 March 2016	29 March 2019	80,400
GISF-3	M1 Motorway	29 June 2017	29 June 2020	71,007
GIS-VRR 17	Jinnah International Airport	30 April 2020	30 April 2025	76.348
GIS-VRR 18	Jinnah International Airport	29 May 2020	29 May2025	74,617
GIS-VRR 19	Jinnah International Airport	24 June 2020	24 June 2025	47,239
22 Issues			Total Values	1,058,282

Source: SBP website and Ministry of Finance, Government of Pakistan

GROWTH OF SHARIAH-COMPLAINT NON-BANKING FINANCIAL INSTITUTIONS (NBFI)

The second important segment of the Islamic finance industry after Islamic banking in Pakistan is the Shariah-compliant Non-Banking Financial Institutions (NBFI) segment, including Islamic mutual funds. The overall NBFI sector in Pakistan comprises of Asset Management Companies (AMCs) operating different mutual and pension funds, Modaraba companies, Real Estate Investment Trust (REIT), leasing companies, investment banks, microfinance companies, private equity funds, venture capital funds, discretionary, and non-discretionary portfolios.

According to the data published by the SECP as on March 2020,[15] the total assets of the NBFI sector stand at Rs 1,298 billion out of which Rs 377 billion is already under the Islamic mode, making the share of Shariah-compliant assets at around 29 per cent of the NBFI sector. Within the NBFI segment in terms of Shariah-compliant assets, the share of Modaraba and the REIT scheme is now at 100 per cent, while Islamic mutual funds are now operating with a market share of 37 per cent of the total mutual fund industry with their asset under management now reached over 256 billion as of March 2020.

Islamic pension funds have also outpaced the conventional pension fund market and with Shariah-complaint pension fund having 63 per cent of the total market share.

Table 5: Overview of the NBFI Sector and Islamic Assets

Sector	Number of Entities	Total Assets (in Billion)	Islamic Assets (in Billion)	% of Islamic
Mutual Funds	216	695.26	256.70	37%
Pension Funds	19	28.09	17.73	63%
Modaraba	28	53.16	53.16	100%
REIT	1	49.55	49.55	100%

Source: Summary of NBFCs, NEs, and Modarabas Sector March 2020 by SECP

These numbers and market share, as per Table 5, present a very encouraging picture for Islamic finance growth in the NBFI segment and also prove that this segment has a significant growth potential and is now well-developed, catering to the needs of the masses.

GROWTH OF TAKAFUL IN PAKISTAN

After the successful introduction of Islamic banking in 2002, the next logical industry to follow is the Islamic insurance or Takaful. In 2005, the SECP issued the Takaful rules and paved the way for the establishment of full-fledged Takaful companies in the General and Family (Life) segment. The SECP also allowed the establishment of Takaful window operations and enabled the existing insurance players in the Pakistani market to start offering Shariah-compliant alternative to the conventional insurance business.

Takaful companies in Pakistan are established on the model of Waqf and Wakalah and offer their services in Shariah-complaint manner by avoiding the impermissible element of gharar, gambling, and Riba present in the conventional insurance product.

As of June 2020, in the non-life segment there are two dedicated Takaful operators: Pak-Qatar General Takaful and Pakistan Takaful.

In addition to the dedicated companies, 19 out of 29 insurance players now have Takaful window operations, including the bigger players like Adamjee, EFU, and NJI with their Shariah-complaint offerings. This shows that gradually with the growth of Islamic banking asset, which is now over Rs 3 trillion, the demand is gearing up for general Takaful and now industry players are responding to this unmet demand.

In the family Takaful segment, there are two dedicated family Takaful operators, including Pak-Qatar Family Takaful and First Dawood Family Takaful while out of seven conventional life insurance companies, four of them, including state-owned State Life Insurance Corporation, have already started offering family Takaful products after obtaining the required license from the SECP.

Table 6: Snapshot of Takaful Players in Pakistan

Total Players (Non-life)	31	Total Players (Life/Family)	9
Dedicated Takaful (Non-life)	2	Dedicated Family Takaful	2
Non-Life Insurance Players	29	Life Insurance Player	7
Total Takaful Windows	19	Life Insurance with Family Takaful Window	4

Source: Security and Exchange Commission of Pakistan

In terms of the market share and net Takaful contribution as compared to the overall insurance market, according to the published data from Insurance Association of Pakistan,[16] the share of Takaful has now reached around 12 per cent of the new policies issued in the country.

THE ESTABLISHMENT OF THE CENTRES OF EXCELLENCE IN ISLAMIC FINANCE

With the fast-paced growth of Islamic finance in the country, one of the main challenges faced by the industry was the availability of trained and skilled human capital that understands the basic concepts, working, and products of Islamic finance. Market players were struggling to acquire trained staff for their operations. The existing staff who switched from the conventional side is being retrained about Islamic finance.

To overcome this challenge, the SBP took the initiative in 2015 to establish Centres for Excellence in Islamic Finance across the country. As a result of this initiative, three centres were established: first at IBA Karachi, second at LUMS, and third at IMSciences, Peshawar. The centres were established with the objective of fulfilling the human resource required by the rapidly growing Islamic banking industry, training of specialised fields within Islamic banking, and conducting research in the field of Islamic banking and finance. After the establishment of these three centres, several other academic institutions across Pakistan also started focusing on imparting Islamic finance education to students to meet the growing demand of Islamic finance in the country.

CHALLENGE FACED BY ISLAMIC FINANCE

The Islamic finance and banking sector still face many challenges and even after decades of successful operation and development of a workable alternative Shariah-compliant financial model, the industry lacks a level-playing environment as compared to the conventional financial industry. The main challenges faced by the industry can be classified as:

Regulatory Issues

In Pakistan, the regulations for Islamic finance are still evolving, the sector needs comprehensive regulation and guidelines by the SBP and SECP for each area of their operations and the ambiguity needs to be removed. The regulations that conflict with Islamic law need to be amended or replaced with Shariah-compliant regulations.

Legal Issues

The industry strongly feels the need of a comprehensive Islamic finance law or act that providse a strong legal cover to Islamic financial institutions, Islamic finance modes, and Shariah governance framework, and to provide clear direction to all stakeholders, including courts of law about the treatment of Islamic finance issues and supremacy of Shariah guidelines for IFIs.

Market Development Issues

The main issue faced by the Islamic finance industry at the operational level is the under development of Islamic money market and Islamic inter-bank market and lack of excess liquidity management instruments and Sukuk as per market demand.

Tax-related Issues

Although tax neutrality has been assured to the Islamic banking sector to a large extent at the federal level, the tax issues related to stamp duty, transfer duties, and tax matters related to specific Islamic modes of finance are still causing problems for the industry players.

Awareness Issues

The awareness of Islamic finance and how Islamic banks, takaful companies, Islamic mutual funds, and other Islamic financial institutions are operating and are Shariah-compliant is still a major challenge for IFIs in Pakistan. A significant segment of society seems to be confused due to dual banking and financial system, use of benchmarks, and lack of clarity at government level about Islamic finance and need to be educated.

RECOMMENDATION FOR ISLAMIC FINANCE

The Islamic finance industry has an immense potential for growth and can contribute to the economic growth of the country by providing a robust and inclusive financial system. Given the right kind of support and level-playing field, Islamic finance can easily reach 50 per cent of market size in the next ten years. It is one of the industries that needs to be supported at all levels for the development of a successful Islamic financial system in Pakistan.

Islamic finance offers a viable alternative to the conventional financial system that is not only against our religious and constitutional requirement but also has created more harm than good to society at large. In order to promote Islamic finance, the following steps are suggested:

- The government needs to accept the strategic importance of the Islamic finance industry and provide wholehearted support to Islamic finance and develop a national policy for the promotion of Islamic finance that not only guarantee a level-playing field for Islamic finance but also provide right incentives to accelerate the growth for the benefit of the economy.
- Comprehensive review of all regulations issued by the SBP and SECP to identify the areas that conflict with Islamic law and their revision with Shariah-compliant regulations.
- Development of Shariah-compliant guidelines for Payment System, FX, trade, and all areas of banking operations and removal of non-Shariah-complaint policies and practices from the SBP regulations, policies, circulars, and notifications.
- The SBP needs to develop and offer Islamic liquidity tools for the Islamic banking sector, including offering of an Islamic finance window, regular Islamic open market operations, and a robust liquidity management framework for IBIs, where Islamic banks could place their excess liquidity.
- The development and launch of Islamic benchmark and development of Islamic monetary policy and fiscal policy guidelines.
- Issuance of a comprehensive Islamic banking act, providing proper legal framework to Islamic banking practices, products, and Shariah governance mechanism.
- The revision of Banking Companies Ordinance 1962 to remove the ambiguity related to dual banking model.
- The revision of Finance Recovery Act to provide separate treatment for Islamic banking modes and clear guidelines for banking courts.
- The revision of Public Debt Act 1944 and regular issuance of regular short-term and long-term Shariah-compliant instrument.
- Establishment of specialised Islamic finance courts.

- The FBR and Provincial Tax authorities to provide tax neutrality for Islamic bank and its customers by amending all required tax laws, particularly related to transfer of property and stamp duties. Moreover, tax incentive to be built for customers opting for Islamic finance to encourage conversion.
- Regular awareness sessions and mass media campaigns at government and institutional levels to educate the masses about the benefits of Islamic finance. The Higher Education Commission (HEC) of Pakistan can support such an academic course for undergraduate students which can enhance awareness.
- To have the right and trained human resource that can contribute to the growth of Islamic finance, introduction of Islamic economics, and finance education at different levels.

* * *

ACKNOWLEDGING THE LEADERSHIP OF DR ISHRAT HUSAIN FOR ISLAMIC FINANCE

The story of success and growth of Islamic finance owes a great deal to the vision and leadership of Dr Ishrat Husain. In 2001, as the Governor of the SBP, he was the person who re-launched Islamic banking in the country and oversaw the development of a robust regulatory framework and also acted as a catalyst for growth. Realising the fact that abrupt change toward Islamic system is not practically possible, he supported the development of workable banking and financial products that can serve the target market in a Shariah-compliant manner. The establishment of a separate Islamic banking department was a right start at the SBP.

During his tenure at IBA as its dean, Dr Husain also worked on the development of Islamic finance in the academic circle. Due to his personal interest, the IBA Centre of Excellence in Islamic Finance (CEIF) was established in 2015, and he is still actively involved with the centre as chairman. Under his leadership, the IBA CEIF has emerged as the regional centre of excellence in Islamic finance by conducting applicative research, providing professional trainings, creating mass awareness of Islamic finance for different segments of society, and offering high-value academic programmes. The centre has provided the much-needed training on various Islamic finance topics to hundreds of industry professionals, regulators, academic, and students. Under his leadership, the centre successfully hosted two World Islamic Finance Forums in 2016 and 2018, respectively.

Dr Husain has also served on several key posts related to Islamic finance, including Advisor to the President of Islamic Development Bank, Jeddah; Chairman AAOIFI Governance & Ethics Board, Bahrain; Member Board of Trustee Islamic Research & Training Institute (IRTI), Jeddah, and has contributed at the international level to the growth of Islamic finance. His vision is to see at least 50 per cent of Pakistan's financial system converted into Islamic finance in the next ten years.

In his last role as ECC member, Dr Ishrat Husain played an instrumental role in the issuance of Pakistan Energy Sukuk worth Rs 400 billion and the revival of the Government of Pakistan Ijarah Sukuk programme. His services for Islamic finance are well recognised by the industry and academia and he has received numerous awards globally as well as a lifetime achievement award for his services for Islamic finance.

Notes

1. See Surah Al Baqarah, 275: 'Those who devour usury will not stand except as stand one whom the Evil one by his touch Hath driven to madness. That is because they say: "Trade is like usury," but Allah hath permitted trade and forbidden usury. Those who after receiving direction from their Lord, desist, shall be pardoned for the past; their case is for Allah (to judge); but those who repeat (The offence) are companions of the Fire: They will abide therein (for ever).' *The Holy Quran*, English translation by Abdullah Yusuf Ali.
2. Types of Riba include Riba Al Nase'ah (excess over loan) and Riba Al Fadhl (excess in sale of homogenous commodities).
3. Like short sale or sale without identification of subject matter of sale.
4. See note 1 above for the prohibition mentioned in Surah Al Baqarah, 275. The Holy Quran further advises the believers to leave all matters related to the dealing of Riba and declared it as an act of War with Allah and the Prophet (PBUH)—'O ye who believe! Fear Allah, and give up what remains of your demand for usury, if ye are indeed believers' (2: 278); 'If ye do it not, Take notice of war from Allah and His Messenger: But if ye turn back, ye shall have your capital sums: Deal not unjustly, and ye shall not be dealt with unjustly' (2: 279).

Similarly, a number of sayings of the Prophet (PBUH) advised the Muslims to keep away from the matter involving Riba and interest in their financial matters. According to Sahih Muslim 1598, Book 22, Hadith 132: 'Jabir said that Allah's Messenger (PBUH) cursed the accepter of interest and its payer, and one who records it, and the two witnesses, and he said: They are all equal.'

5. Muhammad Imran Ashraf Usmani, *Meezan Bank's Guide to Islamic Banking* (Darul Ishaat, 2007).

6. Muhammad Imran Ashraf Usmani, *Islamic Finance* (Maktaba Maariful Quran, April 2015).

7. Islamic Insurance.

8. 'IFSB Industry Stability Report 2019,' Islamic Financial Services Board.

9. 'Quaid-i-Azam's Speech on the occasion of the Opening Ceremony of the State Bank of Pakistan,' July 1, 1948.

10. Section 227 of the 1973 Constitution of the Islamic Republic of Pakistan.

11. Now Pakistan Stock Exchange (PSX).

12. Formerly operating as Al Meezan Investment Bank.

13. 'KAP study: Knowledge, Attitude and Practices of Islamic Banking in Pakistan,' State Bank of Pakistan and Department for International Development (2014).

14. SBP Islamic banking bulletins from 2010 to 2020.

15. Summary of NBFCs, NEs, and Modarabas Sector, SECP (March 2020).

16. For more, see Insurance Association of Pakistan (IAP), http://www.iap.net.pk.

Part

4

SOCIOECONOMIC
CHALLENGES IN PAKISTAN

CHAPTER 13

Women's Economic Empowerment and Financial Inclusion in Pakistan

HADIA MAJID

INTRODUCTION

Women's economic empowerment has become a mainstay in measures of development across the world. Here, economic empowerment is generally encapsulated in the extent and nature of work that women do, i.e., their access to economic resources.[1] In particular, paid employment in the formal sector, and thereto in the manufacturing or services industry, is usually considered more empowering than other forms of employment.[2] This emphasis on economic empowerment stems from its key role in women's well-being, status within the household, and multiplier effects on other domains, both within the household and across the economy as a whole. Not only has women's access to resources, especially earned regular income, been shown to improve their say in household decision-making it has also been shown to affect household consumption patterns, investments in child human capital, and the overall growth trajectory of the economy.[3] The key question then is: how do we ensure women's economic empowerment?

In this chapter, financial inclusion of women has been shown to play the main role. Financial inclusion covers a multitude of financial products, including payment services, current and savings accounts, loans, and insurance.[4] Even more unconventional products, such as digital wallets, can be considered to fall under this broader umbrella. There is plenty of evidence to show that availing financial products increases women's income, reduces dependency on local money lenders, while improving purchasing and bargaining power within the household.[5] This chapter will focus on the role of financial inclusion in women's economic empowerment.

The discussion will present the status of economic empowerment in Pakistan while painting a comprehensive picture of the state of financial inclusion of women in the country. For the latter, the analysis will make use of the Global Findex Database, which records information on savings and borrowing behaviour. Findex is a nationally representative survey of 150,000 adults fielded under the World Bank in over 140 countries in three waves—2011, 2014, and 2017. The chapter will underscore data on women from all three waves while drawing comparisons with men, and where appropriate, South Asia as a whole. Finally, the challenges and steps taken to improve financial inclusion and women's economic empowerment will be highlighted. In this regard, special attention will be paid to the role of the SBP under the stewardship of Dr Ishrat Husain in the crucial steps taken to establish and expand microfinance institutions in Pakistan.

ECONOMIC EMPOWERMENT AND FINANCIAL INCLUSION IN PAKISTAN

The question of women's economic empowerment and the role of financial inclusion in this is especially pertinent in Pakistan's case. With a rank of 150, Pakistan is among the worst performers in the women's economic participation and opportunities index.[6] This is unsurprising as the country has a female labour force participation of only 22 per cent, which is the lowest in the region with the exception of Afghanistan.[7] When women do work, they tend to work primarily in the agriculture sector as unpaid family workers. Even in the manufacturing sector, the majority work on casual contracts that provide no worker benefits and see large wage differentials vis-à-vis men.[8] One way to improve women's economic empowerment would then be to increase labour force participation rates while ensuring that work is well-remunerated. However, women face a multitude of barriers after joining the labour force in Pakistan. Chief among these is familial and mobility restrictions, and the constraints imposed by the reproductive burden.[9]

One solution would be to have women work from home. Many are, in fact, availing this option—some 80 per cent of women who work do so from home.[10] However, the majority of such women are deeply dependent on male kin to connect them with the market, restricting their own networks of access. The dependence on male members also means that payments do not come straight into the women's hands. In fact, fieldwork with home-based women workers indicates that even when they are the only income-earners, many still do not consider themselves to be household heads and do not make financial decisions since they receive payments through male kin.[11] Even when women workers can access their income, their control over it remains limited primarily because of patriarchal structures that supplant women's authority. Hence, many choose to hide their income. However, in a context where the vast majority—more than 95 per cent—have no access to the formal financial sector, the scope for women to do so is limited.[12] Their limited access to the formal financial sector also means that they have little to no recourse to formal credit. This, in turn, curtails their ability to start and scale-up businesses.

THE CONTOURS OF FINANCIAL INCLUSION IN PAKISTAN

Before considering the incidence of account ownership in Pakistan, Figure 1 enumerates some of the main reasons why individuals need credit. This is done by considering the questions in the 2014 round of the Findex data set, asked from the entire respondent sample, about four primary needs: school fees, business, medical purposes, and old age.

It appears that adult men and women primarily borrow for health purposes, highlighting the poor provisioning of state sponsored healthcare. Interestingly, the second most prominent reason why men borrow or save is to invest in their business, whereas for women it is to invest in their education. The primary sources for this credit are provided in Figure 2.

Figure 1: Reasons for Borrowing/Saving

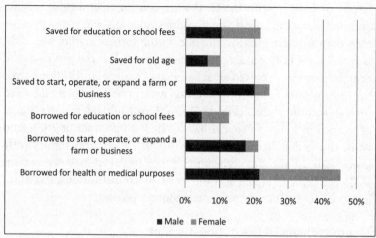

Source: Findex Data: 2014 wave

Figure 2: Source of Borrowed Funds

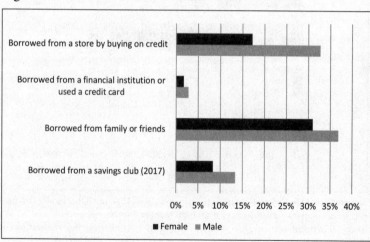

Source: Findex Data: 2014 and 2017 waves

Clearly, when borrowing, both men and women depend largely on family or friends, with the local store coming in at a close second, especially for men. Surprisingly, savings clubs are being used by more men than women. Finally, reliance on the formal market for credit is very low for both genders. Yet, when we consider the percentage of respondents who reported an account at a financial institution across the three waves of Findex we find that nearly one-third of men owned such an account in 2017 (Figure 3). On the other hand, only 6 per cent of women in Pakistan report having such an account in 2017. And while this is double the percentage for 2011, it remains significantly lower than the account ownership of men in Pakistan. It seems then that even if they have an account in financial institutions, Pakistani adults prefer to borrow from other sources instead.

Figure 3: Financial Institution Account

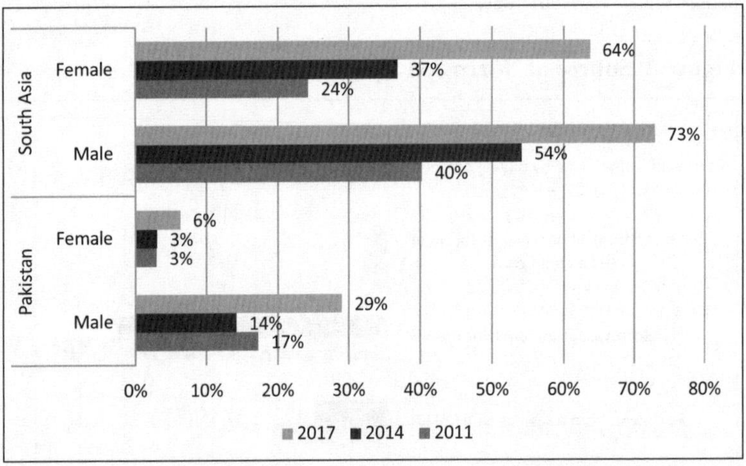

Source: Global Findex Data: 2011, 2014, 2017 waves. Note that the Global Findex database defines account ownership as having an individual or jointly owned account either at a financial institution (bank, credit union, cooperative, or microfinance institution) or through a mobile money provider.

Comparing the account ownership figures to the South Asia average, we find two points of interest. One: the difference between men and women's account ownership in the rest of South Asia is not as large as that found in Pakistan. Two: both the percentage of women and men who do not have accounts in Pakistan is far above that found in the rest of South Asia. In fact, the data shows that no matter which demographics we consider—age, education, income level, or region— the percentage of the unbanked remains significantly higher than that for South Asia. This suggests that the landscape surrounding financial institutions is markedly different in Pakistan's context relative to the rest of the region.

A look at the primary reasons why individuals do not have an account shows that it is a combination of both supply and demand-side factors. The predominant reason seems to be a dearth of sufficient funds for an account. After all, adults who are active in the labour force are more likely to have an account.[13] Even so, the significance of this reason seems strange. Pakistan's GDP per capita in 2017 was significantly higher than that of Nepal yet, 40 per cent of Nepalese as opposed to 44 per cent of Pakistani gave lack of funds as their reason for not having an account.[14] What seems more likely is that the base amount required to open an account in Pakistan is high or that this is the prevailing perception among the population.

Figure 4: Reasons for Not Having an Account

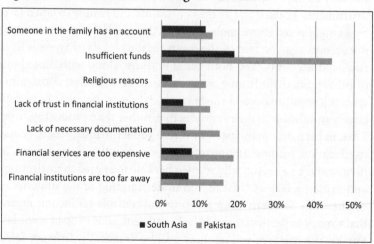

Source: Global Findex Data: 2017 wave

Similarly, financial institutions seem to be sparsely situated, and many lack the necessary identification, such as the national identity cards, to open accounts. Distance and lack of identification are especially pressing issues for women in the country. In 2017, it was estimated that some 12 million women did not have national identification cards, and the lack of identity cards was highlighted as one of the primary public issues faced by women in fieldwork with home-based and domestic workers.[15]

The picture that emerges from the Findex data is that both men and women are unable to meet medical, business, and educational needs through own funds and need to borrow. However, there is very little recourse to the formal financial market to meet this shortfall of funds, even among those who have an account in financial institutions. Finally, as expected, women are largely excluded from having accounts in financial institutions. The question then is: how do we improve their inclusion?

IDENTIFYING THE CHALLENGES

In order to improve women's inclusivity vis-à-vis access to financial instruments we must clarify the constraints and realities women face.

As highlighted above, mobility restrictions and lack of identification documents may be two of the main reasons why few women have financial accounts. Yet, both these reasons, along with a plethora of others, emanate from a socio-cultural context that constraints women's mobility beyond the home and defines their role in society largely in relation to their reproductive, rather than productive, role. This, in turn, has manifested in severe gender inequalities in access to education, income, among others. Poor educational attainment, in turn, could be a reason why women hesitate to approach institutions and exhibit a lack of trust in and understanding of the underlying mechanisms. Similarly, poor access to and control over income means that women in particular would lack sufficient sums to open accounts. Finally, the needs of women may well be drastically different from those being met by the market.

We know that the vast majority of women do not work. Moreover, for many, even when they work, it is unremunerated. Hence, they may not feel the need to have an account. Further, in a context where women do not hold agricultural land and largely work from home often as micro-entrepreneurs, financial instruments offered by the formal, more conventional market, are likely not attractive options for them. What we need then are alternatives to the conventional financial system, such as those offered by microfinance institutions (MFIs), along with features specifically targeted toward women.

THE WAY FORWARD

This section details the many interventions that have taken place in the last few years to improve women's financial inclusivity. The section also highlights more general changes in Pakistan's socioeconomic landscape that may improve women's participation in the financial markets.

1. Microfinance and Microcredit

Pakistan has a long history of micro-lending. Early initiatives by the government largely focused on the rural agriculture poor and provided loans to the needy farmers at rates lower than the market and/or those typically charged by semi-formal and informal sources. Here, examples include the Agricultural Development Finance Corporation and the Agricultural Bank established in the 1950s.[16] Even when it comes to NGOs, we find that bodies, such as the Aga Khan Rural Support Programme and the Orangi Pilot Project, were disbursing small loans to their beneficiaries in the 1980s and 1990s, respectively. It was not until the 2000s that we saw concerted efforts by both the government and NGOs to consolidate and expand their microfinance operations.

The Pakistan Microfinance Network, a collaboration of several different NGOs dealing with microfinance instruments, was established in 2001. While at government level, an apex body that served as both the supplier and intermediary body for funds targeted at poverty alleviation, the Pakistan Poverty Alleviation Fund (PPAF), was established in 2000.[17] Both these developments took place after a crucial turning point in the MFI history in Pakistan.

In 1996, the Kashf Foundation was established as the first specialised microfinance organisation in the country through seed money from the Grameen Bank. Up until that point, micro-lending was just one of the features offered by organisations involved in poverty mitigation. Post 1996, it became the primary purpose of several players both big and small in the MFI landscape, many of the NGOs among whom proceeded to receive funding from such organisations as the PPAF.

By 2017, Pakistan's microfinance sector had more than 40 accredited institutions operating in 106 districts, serving about 5.2 million borrowers with over half of the loans being made to women.[18] These developments, however, were in part only possible due to the SBP. Under the guidance of Dr Ishrat Husain, in 2001, the SBP formulated and established the Microfinance Institutions Ordinance. Under this ordinance, the MFIs were able to set up their operations at lower reserve requirements and equity financing than those in place for other banks.[19] In fact, in his address at the Asia-Pacific Microcredit Summit in 2001, Dr Husain asserted that 'the conventional norms applied to commercial banks and other financial institutions will not be extended mutatis mutandis to MFIs'.

In the same address he also shared his vision of the MFIs as 'sustainable community-based service delivery system(s) ...' for which the SBP would follow a '... learning-by-doing approach ... instead of following a prescriptive approach'. This vision, in effect, set the stage for the subsequent operation of the MFIs in Pakistan. Even today, micro-lending takes place with a high degree of community involvement and in view of community level requirements. Similarly, there remains a fair degree of a bottoms-up approach with recommendations taking into account the specific experience of the MFIs on the ground.

The portfolio of products and lending methodologies used by the sector include both fairly standard and more innovative products. The vast majority rely on group lending, even among those providing agricultural credit. When it comes to women-centric lending, organisations like Kashf lead the charge focusing on women from low-income backgrounds. Regardless of the type of borrower though, one of the primary reasons why clients reach out to the MFIs is for income smoothing, especially since most have only irregular sources of income and/or small businesses. With a loan portfolio of Rs 184 billion in 2018 and considerable growth in the last two decades, the MFI sector then has been a significant mechanism through which small businesses and farms attain credit to sustain themselves and grow.

In this regard, too, Dr Husain has played a key role. Throughout his tenure as SBP governor, he continued to lend his support to not just Small and Medium Enterprises (SMEs) financing but overall business development services for the sector. He was also, and continues to remain, a major proponent of poverty reduction via micro, small and medium enterprise-led growth.

Nonetheless, despite the availability of smaller loans based on mechanisms other than collateral, and even in the absence of interest charged by such organisations as Akhuwat, we continue to lag behind countries such as Bangladesh and Sri Lanka. In a country where more than 90 per cent of companies are SMEs, it is crucial to develop a cohesive strategy to financially include SMEs, cottage industry, and micro-enterprises, particularly those led by women. Similarly, it is worth noting that the Findex includes the MFIs in its definition of finance institutions. Thus, we are witnessing abysmally poor numbers, especially vis-à-vis women's inclusion even 'after' we count accounts with the MFIs. Of course, under-reporting could be one problem. Similarly, there is no clear indication of the state of account ownership among women prior to 2011 and the current levels of 6 per cent could well be a 10-fold increase over where we were two decades ago. Access to finance then is something that both local and international organisations have been working on more aggressively in the last few years. For instance, in 2019, the Asian Development Bank partnered with the Kashf Foundation to give more financing to women and women-led small businesses.[20]

However, it is not enough to earmark financing for women. Concrete steps and strategies need to be promulgated to bring more into the banking fold. With this in mind, several interventions continue to be made.

2. Mobility Beyond the Home and Distance to Financial Institutions

When looking to improve women's access to the financial market, the first order of business may well be to change norms that constrain women's movement beyond home. This could be done through the introduction of role models in social and conventional media that normalise women's presence in the public sphere. In this regard, safety considerations in city and market design, and easily accessible female-specific public transport is also important. One possibility to make the financial sector, banks, and otherwise, more accessible to women with mobility constraints is through branch-less and mobile banking. Indeed, the last five years have seen major changes in this regard with the percentage of Pakistan's adult population using mobile financial services is expected to increase from 2 to 35 per cent by 2020.[21] This change has been precipitated by both rise in mobile money transfer services by the telecommunication and microfinance industry as well as the launch of small, mobile branches by major banks.

However, here it is important to consider gender gaps in mobile phone and internet access. In particular, low-literate, low-income women in Pakistan typically only have access to a family cell phone and its use is closely monitored. In this scenario, even personalised digital wallets would not be enough, especially when women are looking to hide their income in order to maintain more control over its use. What is needed then are mobile applications designed specifically keeping the patriarchal context in mind which allow women to access funds and connect with each other, thereby growing their networks of access. The latter is especially important for business development and financial literacy. Even here, there is a key role for social and conventional media in helping change community perceptions regarding the role of women and norms of female use of technology.

a. *Literacy*

There has been a steady and significant decline in female illiteracy levels since 1990, with gaps between education levels closing between the genders.[22] This rise in education should in theory make financial institutions less intimidating for women. However, education's attainment remains lower for older female cohorts compared to younger ones.[23] Given that it is typically older women who have fewer mobility restrictions, we are back to travelling restrictions as the primary constraints. Besides, education is not the same as financial literacy.

When it comes to financial literacy there are two points to consider. One is that even among the banked, limited knowledge of basic financial concepts limits business development. Hence, organisations like Kashf have been building financial literacy modules for their regular loan disbursements. Two, a lack of financial education fosters financial exclusion. With this in mind, the National Financial Literacy Program (NFLP) was launched by the SBP with support from the Asian Development Bank (ADB) in 2017.[24] One of NFLP's flagship programmes is to provide basic financial education to the unbanked, low-income youth, and women. The NFLP aims to reach its audience not just through conventional print and electronic media but also through a dedicated helpline, social media, while also showcasing its products through theatre groups.

b. *Identifying Documents*

All of the above steps are in vain if women lack the necessary identifying documents to be able to open accounts in either banks or in the MFIs. In this regard, the launch of the Benazir Income Support Programme (BISP) in 2008 saw an increase in the issuance of national identity cards (NICs) to women across the country as the NIC was the only way for women in recipient households to access BISP funds. The National Database and Registration Authority (NADRA) has also been instrumental in the expansion and computerisation of national identification records. Here, the NADRA Mobile Registration Cars Project launched in 2018 which brings registration services to people's doorstep has gone a long way in reaching unregistered women, especially in the context of strict norms of seclusion for women.

CONCLUSION

Women's economic empowerment is increasingly being recognised as a prerequisite to ensure sustained economic growth. This owes to the crucial links between not just women's important role as earners in their own right, but their earnings as instruments for generating positive multiplier and lasting effects throughout the economy. In this regard, there has been documentation of a deep link between women's economic empowerment and financial inclusion. After all, it is only if women have access to the requisite financial instruments that they can generate, control, and grow their income.

Recognising the crucial importance of financial inclusion, in 2018, Prime Minister Imran Khan approved a five-year National Financial Inclusion Strategy plan. The key features of this strategy look to enhance the deposit base and use of digital payments while promoting SMEs, agricultural financing, and the use of Islamic banking. The last in particular has been highlighted by Dr Ishrat Husain as a means to reach those who cite religious concerns as their reason for remaining unbanked. Thus, as was the case in the SBP MFI Ordinance, here too, Dr Husain has played a significant role.

With a third of men and only 6 per cent of women reporting account ownership (either individual or joint) in a financial institution, this chapter has underscored some of the primary reasons constraining women's financial inclusion. There have also been some major recent developments, some as recent as only two to three years ago, such as NADRA's mobile registration vans, a rapid expansion of mobile and branchless banking, as well as national financial literacy programmes that are expected to go a long way in reducing exclusion, especially among women.

However, the discussion in this chapter also underlines that the relationship between financial inclusion and economic empowerment is not necessarily straightforward. Indeed, women's poor access to and control over resources, including education, literacy, even proper state documentation to a large extent stem from a socio-cultural context that severely restricts their mobility. This, in turn, limits their ability to both generate income and access financial instruments. Some tout public transport, and thereto women-only public transport, as a vital factor in enabling and normalising women's presence in the public sphere. As this presence becomes normalised and mobility improves, access to a whole host of other services and socioeconomic factors also increase. Undeniably, there is a role that public transport plays in increasing the use of financial services. However, it is not a solution that can work in isolation, nor is it a quick fix. What is needed is a multi-pronged approach that tackles the issue of financial exclusion from several angles simultaneously—an approach undertaken by successive governmental and non-governmental agencies for many years now.

Notes

1. Naila Kabeer, 'Women's economic empowerment and inclusive growth: labour markets and enterprise development,' Discussion Paper No. 29 (Centre for Development Policy & Research, School of Oriental & African Studies, University of London, 2012).
2. Karin Astrid Siegmann and Hadia Majid, 'Empowering growth in Pakistan?' No 595, ISS Working Papers - General Series from International Institute of Social Studies of Erasmus University Rotterdam (ISS) (The Hague, 2014).
3. Kabeer, 'Women's economic empowerment and inclusive growth'; and Cheryl Doss, 'Intrahousehold Bargaining and Resource Allocation in Developing Countries,' *World Bank Research Observer* 28, no. 1 (2013): 52–78.
4. Asli Demirgüç-Kunt, Leora Klapper, and Dorothe Singer, 'Financial Inclusion and Inclusive Growth: A Review of Recent Empirical Evidence,' Policy Research Working Paper: No. 8040 (World Bank, 2017).
5. Michael Chibba, 'Financial Inclusion, Poverty Reduction and the Millennium Development Goals,' *European Journal of Development Research* 21, no. 2 (April 2009): 213–230; and Md. Nur Alam Siddik, 'Does Financial Inclusion Promote Women Empowerment? Evidence from Bangladesh,' *Applied Economics and Finance* 4, no. 4 (2017): 169–177.
6. 'The Global Gender Gap Report 2020,' World Economic Forum, Technical Report (2020).
7. 'World Development Indicator,' World Bank (2019).
8. Hadia Majid, 'Women's Work and Household Income: Examining 25 Years of Data,' Gender Identities at Work in Pakistan Workshop, January 3, 2019.
9. Hadia Majid, 'Female Labor Supply in Pakistan: Mapping the Last Three Decades,' Forman Christian College Pakistan: The Long View, 2047 Workshop, December 2, 2016.
10. Majid, 'Women's Work and Household Income.'
11. Hadia Majid and A. Malik, 'Who listens to the underprivileged? Vulnerabilities of women workers in an urban informal economy,' Mimeo (Lahore University of Management Sciences, 2019).
12. 'Pakistan Wave 5 report fifth annual FII tracker,' Financial Inclusion Insights, Technical Report, 2018.
13. Asli Demirgüç-Kunt, Leora Klapper, Dorothe Singer, Saniya Ansar, and Jake Hess, 'The Global Findex Database 2017: Measuring Financial Inclusion and the Fintech Revolution' (World Bank, 2018).
14. 'The Global Findex Database,' The World Bank and Global Findex (2018).

15. Aiman Jalil, '12 million women without CNIC,' *The Express Tribune*, November 30, 2017; and Majid and Malik, 'Who listens to the underprivileged?'
16. 'State of Microfinance in Pakistan,' Institute of Microfinance (2018).
17. Ibid.
18. Kaswar Klasra, 'Microfinance is a growing business in Pakistan,' *ACCA*, March 1, 2018.
19. 'State of Microfinance in Pakistan,' Institute of Microfinance (2018).
20. 'ADB, Kashf Foundation Partner to Expand Women's Access to Credit in Pakistan,' Asian Development Bank (2019).
21. 'National Financial Literacy Program,' State Bank of Pakistan (2019).
22. Majid, 'Female Labor Supply in Pakistan.'
23. Ibid.
24. 'National Financial Literacy Program.'

CHAPTER 14

The State of Entrepreneurship in Pakistan

MUHAMMAD ARIF

Entrepreneurs, though different in their own flock, are a rare species. Their efforts to create new enterprises are important because of their contribution in terms of job creation, poverty alleviation, economic development, more equal distribution of wealth, and consequently greater social order in a society.

Entrepreneurship demands continuous reflection to understand the characteristics of entrepreneurs (individuals daring to be different), features of organisations entrepreneurs are creating, the processes used by them to create new enterprises, along with the environment for entrepreneurship. This debate is taken up in this chapter in Pakistan's context. This informed reflection aims to provide some input for legislators, policymakers, and regulators and is based on literature pertaining to entrepreneurship in general and specific to Pakistan.

ENTREPRENEURSHIP: INTRODUCTION IN BRIEF

The period after 2010 remained turbulent for entrepreneurs globally. The fame of renowned unicorns such as Uber, Lyft, and Wework was challenged. In 2019, Lyft's stocks were down almost 40 per cent from its Initial Public Offering (IPO) price. Uber lost 30 per cent of the face value of its shares and a vast majority of its early investors were leaving.[1] Nevertheless, such stumbling of big tech entrepreneurs did not deter countries from restless competition for and desire to see more entrepreneurs flourishing on their turf. The Global

Entrepreneurship Index (GEI) measures this competition. According to the GEI's 2019 ranking, the top 10 countries included:

Table 1: Global Entrepreneurship Index (2019)

No.	Country	Ranking
1	United States	1
2	Switzerland	2
3	Canada	3
4	Denmark	4
5	United Kingdom	5
6	Australia	6
7	Iceland	7
8	Netherland	8
9	Ireland	9
10	Sweden	10

Source: Global Entrepreneurship Index Report 2019

According to Kuratko, Morris, and Schindehutte, 'an entrepreneurial revolution has spread throughout the world.'[2] Competition among countries to attract, nourish, and retain a greater number of entrepreneurs from around the world is because of some understandable reasons. Countries are pursuing this path largely because entrepreneurship has become increasingly associated with innovation, productivity, and jobs.[3] It is also considered as an engine of global economic development and a force for positive change in society.[4]

One of the ways to define entrepreneurship is, 'the capacity and willingness to develop, organize and manage a business venture along with any of its risks in order to make a profit. The most obvious example of entrepreneurship is the starting of new businesses.'[5]

Entrepreneurship is not a new phenomenon, nevertheless, attempts to study it in a systematic way is not very old.[6] However, it is a complex and multidimensional phenomenon. One of the explanations behind this complexity is that 'entrepreneurship' as a discipline emerges on the periphery of other disciplines, including but not limited to sociology, psychology, anthropology, marketing, management, finance, organisational behaviour, engineering, and information technology (IT).

Many frameworks and theories try to explain this phenomenon. These efforts vary from a single framework[7] to multiple frameworks approach.[8] Gartner describes creation of a new venture (or in other words entrepreneurship) with the help of four dimensions: (a) individual(s)—the person(s) involved in starting a new organisation; (b) organisation—the kind of firm that is started; (c) environment—the situation surrounding and influencing the new organisation; and (d) new venture process—the actions undertaken by the individual(s) to start the venture.[9] Figure 1 shows the suggested connection among these.

Figure 1: Framework for describing new venture creation

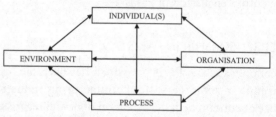

Source: Adapted from Gartner (1985)

This framework adds to our understanding about entrepreneurship in many significant ways. Firstly, it highlights the importance of an individual with the expertise to pursue a risky adventure. Secondly, the 'process' suggests that new venture creation is not instantaneously produced rather 'evolves' over time—hinting towards patience as a desired attribute of an entrepreneur. Thirdly, the organisation structure the entrepreneurs tried to create in terms of, for instance, legal (sole proprietorship or partnership) or strategic orientation (differentiation, cost leadership, or focus) could have implications for sustainability of the organisation. Fourthly, the environment (ecosystem) suggests that entrepreneurship or new enterprises do not emerge from or operate in vacuum.[10] Finally, interaction among these components illustrates the potential for a high degree of complexity of this phenomenon.

Various dimensions of entrepreneurship and their interaction in this model also suggests caution against the tendency of 'researchers researching various but a single aspect of an elephant at one time' that may possibly lead to 'fragmented thinking' and consequently, for instance, less optimal policy interventions. Hence, a discussion around a framework as suggested by Gartner has its value in place.

This model also draws its importance from a comparison between the GEI and this framework. It can be implied that the GEI is structured around or inspired by this model. The GEI measures entrepreneurship (ecosystem) in terms of 14 components which revolve around four dimensions and their interaction as suggested by Gartner. The following sections in this chapter will take Gartner's conceptual framework and will deliberate each component in the context of entrepreneurship in Pakistan.

1. ENTREPRENEURSHIP IN PAKISTAN

For an economy such as Pakistan, which has been facing contractionary trends in its large-scale manufacturing industries,[11] the significance of entrepreneurship/creation of new enterprises can not be over-claimed. Collective capacity of public and private sectors would not be sufficient to accommodate around two million young people who enter into the job market every year.[12]

Three major classifications of enterprises in Pakistan are: creative,[13] social,[14] and enterprises which can be classified as both creative and social.[15] It will be hard to precisely locate the emergence of entrepreneurship in the creative domain in Pakistan. Nevertheless, theater and cinema could be considered as the pioneers which tried to maintain the subcontinent's rich tradition. Later development in services, such as banking, distribution channel, etc. in the 1960s, enriched the creative landscape of Pakistan further.

Not only cinema but other expressions of creative endeavours, including music and theatrical performances by organisations, such as Rafi Peer theatre, Vital Signs, Junoon, and Strings tried to keep vibrancy in a society which has been otherwise facing an increasingly shrinking space for any non-religious expressions. Sharmeen Obaid-Chinoy became the recent figure who put Pakistan on the international creative map by documenting social issues of Pakistan. These groups and individuals' efforts and the consequent acknowledgement were not limited to the national level.

The Hamdard Group, a socially motivated business founded in pre-partition India in 1906, can be classified as among the pioneers in social entrepreneurship area. The social landscape of Pakistan further enriched by organisations, such as The Aga Khan Foundation, Edhi Welfare Organization, and Shaukat Khanum Memorial Cancer Hospital & Research Centre. Lately, Pakistan experienced diversification in the themes where organisations choose to work. The emergence of social entrepreneurship in the areas including education (The Citizens Foundation), microfinance (Aga Khan Rural Support Programme [AKRSP] and Akhuwat Foundation), and women empowerment (Aurat Foundation) suggest not only diversification but also elevation of the social sector from its embryonic stage.

Digital economy became the new testing ground for entrepreneurs in Pakistan. Youths qualified in disciplines, such as engineering, IT, and business turned their novel ideas into promising start-ups, with innovations in areas ranging from e-commerce to music and broadcasting and from food to transportation and entertainment. From 2010 onward, few other start-ups, in both traditional and non-traditional sectors, which mesmerised Pakistan and the world include: Markhor, XGear, Patari, and Finja. This substantiates the studies, such as Arif[16] and i-genius,[17] which argued that the Pakistani society and culture have enormous potential for innovation and social entrepreneurship ventures.

Increased inclination towards entrepreneurship can also be inferred from recent study findings. According to a study, more than 50 per cent of enterprises surveyed in this inquiry started their operations from 2010 onward.[18] Such studies are rare in Pakistan's context as also highlighted by Ali and Darko along with Ahmed, Khalid, Lynch, and Darko.[19] Nevertheless, this also suggests an opportunity to investigate more into this discipline.

1.1. Individual

Pursuing opportunity beyond resources controlled by an entrepreneur[20] sums up perfectly what a very large majority of entrepreneurs would be doing on a day-to-day basis. In order to survive, one needs to be inventive, creative, opportunistic, and persuasive, because it is rare for entrepreneurs to have enough resources.[21]

Demographic and psychographic characteristics of entrepreneurs remained in focus of research. If need for achievement, locus of control, and risk-taking were the key features of entrepreneurs in the 1980s as reported by Brockhaus,[22] then some of the traits which enabled entrepreneurs to become part of 'the most important entrepreneurs of the last decade' are audacity, innovation, disruption, and social responsibility.[23] Not meant for generalisation but variation suggests that the list is unending.

This is a sparsely researched topic in Pakistan's context. Nevertheless, there are some valuable efforts to identify some of the characteristics. Cridge, in her PhD thesis, while using data on firm origins and growth, shows how firm performance (including their ability to diversify) is related to the founder's (or director's) experience which includes education, industry-related employment, and industry exposure.[24] Based on representative case studies in Pakistan's textile sector, she claimed that the experience of the entrepreneur is manifested in the firm's entry strategy, its initial production and organisational capabilities, and persists via its procedures to improve productivity, quality, and marketing.

Further to this, qualities emerged from literature, shedding light on individuals who took a leap of faith to start business include (but not limited to) persistence, willing to face odds, including change of mindsets e.g., running a cafe by a female is a taboo, technical knowledge, creativity, and ability to communicate persuasively.[25]

1.2. Process

Entrepreneurship is an activity or function. This notion suggests entrepreneurs perform certain functions that contribute or help them create a new enterprise. Rigorous literature pertaining to the processes is based on observation, i.e., the activities or functions performed by entrepreneurs include: locating a business opportunity, accumulating resources, producing and marketing products or services, building an organisation, and conforming to or responding to government and society's expectations.

In Pakistan's case, it is hard to find a study which is based on observation or reporting of the entrepreneurs who described what they do. In most cases, discussion drifted to the challenges faced by entrepreneurs in Pakistan. Some of the challenges experienced by entrepreneurs in their process of creating enterprises in Pakistan are documented by authors such as Rizvi.[26] A substantial discussion of these challenges also relates to the ecosystem entrepreneurs have been facing.

1.3. The Organisation

Type of organisations entrepreneurs opt to create vary with respect to their orientation (creative, social, or hybrid), nature of economic activity (manufacturing, service, etc.), legal structure (sole proprietor or partnership), and strategic choice (overall cost leadership, focus, or differentiation). More than 75 per cent of organisations (a majority of these registered in 2010s) were registered entities and a majority as private firms.

1.4. The Ecosystem

The predominant metaphor for fostering self-employment as an economic development strategy is the 'entrepreneurship ecosystem'.[27] Factors associated with 'entrepreneurship ecosystem' have been discussed by Gartner.[28] Pakistan, with its irresistible market potential,[29] invites investors to look at this market with a lot of trepidation.[30]

A recent study, based on in-depth interviews with top 22 MNCs' CEOs, did a Strengths, Weaknesses, Opportunities and Threats (SWOT) analysis of Pakistan (see Table 2).[31] Some of the strengths and opportunities associated with Pakistan could be implied as pull (motivating) factors for entrepreneurs whereas few of the weaknesses and threats can be interpreted as push (inhibiting) factors for entrepreneurship in Pakistan.

Table 2: Pakistan's SWOT Analysis—In Brief

Strengths	Weaknesses
1. Improved security situation 2. Untapped and underutilised Resources 3. Positive attitude of CEOs 4. Gateway to several regional economies	1. National-level governance challenges 2. Age-old structural issues faced by businesses 3. Increased cost of doing business relative to peers 4. Uncertainty faced by CEOs
Opportunities	**Threats**
1. Leveraging on strengths 2. Working on gaps	1. Internal 2. External

Source: Adapted from Arif (2019)

To overcome the weaknesses and manage threats, some reforms have been undertaken under the leadership of Dr Ishrat Husain, for example, Pakistan Regulatory Modernization Initiative (PRMI). There are also some sector-specific steps being undertaken in consultation with the stakeholders. For example, in the IT sector, the Ministry of IT and Telecom's IGNITE initiative is dedicated to promoting innovation and research commercialisation ecosystem in Pakistan by providing venture capital funding to new businesses in IT while focusing on the fourth industrial revolution.[32]

1.4.1. Pull factors

Based on Table 3 major attractions which can possibly excite entrepreneurs about Pakistan are:

1.4.1.1. A large, evolving market

The world does not have many markets equal to or bigger than Pakistan.[33] Pakistan continues to be the sixth most populous country in the world with a burgeoning and increasingly empowered young and educated middle/urban class.[34] This class is increasingly adopting a Western lifestyle, including its love to remain logged-in to the social media platforms, following seasons of various movies/dramas on Netflix, sipping freshly brewed coffees at expensive local and foreign coffee chains, and enjoying energy drinks while watching league matches of football and cricket. All these suggest opportunities.

1.4.1.2. *The industrious and entrepreneurial Pakistanis*

Industrious and entrepreneurial are the two attributes Pakistan's youth is associated with as acknowledged by many CEOs.[35] Some of the entrepreneurial qualities as observed by these CEOs are: being positive, resilient, vibrant, intelligent, and aspiring. Companies also find Pakistan's talent as competitive, i.e., young, high-quality and low-cost as compared to other regional economies, including India and China.[36]

1.4.1.3. *Liberalisation and deregulations*

Since the 1990s, the direction of reforms has been more or less the same. This includes efforts for privatisation, policies to widen the tax base, continuous investment in infrastructure, and incessant deregulations in sectors, including telecom, energy, and banking, giving positive signals to aspiring entrepreneurs. For instance, entrance of telecom firms and consequent start-ups providing financial services to the people of Pakistan has contributed to the emergence of a new industry—fintech.

1.4.1.4. *A gateway—Pakistan's geographical proximity to the regional markets*

As mentioned in Table 3, one of the major reasons Pakistan remained an attractive turf for entrepreneurs is markets it is close to. The country's geographical proximity to the Middle East and Chinese market makes it a lucrative option for aspiring entrepreneurs. In this backdrop of increased inclination of global trade towards regionalisation, the regional economies' interdependencies are expected to increase[37] and so is the attractiveness of Pakistan.

1.4.1.5. *Untapped and underutilised resources*

Many venture-capitalists have this realisation that various technologies which worked successfully in the West could be replicated in Pakistan with reasonable success—a point also emphasised by one of the CEOs heading a subsidiary of a global IT firm in technology-related services.[38] Seventy-four million 3G/4G subscribers and 76 million broadband users with penetration rate of 35.21 per cent and 36.18 per cent, respectively, offer a lucrative set of opportunities for tech entrepreneurs, ranging from medical, agriculture, to the provision of financial services.

1.4.1.6. Incubation centres, accelerators, and networks

There are more than 50 incubation centres in Pakistan[39] both in public and private domain. In public domain, centres such as National Incubation Center and Center for Innovation and Entrepreneurship at Information Technology University, Lahore, along with many other similar centres established under the government's vision to promote entrepreneurship in Pakistan, offer desired facilitation. In the private sector domain, platforms such as the Organization for Pakistani Entrepreneurs (OPEN)[40] offered much-needed help.

1.4.2. Push factors

Following are the major factors which are possibly intimidating entrepreneurs:

1.4.2.1. Pertaining to (un)governable—Red tape

Irrespective of the policies, bureaucracy's ability to exercise 'discretion' is a major issue in Pakistan's business environment.[41] Complexity in the regulatory arena of the country further increased because of the 18th Amendment to the Constitution. This has not only contributed to increased cost of doing business in terms of compliance but also leads to more bureaucratic procedures.

1.4.2.2. Age-old structural issues—Political-social-economic surprises

Pakistan's political instability remained one of the major bottlenecks, which according to entrepreneurs, leads to reluctance, lack of reliability, and trust-deficit when foreign businesses are approached by local entrepreneurs for business transactions.[42] The economic cost of political unrest, such as strikes and sit-ins, affects small businesses as well.

1.4.2.3. Poor quality of human resource

The question of Pakistani educational establishment's capacity to turn out highly trained graduates kept on haunting many stakeholders, including entrepreneurs in this country.[43] The availability of quality human resources is indispensable for not only sustainability but also for scaling up small businesses.

1.4.2.4. The cost of a redundant system

More than ten years ago, one of the major reservations of prospective entrepreneurs was the cost of redundant system against unreliable supply of electricity, water, and other utilities.[44] After more than a decade, such concerns have not been subsided to the desired extent.

1.4.2.5. Grey market

Though the scale and size of grey market has not been measured so far, estimates vary between 40–60 per cent depending upon the sector. Differences in the market for the price of same product because of difference in their channel (legal or illegal) can kill the new-born business that aspires to operate in the legal domain.

1.4.2.6. Taxing financial issues

Taxation, limited access to investors (no relevant contacts, limited network), finding long-term grant opportunities, and demonstrating/achieving revenue/profit for equity investors and banks remained among the major financial concerns of new enterprises.[45] Some of these issues also highlighted by Kearney[46] for digital entrepeneurs in Pakistan.

The morphology of entrepreneurship, in addition to the elements of the model as suggested by Gartner[47] and copied in Figure 1, include some of the important trends which would be shaping the future of entrepreneurship in Pakistan. These include: de-globalisation, increased nationalism (including techno-nationalism), unabated trend of sharp decline in the demand for non-technical labour, and more knowledge-driven economies.[48]

There are many authors with a background of business and economics who wrote on issues pertaining to entrepreneurship in Pakistan. Dr Ishrat Husain is among one of those. The next section reflects on his contribution followed by the concluding section.

DR ISHRAT HUSAIN'S CONTRIBUTION IN PAKISTAN'S ENTREPRENEURSHIP LANDSCAPE

Perhaps in line with Schumpeter,[49] Dr Ishrat Husain is among the pioneer economists in Pakistan who remained strong believers in the private sector (can also be referred to as entrepreneurs) as the primary driving force behind innovation and consequent development. This can be implied from his lamenting reflection on the 1970s regime which nationalised hard-earned enterprises of emerging entrepreneurs in Pakistan.[50] A big disfavour to Pakistan's emerging entrepreneurial spirit could not be more than that. By pursing privatisation drive to date, Pakistan is possibly trying to undo what economic managers did in the 1970s.

Dr Husain's work, including *Governing the Ungovernable*, reflected more on macroeconomic issues which fall in the domain of the 'ecosystem' for entrepreneurship in Pakistan. Dr Husain blamed 'governance' behind the continuous decline of Pakistan's socioeconomic development environment which deters for instance investment and innovation. According to him:

> [...] both theoretical and cross country empirical evidence, as well as Pakistan's own experience, lend a great deal of weight to the argument that poor governance manifested by weak institutions, among many other factors, could be the predominant reason for Pakistan's unsatisfactory economic and social performance over the past quarter of a century, in relation to both, its own last four decades and other countries in the regions.[51]

Again, pertinent to ecosystem for business at large (including for entrepreneurship), Dr Husain also deliberated on how Pakistan has created what can be referred as 'not a level-playing field for non-partisan businesses'.[52] Hence, it can be implied that 'politically' strong businesses and poor governance possibly pushed Pakistan to attain its true potential for entrepreneurship.

UNDERSTANDING ENTREPRENEURSHIP IN PAKISTAN

It is not hard to find cases of entrepreneurial excellence of individuals and organisations and sectors largely because of a supporting ecosystem. Success of thousands of firms operating in Shenzhen (in China) associated more with the support provided by the Chinese government.[53] Long before this, the rise of creative cities, such as the Silicon Valley, and because of a creative leap the bunch of firms were able to make in an increasingly resource-rich domestic market, which is another evidence of supporting entrepreneurship ecosystem.

Nevertheless, firms such as Tata (India) developed itself to challenge global giants from a similar (if not more conducive) ecosystem than offered by Pakistan. It was only in the 1990s when India started liberalisation and introduced major reforms which boosted businesses.

Table 3 summarises and extends the deliberation focused on the entrepreneurship ecosystem pertaining to Pakistan. Based on this table, it can be inferred that Pakistan offered a mixed bundle of attractive and unattractive factors with varying level of sustainability and manageability. This picture does not suggest a conducive entrepreneurial ecosystem.

Nevertheless, history of business in Pakistan offers cases of excellence at industrial, organisational, and individual level. For instance, at the industry level, with varying market share possibly every fourth inflatable ball kicked in this world is manufactured in Sialkot.[55]

At the organisational level, within sports goods industry, Pakistan Forward Sports remained a trusted supplier for Adidas and exported approximately 42 million Brazuca balls from Pakistan in 2014. Forward Sports earned this honour again in 2018 by producing 'Telstar 18'—the match ball for FIFA 2018 World Cup in Russia.[56] The Highnoon Laboratories Pakistan (in pharmaceutical industry) is among the Forbes Asia's 200 companies under $1 billion.[57]

Table 3: Top 5 Push and Pull factors for entrepreneurship in Pakistan

No.	Pull Factors			Push Factors		
	Factor	Strength of attractiveness	Sustainability	Factor	Strength of unattractiveness	Manageability
1	A large, evolving market	***	Reasonably enduring	Pertaining to (un) governable—Red Tape	***	Challenging
2	The industrious and entrepreneurial Pakistanis	***	Reasonably enduring	Age-old structural issues—Political-social-economic surprises	***	Challenging
3	Liberalisation, deregulations, and facilitation (incubation centres, accelerators, and networks)	***	Reasonably consistent	Poor quality of human resource	***	Challenging
4	A Gateway—Pakistan's geographical proximity to regional markets	***	Reasonably enduring	Cost of redundant system	***	Challenging
5	Untapped and underutilised resources	***	Reasonably enduring	Taxing financial issues	***	Challenging

Note: Stars measure attractiveness or unattractiveness of a factor. Allocation of stars is based on subjective interpretation of the authors which is based on reading of the literature[54] and personal experiences.

Source: Arif 2019.

The purpose behind this listing is to, while borrowing the term 'black swan' from Karl R. Popper,[58] substantiate the claim: if one entrepreneur has been able to navigate his/her entrepreneurship in the given entrepreneurship ecosystem of Pakistan then why not others? A partial explanation could be or the credit goes to the strategy and/or entrepreneurial spirit of the entrepreneur or both.

If we brought in the analysis of ecosystem entrepreneurs embedded within Pakistan, with regards to our discussion about the black swan, it can be claimed that entrepreneurs who dare to invest in Pakistan continue to believe in 'pull' factors or giving more heed to factors inducing them to invest than feel threatened by intimidating elements of the ecosystem.

Based on the stories of these black swans in Pakistan, nevertheless, this cannot be implied that future entrepreneurs can also thrive exonerating the legislators, policymakers, and regulators from their obligations to strive and be held responsible for the improvement of the entrepreneurial ecosystem in Pakistan. Table 4 offers a lot to these stakeholders to ponder over the areas of ecosystem, which need to be improved.

Note: Numerator shows Pakistan's ranking denominator indicates the number of countries measured/total score. The lower the score the higher the positiveness associated with the score and vice versa.

Table 4 offers Pakistan's ranking against 10 major indices which can have direct to indirect relevance to entrepreneurship ecosystem. Positive ranking against three indices (3, 4, and 5) vis-à-vis negative ranking against seven indices (1, 2, 6, 7, 8, 9, and 10) does not overall indicate a very promising picture about the entrepreneurial ecosystem in Pakistan.

Among the plethora of issues, legislators, policymakers, and regulators need to pick up on some important threads on a priority basis. These include:

1. In an economy, such as Pakistan's, the government remained the most powerful engine to stimulate economic activities that can make private sector follow suit. As we move into 2022, the country needs megaprojects under the public domain.

Table 4: Pakistan's Ranking Against Select Indices

No.	Index	2015	2016	2017	2018	2019	Comments
1	Ease of Doing Business Index (World Bank)	138/189	144/189	147/190	136/190	108/190	Improving but inconsistent
2	Competitiveness Index (World Economic Forum)	126/140	122/138	115/137	107/140	110/141	Inconsistent
3	Innovation Index (Global Innovation Index Report)	131/141	119/128	113/127	109/126	105/129	Improving
4	Creativity Index (World Intellectual Property Organization)	121/141	114/128	112/127	104/126	104/129	Improving
5	Transparency Index (Transparency International)	126/175	117/168	116/176	117/180	117/180	Improving
6	Quality of Life Index (Quality of Life Index)	74/86	48/56	55/67	53/60	60/71	Deteriorating
7	Technology Adoption Index (World Economic Forum)	113/140	119/138	111/137	127/140	131/141	Deteriorating
8	Political Risk (1 to 7—low to high) (Economist Intelligence Unit)	7/7	7/7	6/7	6/7	6/7	Consistently high risk
9	Global Entrepreneurship Index (Global Entrepreneurship Index)	123/130	109/131	121/136	120/137	108/136	Inconsistent
10	Global Talent Competitiveness Index (Global Talent Competitiveness Index)	103/105		111/118	109/119	108/125	Deteriorating

2. Access to the relevant business network for new enterprises remained a big challenge.[59] On the other hand, because of entrepreneurs' qualities, such as their nimbleness, there's an increasing trend that large businesses (LB) seek collaboration with new entrepreneurs for reasons such as to bring innovation.[60] Possibilities of symbiotic exchange relationships can be explored by encouraging the LB to seek more collaboration with new entrepreneurs. Persuading the LB under their corporate social responsibility or some policy incentives, such as tax exemptions, can derive the desired behaviour.

3. Education has a reasonably well-established correlation with the success of enterprises.[61] While considering the multidisciplinary nature of new products/offering, students from a broad range of disciplines should be exposed to the science of 'creating new businesses'. Hence, entrepreneurship-related courses should be offered as general stream of courses at college and university level, instead of reserving this holy grail only for 'business' discipline.

4. How many entrepreneurs failed in the last 10 years and what were the reasons? What are the major success stories in the last ten years? How can we theorise or develop models based on such studies which can inform, e.g., the policy corridors? These are the jobs that need to be taken more by the academic community. Nevertheless, a very large majority of academic research in Pakistan is focused on 'theoretical research'—turning their back from the socioeconomic issues highlighted above. The academia needs to be persuaded to give equal space to research in applied and policy issues, if not greater than what it has already been allocating to the theoretical research. Policymaking at the Higher Education Commission (HEC) can address this imbalance.

5. Incubation centres remained a major driving force in pushing more individuals to pursue entrepreneurship.[62] These can also be relevant more because of the services they offered, such as mentorship, office space, funding opportunities, and legal advice. These are some of the areas that need to be focused

on to promote a supportive ecosystem for entrepreneurship. Hence, a logical action would be to reinforce the existing incubation centres and establish more.

6. Issues related to taxation, e.g., withholding and provincial income tax remained most troublesome for entrepreneurs.[63] Hence, more conducive policies will be required to motivate and facilitate the new enterprises.

7. A meagre 1.04 per cent technical labour, which is also poor with respect to the number of years in school education and their continuous low enrolment,[64] needs quick attention of policymakers in the era when Pakistan has been facing continuous contraction in jobs in large-scale industries. Turkish enrolment in technical skills is around 35 per cent of the relevant age cohort, for example. Changes such as semi-automation processes, ICT and their convergence suggest complex job descriptions or skill sets required to kick-start one's own enterprise. Hence, the National Vocational & Technical Training Center needs to look at such development and respond accordingly.

8. According to one of the CEOs interviewed during the study,[65] most of the work being performed by Pakistani freelancers are going to be eaten up by Artificial Intelligence (AI), hence, a new set of skills needs to be identified and training should be planned for future IT-related freelancers who are running their virtual enterprises.

9. The quality of education remained a major concern for new enterprises which heavily rely on raw talent because of cost consideration.[66] Pakistan's poor ranking (109 out of 119 countries) on Global Talent Competitiveness Index provides further evidence against this claim. An educational emergency is required to deal with the situation. A shift is also required in the orientation of academia at the higher education institutions which is more engaged in trying to 'manage themselves' published rather than developing their capacity to publish which is strongly linked with substantive reading and reflective sharing with the students and the society at large. The centre

of academia's gravity can be changed only if the HEC revisits its only publication-based criteria for promotion.

10. The availability/cost of suitable premises remained another important barrier for new businesses.[67] At present, sales tax registration does not allow a new business to get registered his/her residence as his/her business premises. A more rationale policy is required on this.

11. Exorbitant interest rates (17 to 23 per cent) on borrowing from banks make it near to impossible for new enterprises to secure loan and return this while sailing smoothly.

CONCLUSION

Top tech unicorns, such as Uber, which contributed towards increased hype about entrepreneurship since their birth have been struggling to find an eraser to erase red parenthesis around the figures in their balance sheet. The cases discussed help us conclude several things about the desired way forward for entrepreneurship in Pakistan.

First, entrepreneurship is emerging on the peripheries of cross-disciplines. Hence, expertise in a single field is bound to fail. The word 'more' will be less if we talk about collaborations between industry, academia, development, and public sector to play an active role in breeding and harnessing entrepreneurship in Pakistan.

A long-term orientation is required so patience is the second important lesson we can draw from these two examples. Entrepreneurship is a moving target. Gaining excellence at one time and in an industry surely is not a guarantee that the leadership/excellence will be enduring. So, the third lesson is keeping stakeholders on their toes to remain vigilant and keep on improving.

Facilitation in financing, exonerating the new enterprises from taxation (during the time of their newly-born status), and saving them from red tape can enable entrepreneurs to think hard about their ventures. All these demand governments to be an active partner, which it is but the implied moral is that without a continuously improving ecosystem, entrepreneurs based in Pakistan surely will not have a level-playing field vis-à-vis their regional and global competitors.

Finally, the government's recently increased efforts to facilitate entrepreneurship in Pakistan needs to remind itself that a shrinking economy cannot be a rich field that can motivate individuals to try their luck in the unchartered waters of entrepreneurship. Megaprojects under the public domain, nevertheless, can be an option to enrich the entrepreneurship landscape of Pakistan.

Notes

1. David Trainer, 'The Unicorn Bubble Is Bursting,' *Forbes*, October 7, 2019.
2. Donald F. Kuratko, Michael H. Morris, and Minet Schindehutte, 'Understanding the dynamics of entrepreneurship through framework approaches,' *Small Business Economics* 45, no. 1 (2015): 1.
3. Zoltán J. Ács, László Szerb, Esteban Lafuente, and Ainsley Lloyd, 'The Global Entrepreneurship Index,' The Global Entrepreneurship and Development Institute (2018).
4. Thomas R. Eisenmann, 'Entrepreneurship: A Working Definition,' *Harvard Business Review*, January 10, 2013.
5. Definition by the Business Dictionary.
6. Kuratko, Morris, and Schindehutte, 'Understanding the dynamics of entrepreneurship.'
7. William B. Gartner, 'A Conceptual Framework for Describing the Phenomenon of New Venture Creation,' *The Academy of Management Review* 10, no. 4 (October 1985): 696–706.
8. Kuratko, Morris, and Schindehutte, 'Understanding the dynamics of entrepreneurship.'
9. Gartner, 'A Conceptual Framework.'
10. Ibid.
11. A. M. M. Khan, *Product Report Sports Goods* (Karachi: Trade Development Authority Pakistan, 2019).
12. Christine Lagarde, 'Pakistan and Emerging Markets in the World Economy,' International Monetary Fund, October 24, 2016.
13. Creative enterprises can be defined as entities that have their origin in individual creativity, skill and talent, and which have a potential for wealth and job creation through the generation and exploitation of intellectual property (British Council, www.britishcouncil.org/arts-creativeindustries-definition.htm). Though entrepreneurship is associated with 'creativity', the term is used for classification purpose which helps us in differentiating various types of enterprises.
14. Definition by the Business Dictionary: A type of non-profit business that employs people and earns income in order to help address perceived social or environmental issues.
15. Nazir, Afridi, Ahmed, Gregory, Arif, and Kazmi, 'Developing Inclusive and Creative Economies.'
16. Work in progress.

17. An organisation that supports ideas pertaining to social entrepreneurship and social businesses in the world.

18. Nazir, Afridi, Ahmed, Gregory, Arif, and Kazmi, 'Developing Inclusive and Creative Economies.'

19. Bushra Ali and Emily Darko, 'Grants, incubators and innovation: a snapshot of social enterprise activities in Pakistan,' Pakistan: ODI (December 2015); and Maryam Mohiuddin Ahmed, Arslan Khalid, Alainna Lynch, and Emily Darko, 'The State of Social Enterprise in Bangladesh, Ghana, India and Pakistan: The State of Social Enterprise in Pakistan,' British Council (2016).

20. Eisenmann, 'Entrepreneurship.'

21. Ibid.

22. Robert H. Brockhaus, 'The Psychology of the Entrepreneur,' in *Encyclopedia of Entrepreneurship*, eds., C. A. Kent, D. L. Sexton, and K. H. Vesper (Englewood Cliffs, NJ: Prentice-Hall, 1982), 39–57.

23. Leigh Buchanan, 'The Most Important Entrepreneurs of the Past Decade,' *INC*, December 24, 2019.

24. Stella Cridge, 'The role of founder experience in industrial development: firm entry, growth and diversification in Pakistan's textile industry during trade liberalization,' PhD Thesis, London School of Economics, 2009.

25. Hina Abidi, Farhan Shafiq, Rimsha Arshad, Maria Pirwan, and Ahmed Hassan, 'Stories of Entrepreneurship,' *Market Forces* 10, no. 2 (December 2015); and Azhar Rizvi, *Entrepreneuring Pakistan: 27 stories of struggle, failure and success* (South Carolina: CreateSpace Independent Publishing Platform, 2018).

26. Rizvi, *Entrepreneuring Pakistan*.

27. Daniel Isenberg, 'What an Entrepreneurship Ecosystem Actually Is,' *Harvard Business Review*, May 12, 2014.

28. Gartner, 'A Conceptual Framework.'

29. 'It has become harder for the Asian tigers to prosper through exports,' *The Economist*, December 5, 2019.

30. Clayton M. Christensen, Efosa Ojomo, and Karen Dillon, 'Cracking Frontier Markets,' *Harvard Business Review* (January–February 2019).

31. Muhammad Arif, 'Understanding a Big Elephant and its Small Chain: Pakistan's SWOT Analysis,' unpublished report (2019).

32. Vaqar Ahmed, M. Javed, R. Tabassum, A. Javed, M. F. Ferracane, and W. Anukoonwattaka, 'National Study on Digital Trade Integration in Pakistan,' United Nations Economic and Social Commission for Asia and the Pacific, Bangkok, 2021 (unpublished).

33. Arif, 'Understanding a Big Elephant.'

34. Peter Ellis and Mark Roberts, 'Leveraging Urbanization in South Asia: Managing Spatial Transformation for Prosperity and Livability,' World Bank (2016).

35. Arif, 'Understanding a Big Elephant.'

36. Ibid.

37. Susan Lund, James Manyika, Jonathan Woetzel, Jacques Bughin, Mekala Krishnan, Jeongmin Seong, and Mac Muir, 'Globalization in transition: The future of trade and value chains,' *McKinsey Quarterly* (2019).

38. Arif, 'Understanding a Big Elephant.'

39. Qahafa Azhad, 'List of Startup Accelerators, Incubators, and Venture Capital Firms in Pakistan,' *Ideagist*, November 18, 2018.
40. A voluntary non-profit organisation formed by a group of US-Pakistani entrepreneurs at MIT in 1998 to facilitate and encourage the growth of Pakistani entrepreneurs and professionals.
41. Arif, 'Understanding a Big Elephant'; and Nazir, Afridi, Ahmed, Gregory, Arif, and Kazmi, 'Developing Inclusive and Creative Economies.'
42. Abeer Pervaiz and Mohammad Saud Khan, 'Entrepreneurial Relations of Pakistani Entrepreneurs: A Macroeconomic and Cultural Perspective,' *SAGE Open* (October 2015): 1–13.
43. A. T. Kearney and Jazz, 'Digital Entrepreneurship Ecosystem in Pakistan 2017: How Pakistan can build a world class digital ecosystem' (Islamabad: A. T. Kearney, 2017).
44. Sameer Sabir, Tania Aidrus, and Sarah Bird, 'Pakistan: A Story of Technology, Entrepreneurs and Global Networks–A Case Study,' MIT Sloan Management Review (2010).
45. Nazir, Afridi, Ahmed, Gregory, Arif, and Kazmi, 'Developing Inclusive and Creative Economies.'
46. 'Digital Entrepreneurship Ecosystem in Pakistan 2017.'
47. Gartner, 'A Conceptual Framework.'
48. Number of words limitations confined author's inclination to reflect more on these. For more, see Joseph A. Schumpeter, *Capitalism, Socialism and Democracy* (New York: Harper & Brothers, 1950).
49. The economist ascribed firms as the driving force behind economic growth.
50. Ishrat Husain, *Governing the Ungovernable: Institutional Reforms for Democratic Governance* (Karachi: Oxford University Press, 2018).
51. Ibid., 17.
52. Ishrat Husain, *Pakistan: The Economy of An Elitist State* (Karachi: Oxford University Press, 1999).
53. An Xiao Mina and Jan Chipchase, 'Inside Shenzhen's race to outdo Silicon Valley,' *Technology Review*, December 18, 2018.
54. Arif, 'Understanding a Big Elephant.'
55. Joe Pinsker, 'One City in Pakistan Makes Nearly Half of the World's Soccer Balls,' *The Atlantic*, July 2, 2014.
56. Khan, *Product Report Sports Goods*.
57. See 'Highnoon laboratories,' *Forbes*, 2019.
58. Mark Easterby-Smith, Richard Thorpe, and Paul Jackson, *Management Research* (Los Angeles; London: SAGE Publications, 2008).
59. Nazir, Afridi, Ahmed, Gregory, Arif, and Kazmi, 'Developing Inclusive and Creative Economies.'
60. Shameen Prashantham, 'Partner with entrepreneurs inside and out,' MIT Sloan Management Review (2019).
61. Jerome A. Katz, 'The chronology and intellectual trajectory of American entrepreneurship education, 1876–1999,' *Journal of Business Venturing* 18 (2003): 283–300.
62. Naved Hamid and Faizan Khalid, 'Entrepreneurship and Innovation in the Digital Economy,' *The Lahore Journal of Economics* 21 (2016): 273–312.

63. Nazir, Afridi, Ahmed, Gregory, Arif, and Kazmi, 'Developing Inclusive and Creative Economies'; and Hamid and Khalid, 'Entrepreneurship and Innovation.'
64. Khan, *Product Report Sports Goods.*
65. Arif, 'Understanding a Big Elephant.'
66. 'Digital Entrepreneurship Ecosystem in Pakistan 2017.'
67. Nazir, Afridi, Ahmed, Gregory, Arif, and Kazmi, 'Developing Inclusive and Creative Economies.'

Part

5

REGIONAL INTEGRATION

CHAPTER 15

Pakistan's Trade with Central Asia

GHULAM SAMAD AND GHULAM NABI

INTRODUCTION

The geo-strategic location of Pakistan places it in an inevitably important position for economies in the region, especially for Central Asian countries, including Afghanistan, Kazakhstan, the Kyrgyz Republic, Tajikistan, and Uzbekistan. Relations with Afghanistan remain tense, but Pakistan remains its largest trading partner.[1] Pakistan can provide a route for trade and also serve as an energy corridor for Central Asian countries that are landlocked[2] not only intra-regionally but also through shortest routes to the international markets.[3] Anwar points out how Central Asian Republics (CARs) are important for Pakistan in terms of supplying raw materials and manufactured goods through regional and bilateral trade.[4] Unfortunately, Pakistan has not yet leveraged the trade advantage of these energy-rich countries.

Pakistan also has bilateral and regional trade agreements with China, Malaysia, Sri Lanka, South Asian Association for Regional Cooperation (SAARC), and the Organization of Islamic Countries (OIC).[5] In January 2020, China agreed to eliminate duties on 313 high-priority tariff lines of Pakistan's export under the second phase of the China-Pakistan Free Trade Agreement (CPFTA),[6] which will boost Pakistan's exports by $4–6 billion.[7] Trade balance remains in favour of Pakistan against Sri Lanka since the signing of the Free Trade Agreement (FTA). In 2018, Pakistan recorded the largest exports to Sri Lanka since 2005 (worth $356 million) and a surplus balance of $256 million.[8] According to the Trade Map database, trade liberalisation with Malaysia stood at $1,316.8 million of trade volume in 2018. Malaysia is exporting a large number of goods and services to Pakistan worth $1,164.3 million. Major exports include palm oil (52 per cent) and machinery (7.85 per cent). Pakistan is exporting only 86 per cent of the top 10 items, including cereal, cotton, textiles, and articles of apparel and fish to Malaysia.[9]

Pakistan's total trade volume was $28,505 million with OIC in 2018 for all products while imports were $22,865 million, thereby having a negative trade balance of $172,26.9 million. The top potential items which Pakistan exports are cotton, cereals, sugar, textile, meat, etc.

Pakistan, like other developing countries, is suffering from a trade deficit and dependence on a variety of imports increasing foreign debts. There was an increasing trade deficit in the period from 2010 to 2018. The imports in 2010 were $37.54 billion whereas exports amounted to $21.41 billion, thus creating a trade deficit of $16.12 billion (which increased to $36.53 billion in 2018).[10] Imports by Pakistan are heavily dominated by food items, machinery, petroleum, consumer durables, raw material, telecom, and transport, constituting 70 per cent of total imports.[11] Petroleum and raw materials have the highest share in total imports around 36 per cent.

Exports are considered a critical indicator for an economy. They not only provide foreign earnings but also create employment, support balance of payment, and improve the term of trade to the international market, thus achieving sustainable growth for the country. The Government of Pakistan is focusing on exports as a driver of economic growth and trying to improve competitiveness, productivity, and efficiency of the local industry by boosting exports via substituting imports. According to the *Economic Survey 2018–19*, the export items are food products, textile, petroleum, and other manufactures with export shares of 19.6, 58.51, 0.9, and 14.75 per cent, respectively. Textile products have the highest share in total exports which include cotton cloth, knitwear, bed wear, ready-made garments, etc.[12]

The pattern of trade growth for Pakistan shows fluctuations overtime in Figure 1. In 2018, trade growth for Pakistan was 6.73 per cent while world trade growth was 3.5 per cent. Trade growth remains more than 25 per cent of GDP overtime whereas the total value of imports and exports in 2018 was 28.5 per cent of GDP. Total value of imports and exports in India and Afghanistan are 43.1 per cent and 51.2 per cent of GDP, respectively.

Figure 1: Pakistan's Economic Growth and Trade

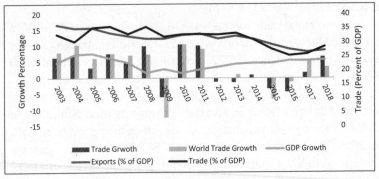

Source: WDI and WITS

Compared to the neighbouring countries, exports from Pakistan have fallen from 16.72 per cent in 2003 to 8.71 per cent of GDP in 2018.

REGIONAL TRADE INTEGRATION AND PAKISTAN

Economic integration has led countries to liberalise the flow of goods and services across borders.[13] Regional integration is a process in which countries share benefits of economies of scale, promote intra-regional trade, new markets, exchange of technical know-how, etc. Akın further argues that trade integration has a significant impact on the degree of specialisation.[14] For Pakistan, trade integration increases its access to international and regional markets which enables the business environment, and increases the capacity to remove barriers to exports efficiently.

To enhance trade performance, Pakistan negotiated many regional/bilateral trade agreements with countries in the region. These regional/bilateral trade agreements between countries help reduce trade barriers for the free flow of goods and services in the region. The Pak-Afghanistan Transit Trade Agreement, SAARC, Economic Cooperation Organization (ECO), and Association of Southeast Asian Nations (ASEAN) are few examples of economic integration.[15]

Countries around the world are signing trade agreements to promote economic growth. While these agreements encourage production for exports, they may be harmful for domestic production due to low-cost import substitution, which reduces the incentive for local production.[16]

Pakistan is a member of the Central Asia Regional Economic Cooperation (CAREC) programme,[17] comprising of 11 countries promoting sustainable development, growth, and poverty reduction through cooperation. The CAREC institute designed a CAREC Regional Integration Index (CRII)[18] to measure the strength of economic cooperation among member countries,[19] and produced a working paper which normalises the indicators and quotes the measured indexes.[20] The CRII scores quoted in the paper are Afghanistan (0.211), Kazakhstan (0.444), Kyrgyzstan (0.408), Pakistan (0.344), Tajikistan (0.369), Turkmenistan (0.400), and Uzbekistan (0.361) for all CAREC countries. Research further reveals that there is relatively more integration among Kazakhstan, Kyrgyz Republic, Pakistan, Tajikistan, and Uzbekistan.

The database of the Asia Regional Integration Center shows normalised data in six dimensions.[21] In 2016, the CAREC member countries' trade and investment index were as follows: Kazakhstan (0.156), Kyrgyz Republic (0.398), Pakistan (0.323), Tajikistan (0.194), Turkmenistan (0.350), and Uzbekistan (0.0322). The data shows that regional value chain index was also higher than other dimensions. For Pakistan, a policy intervention is required for higher regional integration with CARs. The CARs are enriched with hydrocarbon resources which has a great potential for trade in energy within the region. In addition to this, most of the Central Asian countries are landlocked and need a transit route to access the international market.

TRADE WITH CENTRAL ASIAN COUNTRIES

According to the World Integrated Trade Solution (WITS) database, the trade volume of Pakistan with the Central Asian countries, including Afghanistan, stood at $2,000.2 million out of which $1,463.8 million worth of exports and $536.4 million worth of imports to and from the Central Asian countries were carried out for the year 2018.

Table 1: Pakistan Trade Volume (Thousand $)

| | Export | | | Import | | | Trade Balance | Trade Volume |
	2006	2011	2018	2006	2011	2018	2018	2018
Afghanistan	991503	2660295	1347934	64943	199529	508361	839,573	1,856,295
Kazakhstan	8516	5770	86898	2549	7769	3310	83588	90209
Kyrgyz Republic	1028	922	1511	388	4	121	1390	1632
Tajikistan	472	623	9405	3506	124	3344	6061	12750
Turkmenistan	762	1075	797	8769	28595	17996	-17199	18794
Uzbekistan	2089	3512	17282	18247	10692	3330	13951	20613

Source: Compiled by authors (WITS, 2018)

Table 1 shows Afghanistan as the largest trading partner in the region to Pakistan (with exports worth $1,347.9 million). The table also shows that Pakistan exported the largest share of goods and services to Afghanistan in 2011, and this share has declined thereafter by approximately 50 per cent.

Dr Ishrat Husain highlighted a number of factors for the declining exports to Afghanistan, including 'instability, customs delays, suspension of North Atlantic Treaty Organization (NATO) supply shipments, and other issues'.[22] Husain and Elahi also suggested that Pakistan should expedite measures which could bring about deeper trade integration between the two countries.

Pakistan, being the largest trading partner of Afghanistan, had a trade share of 42.86 per cent and 14.67 per cent for all its exports and imports, respectively, to Pakistan in 2018. The total trade volume is $1,856.29 million. Pakistan has exported 5.7 per cent of all export products to Afghanistan, amounting to $1,347.92 million (Table 1).

Kazakhstan is a landlocked country and its trade with Pakistan is very limited. The total trade volume between both countries was worth $90.2 million in 2018, which is considerably higher compared to the export volume in 2003 (when exports amounted to $8.52 million). Kazakhstan carries out 5.24 per cent of total imports and 0.37 per cent of total exports to and from Pakistan, whereas Pakistan imports $3.31·million of goods and services from Kazakhstan (0.01 per cent of all imports). Pakistan enjoys a favourable trade balance with Central Asian countries, except for Turkmenistan (with which it has a negative trade balance of $17.19 million).

Trade with Afghanistan

Historically, relations between Pakistan and Afghanistan have remained tense due to cross-border infiltration, refugees, militant groups, disputes over policies, drug smuggling, and terrorist activities.[23] Despite this, Afghanistan is listed as Pakistan's fifth-largest trading partner while Pakistan is the largest importer of products from Afghanistan.

Afghanistan imported goods and services worth $1,347.93 from Pakistan in 2018, including capital goods ($38.27 million), consumer goods ($757.56 million), intermediate goods ($300.44 million), and raw material ($251.65). Among the top ten products exported by Pakistan to Afghanistan, vegetables have been listed as the most-exported product (38.27 per cent of total exports), followed by food products (20.29 per cent), and fuels (12.22 per cent). The calculation shows an absolute increase in export products when compared to 2010. Export of vegetables has increased by 17.39 units of the total share, whereas food products and chemicals increased by 16.31 units and 4.9 units, respectively. Simultaneously, fuel exports decreased by 27.11 units. The main decline was seen in consumer goods and intermediate goods, which collectively contribute approximately 80 per cent of total exports.

In 2018, Afghanistan exported $508.36 million worth of goods and services to Pakistan, including raw material (86.81 per cent of total Afghan exports), intermediate goods (12.32 per cent), consumer goods, and capital goods.

The top import products from Afghanistan based on the 2018 product-wise distribution include vegetables as a top commodity that constitutes approximately 54.46 per cent of total imports, which is considerably higher than its import share in 2010.

Fuel is the second most imported product (18.57 per cent of total imports), which is a significant rise from its share in 2010 of only 1.38 per cent of total imports. Likewise, the import shares of some products have shrunk over time, including those of textiles and clothing, although in 2010 it was the top most imported item.

There is a great potential for trade with Afghanistan and both countries cannot deny their dependence on each other. A huge trade volume between both the countries exists and the potential import and export goods for bilateral trade include: sugar, mineral fuel, mineral oil, and cereals among many others. Dr Ishrat Husain rightfully said that 'peaceful economic cooperation between Afghanistan and Pakistan and improved trade and transit facilities would help connect South Asia with Central Asia'.[24]

Trade with Kazakhstan

According to the World Bank (WB) database, Kazakhstan has a GDP of $179,340 million, 4.1 per cent GDP growth rate in 2018, and 62.82 per cent trade volume of GDP. However, Kazakhstan's bilateral trade volume with Pakistan is $90.21 million, which is approximately 0.38 per cent of total trade volume. Kazakhstan has cyclical trends for imports from 2006 to 2012. Both countries have enjoyed bilateral trade relations since independence. Although trading volume was very low, Kazakhstan has enjoyed a positive trade balance with Pakistan till 2013 when imports from Kazakhstan drastically declined from $13.20 million to $4.23 million and the exports share increased from 0.022 per cent in 2013 to 0.37 per cent in 2018. The WB's estimations show that there is a great potential for bilateral trade between Pakistan and Kazakhstan.[25] The predicted trade estimation was $24.44 million in 2015 when the total volume was $16.56 million.

In 2018, data indicates that Kazakhstan's major import was consumer goods (74.16 per cent of total imports), amounting to about $64.45 million. Kazakhstan is exporting $3.31 million worth of goods and services to Pakistan. The major goods exported from Pakistan to Kazakhstan in 2018, with the top export item being vegetables (mandarins, potatoes, etc.). A report published by the Pakistan Business Council (PBC) in 2017 indicated medical appliances ($73.95 million), medicaments for therapy and hormones ($99.54 million), and bandages ($4.25 million) as potential export items for Pakistan.[26]

The major products imported by Pakistan in 2018 were chemicals (61.24 per cent) being the most imported product in 2018 (as opposed to it being the fourth most least-imported in 2010). According to the above-mentioned PBC report, the highest import potential products for Pakistan include: dried lentils ($33.59 million), boring or sinking machinery ($20.23 million), and boards and cabinets for electric control ($12.13 million).

There are countless other potential goods for bilateral trade between Kazakhstan and Pakistan, including inorganic chemicals, organic or inorganic compounds of precious metals, and leather among many others.

Trade with the Kyrgyz Republic

The Kyrgyz Republic is another landlocked country in the region. It is bordered by four countries: Kazakhstan (north), Uzbekistan (west), Tajikistan (southwest), and China (east). Agriculture is a dominant sector in the Kyrgyz Republic but its economy heavily depends on gold exports. In 2018, Kyrgyz Republic's GDP amounted to $8,092.84.

Pakistan has established relations with the Kyrgyz Republic since after independence. Both countries are cooperating in various fields for the promotion of political and economic relations. The total trade volume between the Kyrgyz Republic and Pakistan in 2018 was $1.63 million.

The product-wise comparison of exports and imports between 2010 and 2018 indicates that consumer goods were the highest exported item in 2018 and their export also increased by approximately 15.8 per cent as compared to 2010. Unfortunately, the export of raw materials only decreased over time and no exports of said product was carried out in 2018. A World Bank report predicted the trade volume between the Kyrgyz Republic and Pakistan to be $3.81 million when the actual trade volume was 0.91 million in 2015.

There is great potential and resources in both countries when it comes to bilateral trade. Both direly need to make good use of this opportunity and thereby strengthen their economies.

Trade with Tajikistan

Tajikistan, too, is a landlocked country and shares borders with Afghanistan, Uzbekistan, Kyrgyz Republic, and China. Its annual GDP growth was 7.3 per cent in 2018. The relationship between Pakistan and Tajikistan grew in different phases. Several summits were held to improve bilateral trade relations between the two.

The bilateral trade volume between Pakistan and Tajikistan in 2018 was $12.75 million. The highest trade volume was in 2016 when exports amounted to $18.96 million and imports $4.37 million. The exports have greatly increased over time, with the highest exports being that of consumer goods (amounting to $9.32 million that is 99.14 per cent of total exports). No export of raw materials was carried out in 2010, whereas raw material imports were the highest. However, raw material exports rose to $0.02 million (0.22 per cent of exports) in 2018 and one hopes to see this positive trajectory continued in the coming years.

The trade share as a partner is very low between the two countries. Tajikistan's export share is 0.039 per cent in 2018 while the import share is 0.0056 per cent of total exports and imports. In 2018, animals, chemicals, textiles and clothing, and vegetables constituted 13.17 per cent, 5.73 per cent, 4.73 per cent, and 0.74 per cent of exports from Pakistan to Tajikistan, respectively. The top imports from Tajikistan were textiles and clothing, vegetables, machinery, and electronics—95.05 per cent, 2.22 per cent, and 0.41 per cent, respectively.

Pakistan has the opportunity to enhance trade relations with Tajikistan and also offer access to its trade route, which will generate great revenues for the two countries. Tajikistan has cheapest electricity in the world and can immensely help Pakistan in overcoming the energy shortfall that it currently faces.

Trade with Turkmenistan

Turkmenistan is enriched with agriculture, irrigated oases, and huge gas and oil reserves. It is mostly a desert and shares borders with Iran, Afghanistan, Uzbekistan, and Kazakhstan. According to the WB database, Turkmenistan's annual GDP growth was 6.2 per cent in 2018.

Relations with Turkmenistan were also established after its independence. The two countries have had a favourable trade relationship with each other since 2010 but a comparison shows exports and imports to have dropped since then. The total volume of trade was $18.7 million in 2018 and the highest trade volume was in 2010 (imports and exports amounting to $31.88 million and $1.5 million, respectively).

The major export groups from Pakistan to Turkmenistan are intermediate and consumer goods worth $0.37 million and $0.34 million in 2018, besides extensive import of raw material worth $16.89 million.

The potential that exists for bilateral trade between Pakistan and Turkmenistan cannot be ignored. There is a variety of products that can be made use of to conduct trade activities and, thus, contribute to the economic prosperity of both the countries in particular and of the region as a whole.

Trade with Uzbekistan

Uzbekistan, another landlocked country in Central Asia, has only 11 per cent of cultivated land and is bordered by Kazakhstan, Kyrgyzstan, Tajikistan, Afghanistan, and Turkmenistan. In 2018, its current GDP growth was 5.12 per cent.

The trade volume in 2010 stood at $21.9 million—imports amounted to $19.18 million and exports $2.73 million. According to WITS, the import and export trade share of Uzbekistan with Pakistan was 0.005 per cent and 0.073 per cent, respectively. Consumer goods ($12.03 million, 71.18 per cent) and raw materials ($3.45 million, 20 per cent) were the top export product groups from Pakistan to Uzbekistan in 2018 while raw materials ($2.5 million, 75.08 per cent) and intermediate goods (0.81, 24.37 per cent) were top two import product groups.

The export and import comparison between 2010 and 2018 for the two countries shows an overall increase in trade volume since 2010. Consumer goods had the greatest share in exports of 2018 while raw material was the most imported product group.

There are several opportunities that can be availed in order to establish beneficial trade relations with Uzbekistan. The two countries are rich in various resources and can greatly contribute to each other's economies.

PAKISTAN'S SELECTED TRADE INDICATORS

Revealed Comparative Advantage

Our exploratory analyses show that Central Asia's Revealed Comparative Advantage (RCA) is mainly in primary commodities that are fuel and mining products. Similarly, Pakistan's comparative advantage is in agricultural primary products. Unfortunately, the above product level analysis did not support the RCA in technology related skills and products. Our exploratory analysis is supported by the CAREC 2018 study.[27] If we look into the historical disaggregated product-wise categorisation, the comparative advantage also remains static.[28]

Table 2 shows that in one decade, the variation in products with RCA>1 has slightly increased for all, except the Kyrgyz Republic. We can see the concentration and diversification of products in these economies, mainly in primary resource products, and diversification is again very limited. The low comparative advantage and concentration of exports may not help to fully achieve the perceived benefits of FTAs, and thus, there is a need to amplify specialisation in the second tier of products.

Table 2: Product RCA and Share of top 15 exports

	2006		2016		Variation 2006/16 (no. of new product categories with RCA>1)
	Total Products RCA>1	% of top 15 exports with RCA>1	Total Products RCA>1	% of top 15 exports with RCA>1	
AFG	34	100	24	86.7	7
KAZ	33	86.7	34	93.3	7
KGZ	54	100	54	93.3	23
PAK	44	100	51	100	15
TAJ	23	93.3	29	100	10
TKM	14	66.7	14	66.7	2
UZB	31	93.3	23	93.3	7

Source: Regional Trade Dynamics and Selected Indicators in the CAREC region (CAREC, 2018)

Trade Complementarity

The bilateral trade figures are also not supporting trade complementarity. Our exploratory analysis is also supported by CAREC 2018—the trade complementarity index for Pakistan is low with the Central Asian countries (Table 3). This index takes a value between 0 and 100, with zero indicating no overlap and 100 indicating a perfect match in the import and export pattern. The highest trade complementarity that Pakistan has is with the Kyrgyz Republic and Kazakhstan. However, the overall magnitude is limited. The disaggregated product-wise categorisation shows that Pakistan's agriculture products have relatively more trade complementarity. The exploratory and empirical analyses support having an FTA to achieve these perceived benefits.

Table 3: Bilateral Trade Complementarity Indices

		Exporter						
		AFG	KAZ	KGZ	PAK	TAJ	TKM	UZB
Importer	**AFG**	–	0.13	0.31	0.25	0.15	0.08	0.10
	KAZ	0.10	–	0.35	0.20	0.11	0.09	0.12
	KGZ	0.11	0.15	–	0.26	0.10	0.11	0.11
	PAK	0.17	0.23	0.29	–	0.10	0.20	0.15
	TAJ	0.09	0.19	0.31	0.28	–	0.11	0.10
	TKM	0.09	0.11	0.29	0.16	0.08	–	0.08
	UZB	0.13	0.19	0.29	0.20	0.12	0.09	–
	Average	0.10	0.15	0.31	0.21	0.10	0.10	0.10

Source: Regional Trade Dynamics and Selected Indicators in the CAREC region (CAREC, 2018)

Trade Similarity

From the product categorisation, we deduce that product similarity is low. Pakistan mainly relies on agriculture-related products while Central Asia mostly relies on minerals and fuels. Based on the existing product similarity, literature indicates that Pakistan has the potential to export agriculture and agriculture-related products and can import minerals and fuel-related products, despite low values of export similarity index (Table 4). An index value close to zero suggests no competition between two countries. CAREC explores Pakistan's similarity indices with Central Asia. Except for the Kyrgyz Republic, Uzbekistan, and Afghanistan (where agriculture is one of the main export products), the similarity indices are low. Our exploratory analysis is in line with CAREC (2018).[29]

Table 4: Export Similarity Indices

	AFG	KAZ	KGZ	PAK	TAJ	TKM	UZB
AFG	–	0.04	0.09	0.09	0.18	0.02	0.22
KAZ	0.04	–	0.15	0.15	0.12	0.05	0.17
KGZ	0.09	0.15	–	0.22	0.21	0.04	0.10
PAK	0.09	0.15	0.22	–	0.11	0.03	0.21
TAJ	0.18	0.12	0.21	0.11	–	0.02	0.20
TKM	0.02	0.05	0.04	0.03	0.02	–	0.35
UZB	0.22	0.17	0.10	0.21	0.20	0.35	–

Source: Regional Trade Dynamics and Selected Indicators in the CAREC region (CAREC, 2018)

CONCLUSION

Analysis shows that the trade potential of Pakistan with Central Asian countries does exist. However, the trade volume is minimal. If we look at Pakistan's export intensity index, it has been less than one since 2000 for most of the years, except with Afghanistan. Similarly, the trade intensity index has also been less than one for most of the Central Asian economies. The overall trade volume of Pakistan in the early 1990s was promising. However, the data shows a gradually decreasing trend in trade volume with most of the Central Asian economies.

Central Asian exports are mostly resource-based. The technological content is minimal. Therefore, Pakistan may not get the value proposition in its export contents by importing goods that have high value-addition. The Central Asian economies' value and supply chains are also not well-developed and have limited regional connectedness. As has been mentioned earlier, Pakistan's revealed comparative advantage and trade complementarity is quite low for most of the products, except agriculture, in addition to the low product similarity, which to some extent, supports Pakistan's trade potential with Central Asia.

A regional FTA with Central Asian economies may not bring about desired benefits (building a competitive environment, developing regional integration, increasing trade volume) to Pakistan's economy, however, Central Asian economies are still unexplored. If Pakistan establishes good trade relations with this region, it may be the beginning of a much-needed diversification of its export market that has, unfortunately, targeted only a few economics historically. Furthermore, connecting with Central Asia provides an opportunity to gain access to the Eurasian Economic Union countries. Energy cooperation with energy-rich Central Asia will also benefit Pakistan greatly while simultaneously providing direct sea access to the landlocked countries.

Before developing a regional FTA with Central Asia, there is a need to revisit Pakistan's barriers to trade (tariffs structure, non-tariff measures, and trade facilitation measures). In addition to this, Pakistan must also revisit the existing FTAs/Preferential Trade Agreements (PTAs). Unfortunately, former FTAs/PTAs were not based on solid research and evidence that should have proposed commodity-wise categorisation to highlight product-wise comparative advantage and trade complementarity. Detailed technical work on tariff structure at commodity level was superficially conducted. The RCA, low level of trade complementarity, and low-level export similarity (that does not match with country's import demand) are adding little value to the traditional regional trade agreements (RTAs).

We offer three recommendations to develop a new generation of RTAs. First, inclusion of Trade in Services in the RTAs. This may be done after a thorough analysis. Second, inclusion (limitedly included so far) of the Trade-Related Investment Measures (TRIMs) in the RTAs, and third, e-commerce clauses, which are almost non-existent in the RTAs currently.

Annex–1: Regional/ Bilateral Trade Agreements

S. No.	Regional/ Bilateral Trade Agreements
1.	Agreement on South Asian Free Trade Area
2.	Sensitive List of SAFTA member (Phase-II)
3.	Draft Offer & Request Lists of Pakistan under SAFTA (Phase-III)
4.	Pak-Malaysia Trade Agreements, Pak-Malaysia Early Harvest Programme
5.	Pak-China Free Trade Agreement in Goods & Investment
6.	Pak-China Free Trade Agreement in Services
7.	Pak-China Early Harvest Programme
8.	Phase-II China Pakistan FTA
9.	China-Pakistan FTA (CPFTA) Phase-II FAQs
10.	Pak-Sri Lanka Free Trade Agreement
11.	Pak-Iran Preferential Trade Agreement
12.	Pak-Mauritius Preferential Trade Agreement
13.	Pak-Indonesia Preferential Trade Agreement

Source: Ministry of Commerce

Notes

1. Ishrat Husain and Muhammad Ather Elahi, 'The Future of Afghanistan-Pakistan Trade Relations,' United State Institute of Peace (2015).
2. Saleem Khan, Sher Ali, and Saima Urooge, 'The Analysis Of Regional Bilateral Trade Between Pakistan and Central Asian Republics,' *Pakistan Journal of Applied Economics* 29, no. 1 (2019): 93–106.
3. Manzoor Ahmad, 'Improving Regional Trade to Support Pakistan's Economic Growth,' *The Lahore Journal of Economics* 19 (September 2014): 461–469.
4. Z. Anwar, 'Central Asia in World Attention,' *Central Asia* 41 (1997): 183.
5. See Annex-1 for details.
6. While reduction on 313 items will be in effect from January 1, 2020, for other items, a period of five years is provided within which duties will be rationalised.
7. 'China-Pakistan trade under renewed Free Trade Agreement to come into effect today,' *The News*, January 1, 2020.
8. Pakistan Business Council, 'A Review of the Pakistan-Sri Lanka Free Trade Agreement,' (2018).
9. Pakistan Business Council, 'An Assessment of the Pakistan–Malaysia Free Trade Agreement,' (2015).
10. The World Integrated Trade Solution is a trade software provided by the World Bank for users to query several international trade databases.

11. 'Pakistan Economic Survey 2018–19,' Ministry of Finance.
12. Ibid.
13. See Farzad Karimi and Akbar Tavakoli, 'The Analysis of Tade Integration and Business Cycles Synchronization with Emphasis on Regional Arrangements among OIC Nation,' Global Trade Analysis Project (2010); and Çiğdem Akın, 'Multiple Determinants of Business Cycle Synchronization,' SSRN (2012).
14. Akın, 'Multiple Determinants of Business Cycle Synchronization.'
15. See Annex-1 for more examples.
16. Anne Krueger, 'Why Trade Liberalisation is Good for Growth,' *The Economic Journal* 108, no. 450 (September 1998): 1513–1522.
17. The CAREC Program is a partnership of 11 countries including Afghanistan, Azerbaijan, China, Georgia, Kazakhstan, Kyrgyz Republic, Mongolia, Pakistan, Tajikistan, Turkmenistan, and Uzbekistan.
18. In 2017, the CAREC Institute designed the CAREC Regional Integration Index (CRII) based on the Asia-Pacific Regional Cooperation and Integration Index (ARCII). Like ARCII, the CRII includes 26 indicators that measure various aspects of regional integration along six dimensions: (i) trade and investment integration, (ii) money and finance integration, (iii) regional value chains, (iv) infrastructure and connectivity, (v) free movement of people, and (vi) institutional and social integration. The indicators are normalised and aggregated using principal component analysis to yield index range from 0 to 1, near to 1 showing higher levels of integration.
19. The focus of this chapter is Pakistan's Trade with Central Asia (countries including Afghanistan, Kazakhstan, Kyrgyz Republic, Tajikistan, Turkmenistan, and Uzbekistan).
20. 'CAREC Regional Integration Index (CRII): Interpretation and Policy Implications,' CAREC Institute, Working Paper (December 2019).
21. 'Asia-Pacific Regional Cooperation and Integration Index,' Asia Regional Integration Center.
22. Husain and Elahi, 'The Future of Afghanistan-Pakistan Trade Relations.'
23. Ibid.
24. Ibid., 4.
25. 'Pakistan@100 Regional Connectivity,' World Bank Group, Policy Note (March 2019).
26. 'Republic of Kazakhstan: The Central Asia Country Series,' Pakistan Business Council (2017).
27. 'Regional Trade Dynamics and Selected Indicators in the CAREC region,' CAREC (2018).
28. Ibid.
29. Ibid.

CHAPTER 16

Leveraging CPEC for Industrial Development

Liaqat Ali Shah

INDUSTRIAL DEVELOPMENT: AN INTRODUCTION

Industrialisation has undoubtedly become a global phenomenon no longer confined to a privileged group of leading countries. It embodies the technology and the organisation which have transformed production methods and the way of life at an unprecedented rate in the last two centuries, leading to improved living standard across the globe.[1]

The phenomenon started markedly in Britain in the eighteenth century, with mechanised spinning machines, followed by steam engines and internal combustion engines which powered the wheels of newly emerged industries during that period. The phenomenon has evolved significantly since then. It has penetrated every part of the world with some parts having a more pronounced industrial footprint than others and has touched the lives of billions of people.

Deeper footprints of the industry are reflective of the economic development because industrial development spurs economic growth. Moreover, industry has historically led the process of structural change. It has played an outsized role in East Asia and has turned the region into the world's factory. It would be fair to say that the East Asian Miracle is a manufacturing miracle. The eventual outcome of industrial development in East Asia, like anywhere else, is the achievement of social objectives, including employment, poverty eradication, labour standards, and greater access to education and healthcare. As opposed to East Asia, South Asia's manufacturing share in GDP, with the exception of Bangladesh, has rather remained stagnant since the 1980s and Pakistan is no exception.

The industrial development across Pakistan has had a chequered history. The industry boomed and became a major contributor to the economic growth in the 1950s and the 1960s, but then again went into recession during the period of nationalisation. From then on, the industry experienced boom and bust cycles. Later, bust began with severe power outages and deteriorating security situation in the country. Since the 1960s, there have been experiments with import substitution strategies with weak success. The situation further exacerbated with the global economic recession in 2008.

With the advent of CPEC, Pakistan's hope for the revival of industry, and industrialisation has been rekindled. However, there will be challenges to overcome in order for this to occur. This chapter focuses on this hope as well as the challenges. But before that, let's take a quick look at Pakistan's industrial development.

INDUSTRIAL DEVELOPMENT IN PAKISTAN: AN OVERVIEW

At its inception, Pakistan inherited a predominantly agrarian economy, with agriculture accounting for 53 per cent of the GDP while employing 65 per cent of the labour force, contributing to 99 per cent of the country's exports and earning 90 per cent of foreign exchange earnings. In the industrial sector, Pakistan inherited only 34 industrial units out of 921 industrial units in the subcontinent, primarily agriculture processing, such as jute bailing, textile, cigarettes, sugar, rice-husking, cotton-ginning, and flour-milling industries. There was virtually no modern manufacturing industry, except an oil refinery in West Pakistan and together they contributed only 5.9 per cent of the GDP and employed a little over 26,000 employees.[2]

Since then, the economy has undergone significant changes. Agriculture currently contributes 18.5 per cent, manufacturing ~13.8 per cent; and service industry 61.2 per cent to the GDP and its contribution in terms of employment is 38.5 per cent, 17 per cent, and ~36.8 per cent, respectively. Textiles, leather, food processing, pharmaceuticals, construction materials, paper products, fertilisers, and shrimp are the most important industries. The industrial production growth rate was 5.4 per cent (2017 est.). Textiles account for most of Pakistan's export earnings.

The transition from agrarian to industrial to primarily service economy occurred because of a multitude of factors, including but not limited to political, social, geo-economic, and geo-strategic reasons. Regardless of the factors that played a significant role, industrial growth has remained stagnant over the years. The industrial mix continues to be dominated by resource-based industries, primarily agriculture and mineral processing industries with low technological sophistication. Lack of research and development, low literacy rate, complicated regulatory environment, and inconsistent trade policies have prevented the industry from taking root and upgrading.

On the innovation index, Pakistan was ranked 105 out of 129 economies for the year 2019. Low innovation leads to low value-added exports which are mostly commodity exports. High-tech exports' share of the manufactured items is merely 2.2 per cent for 2018 as compared to India whose share stands at 9.1 per cent for the same year. Unfortunately, the overall performance of the industrial sector over the years has been dissatisfactory.

KEY CHALLENGES TO INDUSTRIAL EXCELLENCE

To remain competitive in an increasingly globalised industrial world, Pakistan's industrial sector faces a number of challenges. Over and above the macro-investment climate challenge, the challenges can be broadly be classified as poor infrastructure in both the transportation and energy sectors, a lack of robust logistic services, industrial and trade policy distortions, low industrial base, low productivity levels, poor quality of products, and complications in the regulatory framework.[3] These challenges have been stifling the growth of the industrial sector and some of them merit closer consideration.

POOR TRANSPORT INFRASTRUCTURE

Well-functioning cities that enjoy agglomeration economies require world class services, such as reliable and low-cost energy, better connectivity in terms of roads, rails, and airways to lower the cost of production to remain competitive in the global industrial arena. However, surveys and indices covering the quality of physical infrastructure indicate a rather poor picture in Pakistan. Road density was 33 km/100 square km with a meagre growth rate of 0.47 per cent during the period 2002–2011, showing a marked underinvestment in the transportation infrastructure.

Railways, despite being a safe, reliable, and fast mode of transportation in the world, performs poorly in Pakistan. The railways as mode of transportation deteriorated overtime in the country. The freight transport share of the railways dropped from 73 per cent in the 1960s to just 4 per cent in 2011.[4] Globally, rail freight transport accounted for 17.3 per cent of total freight transport in 2017 while road took 76.7 per cent of the share.[5] The drop in the share can be attributed to poor infrastructure as well governance issues affecting the operational efficiency of the railways in Pakistan. The 'Vision 2025' targets Pakistan's railways share in freight transport to be increased to 20 per cent through upgradation of Pakistan railways infrastructure.

In the port category, 95 per cent of export and import bulk is handled through Karachi Port Terminal (KPT) and Port Qasim. The two ports lack the required infrastructure and performance in terms of operational efficiency, and are becoming congested. The same can be said for airports. Of 46 airports, only 10 are open for international operations, 22 airports have been scaled back or closed with only 11 airports being used both for national and international operations. However, air cargo is negligible because of multitude of factors, including high freight rates, and cumbersome customs procedures.

In short, the transportation sector infrastructure in Pakistan is relatively weak by international standards. As per the *Pakistan Infrastructure Report* of the SBP, Pakistan loses 4–6 per cent of its GDP due to infrastructure deficiencies (power infrastructure included). Inefficiency in the transportation sector, which includes rail, road, port, and aviation, costs Pakistan 4 per cent of its GDP.[6]

INEFFICIENT LOGISTICS SERVICES

Closely associated with physical infrastructure is the logistics industry because an efficient logistics industry heavily relies on robust infrastructure and improved connectivity. Moreover, industrial growth necessitates the need for efficient logistics. The development of logistics development plays a supporting role in the overall economic development.

Efficient logistics service is vital to economic competitiveness. However, it suffers from a number of inefficiencies in Pakistan caused by outdated processes and lack of regulatory framework. Even this sector has not been formally recognised as an industry in Pakistan. Inefficiencies exist in the system's services, such as warehouses, packaging, multi-modal integration, facilitation centres for transporters, and seamless coordination among institutions, such as customs, immigration, quarantine, anti-narcotics, and highway police forces, among others. As a result, the system performs poorly. On the logistics performance index indicator, Pakistan is ranked 122 out of 167 countries, lagging behind other South Asian economies. Customs procedures (139) receive the lowest scores, followed by tracking and tracing (136), and timeliness (136).

Despite a low score of Logistics Performance Index (LPI), the sector was valued at $34 billion and grew by 18 per cent in the year 2017–2018, according to the Ministry of Communications. Inefficiencies on so many fronts in the sector that contributes around 10 per cent to the GDP (infrastructure included) means a lot to the country. Poor regulatory harmonisation is visible in the customs. For instance, a container, if processed at the Sialkot dry port, is again lined up for processing at the Karachi port, causing delays and incurring high shipment costs.

Therefore, a lack of strategies to develop this sector would negatively affect the future corridor efficiency and the economic zones that are expected to serve Western China, Central Asian Republics, and Afghanistan, to say the least. Modernisation of the sector is urgently needed in order to generate high payoffs in terms of strengthening Pakistan's industry and making it more competitive on a global scale.

ENERGY INFRASTRUCTURE BOTTLENECK

Access to affordable and reliable energy is as important as ever to industrial development. Over the last two decades, Pakistan's energy demand-supply has had negative impact on the country's economy. The cumulative effect of energy shortfalls could be observed both in the social development and industrial productivity of the nation[7] (and caused many industries to shut down operations and flight of capital to other countries.[8]

Because of poor energy planning on the part of successive governments, Pakistan went from being an energy-surplus country in 2001 to an energy-deficient one in 2006, and the gap between demand and supply widened thereafter. The rate of growth in the net energy supply remained 1.8 per cent, while the rate of consumption stayed at 2.9 per cent for the past six years.[9]

Moreover, reliance on thermal power generation using furnace oil coupled with volatile international oil prices has had adverse implications for the cost structure of electricity production, further undermining the competitiveness of the industry. Costly energy, in turn, adversely impacts the manufacturing sector, making it non-competitive. In addition to fuel charges causing inefficiencies in the energy market, transmission and distribution infrastructure inefficiencies are also adversely impacting the energy market and, as a result, the industrial sector.

HUMAN RESOURCES QUALITY

Quality human resources is critical for the economic prosperity of a country. As per the labour market survey 2017–2018, Pakistan has the ninth largest labour market, with 65 million workers. However, the quality of the resources falls short of that of the international market.

To equip the burgeoning working population with skills, a number of organisations are involved in Pakistan both at federal and provincial level. National, Vocational & Technical Training Commission (NAVTTC) is the apex body at federal level, and it has assumed the role to carry out skill planning, define skills standards, and develop policies and curricula, among the other things, in the sector. Other organisations include: Technical Education and Vocational Training Authority (TEVTA) in each province and Skills Development Council, and others.

However, lack of sufficient resources, weak liaison of the sector with industry and social support for students joining the TEVTA stream present the sector with many challenges. Moreover, low literacy rate in the country has become an impediment in the development of a large pool of skilled workers. Primary education rate in Pakistan is 67 per cent, far below the regional countries, such as India where the rate is 96 per cent and Turkey's rate is 100 per cent.[10] The secondary level education in Pakistan is just 35 per cent, making it hard for the institutions to play their role effectively and efficiently.

Low literacy rates, combined with other issues for the sector, result in less productive labour which, in turn, affects productivity levels and thus represents a bottleneck for the competitiveness of the industry.

FINANCIAL SYSTEM PERFORMANCE

Financial development and liberalisation in terms of capital account openness, equity openness, trade openness, and better governance of the financial system all play an important role in the industrial development of a country, ultimately fostering overall economic stability.[11] The financial sector underdevelopment and information asymmetries may cause frictions that impede financial liberalisation, affecting the industrial sector development.

Historically, Development Financial Institutions (DFIs) such as the Pakistan Industrial Credit and Investment Corporation (PICIC) and the National Development Finance Corporation (NDFC), the Industrial Development Bank (IDB), and others played an important role in providing the much-needed assistance to newly established industries. However, as a result of the significant losses sustained during the East Pakistan Strategy, they became less efficient.

The DFIs are no longer in existence and the government has taken on the role of a loan provider. Access to finance has become an issue for industrialisation and there is virtually no long-term lending instrument available. However, these DFI have been privatised and merged with banks that focus on lending to government or provide credit facility/access for short-term financing.

LEGAL AND REGULATORY ENVIRONMENT

The field of law and development holds that rapid industrial growth largely depends on simplified and transparent procedures, rules and regulations, their consistent interpretation and enforcement, just and rapid resolution of conflicts, and a social attitude of respect for legal and regulatory institutions.[12] In the case of Pakistan, regulatory framework is stringent and the cost of entry, compliances with regulations, be it in the labour, financial market, or with tax system requires time and effort and incurs a high cost of doing business. Moreover, price control mechanisms, rationalised tariff structure, subsidies to non-productive sectors, high rate of protectionism, and Statutory Regulatory Orders (SROs) to favour industries are among the issues that must be addressed to improve market efficiency and spur innovation and growth.

To improve efficiency, some regulations should be repealed and others should be reformed. Under the auspices of Dr Ishrat Husain, the government initiated a reform plan that included regulatory and civil reforms in order to strengthen the country's institutional quality. In the civil service reform plan, right from recruitment of officers to post-induction and/or in-service training, performance appraisals, and domain-specific clustering and beyond are areas in the reform agenda. Moreover, lateral entry of technical advisors from private sectors is also under consideration. In the regulatory reforms, being led by the federal Board of Investment, the purpose is to simplify and streamline regulations and create ease for conducting businesses. These reforms would enhance the capacity of the institutions for managing the affairs of the state, including economic and industrial affairs. Lack of capacity of the institutions in Pakistan has made state-owned enterprises into loss-making enterprises and Pakistan Steel Mill (PSM) is one such example.

In addition to these challenges, a lack of focused industrial policy and its relevance to the ever-changing international arena was another area that did not allow the industrial sector to diversify and to upgrade because industrial policies preferred some sectors over others. That was not based on economic rationale but rather on political expediency or vested interest. This resulted in distortions in the market that is witnessed even to this date.

In a nutshell, a lack of supportive structure coupled with inconsistent trade and industrial policies, and a myriad of other issues, including the geo-political situation, economic ties with trade partners, and missing opportunities in the wave of regionalism are among the factors that stifled Pakistan's industrial growth, particularly in the last four decades.

INDUSTRIAL REVITALISATION UNDER CPEC

Pakistan sees the signing of CPEC framework as an opportunity to revive its industry. The framework with 1+4 portfolio that kept Gwadar, energy, infrastructure, and industrial cooperation at the centre of bilateral cooperation under CPEC was meant to propel Pakistan towards a sustained economic growth. In the early harvest phase, energy and transportation infrastructure sectors were prioritised to remove the economic bottlenecks and pave the way for sustainable industrialisation.

In the 6th Joint Coordination Committee Meeting (JCC) held at Beijing on December 29, 2016, both sides agreed on industrial cooperation under CPEC. Following that, nine Special Economic Zones (SEZs) were identified and prioritised for establishment under the SEZ Act 2012 (Amended 2016).

As of now, three of the nine prioritised SEZs, namely Rashakai SEZ in Nowshera, Allama Iqbal SEZ in Faisalabad, and Dhabeji SEZ in Thatta are nearing completion. The remaining SEZs are in their early stages of development. It is worth mentioning that industrial cooperation is not confined to the nine prioritised zones but evolves over time, with more SEZs being added to the cooperation framework. In addition to the prioritised SEZs, Gwadar Free Zone with a total area of 2,200 acres of land is being established in the prospective port city of Gwadar to strengthen industrial cooperation.

On the policy front, the SEZ Act 2012 per se instils confidence in investors, while also signalling the government's commitment towards a stable SEZ policy regime. The Act offers indiscriminate fiscal concessions to both foreign and local investors. More concessions and incentives are under consideration to offset few impediments in the way of doing business in Pakistan and to make the country competitive with respect to other regional countries.

Moreover, a Joint Working Group (JWG) on industrial cooperation has been formed and the BOI has been designated as the lead agency to oversee CPEC industrial cooperation with China. Furthermore, Pakistan Steel Mill's revival is also under consideration in the CPEC framework.

Furthermore, steps are being taken to improve the technical capabilities within the country to increase productivity and supply of skilled labour to the industry in the domestic economy and to the zone enterprises alike. Delegations are facilitated on both sides of the border to boost industrial cooperation. All of these strategies and efforts are intended to kick-start industrialisation in the country.

To create an enabling environment for industrial development in the country and to attract foreign investors in the CPEC SEZs, a number of interventions have been made so far. These interventions are being executed in the order of priority that is: removing the infrastructure bottlenecks in transportation system, energy, and ICT sectors, and followed up by the development of the SEZs. Social sector development that includes interventions in the vocational and technical education, agriculture, poverty alleviation, tourism, etc., will go hand in hand with the development of the SEZs in order to make development sustainable and inclusive.

TRANSPORT INFRASTRUCTURE DEVELOPMENT UNDER CPEC

Projects in transportation infrastructure are being implemented as per the monographic study conducted in 2013–2015 in partnership with China's Ministry of Transport (MoT) to formulate a long-term plan (2015–2030) for the sector. The construction and upgradation work in the northern alignment (Khunjerab-Burhan), Trans-Pakistan north-south motorway link (Peshawar-Karachi), and western alignment (Islamabad-Quetta-Sorab) were made part of the plan. Central alignment from Pindigheb to Wangu Hills via DG Khan is also included in the long-term plan. So far, major projects completed in the infrastructure include: Multan-Sukkur Motorway (392 km) and Havelian-Thakot (118 km), Hakla-DI Khan Road (210 km), Eastbay Expressway, and other segments on the western corridor.

Moreover, the railways main line ML-1 is also part of the transportation infrastructure projects under CPEC. The upgradation of railways will give a new impetus to the logistics industry in

Pakistan. The completion of these projects would greatly improve the quality and accessibility of Pakistan's infrastructure. Moreover, natural resources along the corridors with improved infrastructure access would boost the value proposition of the region and could trigger economic activities. Additionally, New Gwadar International Airport (NGIA) would greatly improve the connectivity of the city. Overall, the transportation infrastructure projects would improve the infrastructure required for reliable logistics.

ENERGY INFRASTRUCTURE UNDER CPEC

In the energy infrastructure, significant development has been made as a result of CPEC. From energy deficiency with a shortfall that exceeded 6,000 MW in 2013, currently Pakistan is an energy-surplus country. More projects are being planned to improve the energy mix and rely more on indigenous resources to reduce the cost of electricity. Matiari to Lahore ± 660kV HVDC Transmission Line Project with 4,000 MW evacuation capacity has improved the country's transmission line capacity to some degree. Projects in the energy sector are being carried out in the Independent Power Producers (IPPs) mode under Power Policy 2015, with the exception of hydropower projects, which are being implemented under Power Policy 2002. To synchronise the energy supply-demand gap, a power market study has been carried out to forecast the energy need till 2030. More energy projects would be included as per power market study.

In addition to power generation and distribution, oil and gas sector development has also been included in CPEC. To that effect, plan entitled 'Oil and Gas Sector Development of Pakistan' has been developed in partnership with China to estimate the energy requirements in the petroleum sector of Pakistan. The plan's implementation has been delegated to a sub-group under Energy Working Group of CPEC.

HUMAN RESOURCES DEVELOPMENT UNDER CPEC

There is a strong emphasis on improving the quality of human resources in the country in order to manage the most complex projects ahead, such as ML-1 or to operate, maintain, and upgrade the special economic zones with the ever-evolving business environment in the region and beyond. Sustainability would not be achieved without quality human resources on our side.

In the context of CPEC, upgradation of vocational institutes, Punjab Tianjin University of Technology, Pak-China Technical & Vocational Institute in Gwadar, Pak-Austria Fachhochschule: Institute of Applied Sciences & Technology are among the initiatives being undertaken to improve the skill sets to meet labour market challenges.

In addition, workshops and trainings are being planned as part of the socioeconomic framework in order to improve the capability of Pakistan human resources. Seventy-two vocational institutes in the vicinity of the prioritised SEZs have been identified for upgrade at the cost of more than $100 million in order to supply skilled labour to meet the need of the SEZs under CPEC and outside. All of these efforts and those that will follow in the future are aimed at ensuring a steady supply of quality workforce for industrial development, innovation, and for staying competitive.

SPECIAL ECONOMIC ZONES UNDER CPEC

All the above-mentioned efforts would be futile unless the SEZs achieve the desired objectives of FDI inflow, export promotion, employment generation, technology transfer, industrialisation, and diversity in the country's industrial base.

Generally, the SEZs have proven to be an effective instrument in promoting these objectives. However, based on global experience, not all objectives can be achieved with a single SEZ. Some SEZs have been developed primarily to generate employment as is the case of the SEZs in Cambodia. Others were developed to diversify economy, such as in Jebel-Ali special economic zone in the UAE, to act as growth strategy as in Malaysia, Indonesia, and the Philippines, and to foster overall development like India. Some SEZs have been developed to provide a platform for innovation as is the case with innovation and technology parks worldwide.

Therefore, the SEZs in Pakistan must be developed with clear objectives in mind. One strategy for all SEZs, ignoring the investment climate which varies considerably across the country, would land some SEZs in a challenging situation. The nine prioritised SEZs under CPEC have been planned in all provinces, including special regions like AJK and Gilgit-Baltistan.

The prime objectives of these SEZs under CPEC are to industrialise the country (diversify industrial base), promote exports, substitute imports, and generate employment. Moreover, the prioritised SEZs are planned in areas to make use of the natural endowments of the region in order to spread economic activities along the corridor and away from the major urban centres. For example, the marble city in Mohmand district of KPK is to capitalise on the area's marble potential. Similarly, Moqpondass SEZ in Gilgit-Baltistan is proposed under CPEC to provide a platform to entrepreneurs to add value to the natural resources of the region; i.e., mines and minerals, gems and jewellery, fruit and vegetables, and beyond. With the completion of these SEZs, and many more in the pipeline, economic activities would be generated along the corridor, effectively transforming the transport into an economic corridor.

Furthermore, these SEZs are important at this point in time because the Chinese economy is transforming and its industries are upgrading. Also, the Chinese government's policy is to discontinue support to light engineering and labour-intensive industries as these industries are no longer competitive because of increasing wages and business cost in China. In addition, the Chinese government aims to generate demand for Chinese machineries and equipment, and to manage the trade barriers Chinese companies experience due to trade-related tensions with trade partners. With these policy objectives, the Chinese government is encouraging their entrepreneurs to relocate abroad and go global. Despite this, Chinese industries have not relocated to other countries at the expected rate. Some industries have relocated from the coastal region to inland China, particularly to the Central and North-Western regions.

RECOMMENDATIONS AND WAY FORWARD

Indeed, the Chinese economic transformation provides Pakistan with opportunities to benefit from and achieve variety of economic and social objectives. However, this would not come without a fair share of challenges. More measures are needed to speed up industrialisation and SEZs colonisation. These measures have been proposed in the form of recommendations listed below:

Focus on Logistics under CPEC

Little progress has been made in this area as a result of CPEC. However, there is a chance that the private sector will step in and take the lead. Interventions would be required to give the private sector the opportunity to invest in the sector.

Hard infrastructure would not improve the dividends of investment to the general public if it did not include logistics. The Economic and Trade Corridor Programme (ETCP) was launched in the eleventh-year plan with the following goals:

- develop an integrated inter-modal transport and logistics sector that efficiently meets requirements of the growing population and expanding economic activities.
- modernise management to ensure harmony and coordination among different transport systems, i.e., ports, railways, highways, inland waterways, and airways, and reduce costs to the economy.
- make a sustained effort to achieve world class transport infrastructure and logistic services to facilitate domestic and international trade through private sector participation.

There is a focus on infrastructure under CPEC, but integrated inter-modal transport, as well as soft skills required for model operation, has not yet been planned. Furthermore, railway projects under CPEC are expected to make significant progress in the near future. However, transforming railways to bring about change in the logistics industry is a difficult task. Either we reform the entire railway system to increase its capacity and enable it to make a difference in the sector, or we seek another authority to achieve the desired results. These are the questions that will occupy us throughout the ML-1 project's implementation.

Multiple Strategy Approach to Industrialisation via SEZs

Different strategies for developing SEZ should be used depending on the investment climate. The underdeveloped region with characteristics of poor infrastructure, including poor education and health facilities, and marred by unemployment should be developed using the First Stage SEZ concept, based on the region's comparative advantage, if any.

The developed region, which has good infrastructure and industrial footprints as well as labour availability, requires the Second Stage SEZ, whereas the leading region, which has competitive industry presence, research and development facilities, and the availability of pre-conditions for innovation, requires the Third Stage SEZ. Incentives for the First Stage should be more liberalised, as the goal is to exploit the region's resources and bring the region up to speed with the rest of the country. The hassle-free environment is more important than fiscal incentives in Second Stage SEZs. As for the Third Stage SEZs, they need comprehensive and long-term legal and institutional framework to attract investors.

Establishing Business-to-Business (B2B) Linkages

Several forums have been established so far to help the business community on both sides promote businesses, including those in SEZs. For instance, CPEC Business Council under the BOI was constituted in March 2019. The business council comprised of members from the public and private sector. Another platform by the name of Pakistan-China Business Forum was formed on July 2019 by the Ministry of Planning and Development. Another forum, Pak-China Business Forum, with the aim to bridge academia-industry linkages between local and Chinese firms was formed in 2012 under the Ministry of Science and Technology. It was specifically designed to address the most important subject of breaking the barriers of academia-based, research-driven outputs and their translation into products for industrial and corporate sectors.

Overall, these platforms have been established to provide highly sought-after linkages between the business communities and other stakeholders to form a solid foundation for technology transfer, business alliances, and sharing their experiences to form a more robust partnership in the path to industrial development. However, these platforms are not well-coordinated and very much functional. Wider support of the business community in addition to public support would be required to make them a platform for growth, innovation, and increased business agility.

Forward and Backward Linkages

The benefits of SEZs can be maximised only if they establish linkages with the domestic economy. Enclave-type SEZs that lack business alliance with firms in the domestic economy will not serve the purpose of technology and knowledge spillover in addition to making domestic firms a part of the global value chains. The linkages can be established at several levels with diverse objectives, such as technology transfer to local firms in the form of managerial know-how, product and process-specific knowledge transfer, technology spillover, international market access, and improving firms' agility and reactivity to respond to the market demands and shocks.

A balanced approach to developing synergy between the SEZs and SMEs is required for this to occur. SEZ enterprises should be located downstream in the supply chain, allowing SMEs in the upstream to connect with and become partners in the value chain. More interaction and alliances between SEZ enterprises and the domestic economy will result in the desired outcomes.

One-window Facility Provision

Clarity and ease of procedures are critical for attracting investment and significantly lowering transaction costs. This is mostly accomplished through the much-touted One-Stop Shop or One-window facility. The overall goal is to provide a hassle-free environment for investors while lowering the cost of doing business. Currently, more than 23 processes are involved in getting an enterprise started in the economic zone, and these processes and procedures are fragmented and related to institutions that fall under the purview of provincial, federal, and local governments.

Mapping and modelling of existing procedures (AS-IS) is required for one-window facility design. Multiple future scenarios (to-be) must then be evaluated and determined to be the most viable option for designing and deploying the one-window facility. For this purpose, information systems modelling tools (BPMN, IDEF1x...) and Business Process Reengineering methodologies can be used.

Industrial Policy

According to renowned economist and Nobel laureate Joseph Stiglitz, every country has an industrial policy, but some countries are unaware of it. He goes on to say that 'not having an industrial policy—leaving it to the market, which is so often structured by special interests—is itself a special-interest agenda'. Without a well-defined industrial policy, the East Asian miracle would not have occurred. In Pakistan, an industrial policy with a clear economic rationale must be developed. Furthermore, the policy should be used as a tool to define and develop the appropriate economic structure for the country while keeping regional economic development in mind. Moreover, the policy should be used as an instrument to define and develop the right economic structure for the country while keeping the regional economic development in perspective. Also, the industrial policy should be aligned with other policy strands to synergise efforts for sustainable industrial development.

Accreditation and Certifications

Non-compliance with international standards may result in non-tariff barriers (NTBs). Pakistan's exports suffer primarily as a result of NTBs, which include sanitary and phytosanitary (SPS) measures as well as technical trade barriers (TBT). Relevant institutions should be strengthened in order to guide the business community in meeting international standards and complying with their regulations. Best practises should be learned and put into action through vigorous programmes. Laboratories, in collaboration with China and other partner countries, should be established to certify products and processes in accordance with international standards and regulations.

To summarise, CPEC-related industrial development will only be realised if Pakistan approaches development from a broader perspective rather than focusing solely on the SEZs. The development of SEZs in isolation would not result in the country's industrialisation. It would necessitate both hard and soft infrastructure to make it happen. In the soft infrastructure, institutions that govern the economic engine must be reformed on a continuous basis and should be tuned in and adjusted as needed. Freight transportation policies must be implemented as soon as possible. For example, containerisation via railways could help bring down costs of doing business and maximise gains for CPEC, including SEZs.

The PTI government's reform agenda, previously spearheaded by Dr Ishrat Husain and others, sought to improve the operational efficiency of institutions by eliminating all redundancies and deficiencies in the system. Improving service delivery in institutions, combined with hard infrastructure in the transportation, logistics, and energy sectors, as well as the right policy instruments, would set Pakistan on the path to industrial excellence. East Asia's manufacturing excellence was only possible because they did many of the right things at the right time. Pakistan must do the same in order to become a popular destination for entrepreneurs and investors and to transform into an industrial powerhouse.

Notes

1. Tom Kemp, *Industrialization in the Non-Western World* (London: Longman, 1989).
2. Swadesh R. Bose, 'The Pakistan Economy since Independence (1947–70),' *The Cambridge Economic History of India* 2, c.1757–c.1970, eds., Dharma Kumar and Meghnad Desai; and Amjad Saeed, *The Economy of Pakistan*, Third Edition (Karachi: Oxford University Press, 2010).
3. A. R. Kemal, 'Key Issues in Industrial Growth in Pakistan,' The Lahore Journal of Economics (September 2006).
4. Xuemei Li, Khalid Mehmood Alam, and Shitong Wang, 'Trend Analysis of Pakistan Railways Based on Industry Life Cycle Theory.' Journal of Advanced Transportation (January 2018).
5. 'Freight Transport Statistics–Modal Split,' *Statistics Explained*.
6. Vaqar Ahmed, Ahsan Abbas, and Saira Ahmed, 'Public Infrastructure and Economic Growth in Pakistan: A Dynamic CGE-Microsimulation Analysis,' in *Infrastructure and Economic Growth in Asia. Economic Studies in Inequality,*

Social Exclusion and Well-Being, eds., J. Cockburn, Y. Dissou, J. Y. Duclos, and L. Tiberti (Springer, 2013), 117–143.

7. Ahmad Bilal Awan and Zeeshan Ali Khan, 'Recent progress in renewable energy–Remedy of energy crisis in Pakistan,' *Renewable and Sustainable Energy Reviews* 33 (May 2014): 236–253.

8. Khanji Harijan, Muhammad Aslam Uqaili, and Mujeebuddin Memon, 'Renewable Energy for Managing Energy Crisis in Pakistan,' in *Wireless Networks, Information Processing and Systems. IMTIC 2008. Communications in Computer and Information Science*, Volume 2, eds., D. M. A. Hussain, A. Q. K. Rajput, B. S. Chowdhry, and Q. Gee (Springer, 2008), 449–455.

9. 'Economic Survey 2017–2018,' Government of Pakistan, Finance Division, Economic Advisor's Wing (Islamabad: Government of Pakistan, 2018), 10.

10. 'World Development Indicators (database),' Washington, DC: World Bank, 2013.

11. Zaib Maroof, Shahzad Hussain, Muhammad Jawad, and Munazza Naz, 'Determinants of industrial development: a panel analysis of South Asian economies,' *Quality & Quantity: International Journal of Methodology* 53, no. 3 (May 2019): 1391–1419.

12. Andrew Stone, Brian Levy, and Ricardo Paredes, 'Public Institutions and Private Transactions. The Legal, and Regulatory Environment for Business Transactions in Brazil and Chile,' No 891, Policy Research Working Paper Series (The World Bank, 1992).

CHAPTER 17

Regional Trade Integration

MAAZ JAVED

INTRODUCTION

Pakistan is currently facing challenges in boosting trade with its neighbours which is mainly attributed to regional political differences and low levels of competitiveness vis-à-vis competitor economies. The country has yet to realise the benefits of its geographic location as it connects Middle East to South Asia on one hand and Central Asia with South Asia on the other.

These issues are not new. The writings of Dr Ishrat Husain are of significance in this regard. He has highlighted the need to integrate in regional trade and investment value chains across his scholarly works. According to him:

Pakistan was one of the top 10 fastest growing developing countries between 1960 and 1990 recording an annual average growth rate of 6 per cent. The structure of the economy was also transformed during this period with the share of agriculture coming down from 50 to 20 per cent. The subsequent 25 years have, however, brought about a significant decline in growth rates and in more recent seven years, it has lagged behind other South Asian countries. A combination of political instability and disruption of evolving democratic process, lack of continuity in policies and poor governance have contributed to this outcome. Pakistan has also not utilized its geographic location to take advantage of intra-regional trade and investment. Many promising opportunities were lost due to lingering tension with India. The future potential can only be realized if Pakistan is able to position itself for meeting the future challenges of integration into the regional and global economy, reaping demographic dividends because of youthful population and moving up the ladder of technology. The realization of these goals will depend upon sound macroeconomic policies, strong institutional and governance framework, investment in infrastructure and human development and political stability.[1]

AFGHANISTAN-PAKISTAN ECONOMIC COOPERATION

There is a need to revisit regional integration scenarios considering recent Afghanistan peace negotiations. In the past five years (2016–2021), Pakistan's export to Afghanistan dropped by 36 per cent. The lost share in exports to Afghanistan was captured by Iran, India, and other regional economies.[2] The same pattern is observed for the transit trade under the Afghanistan-Pakistan Transit Trade Agreement (APPTA). As a landlocked country, Afghanistan relies on transit trade route to meet its trade requirements. The APPTA was reformed in 2010 to allow Afghan exports to India and Indian exports to Afghanistan through Wagah and seaports of Karachi and Gwadar. Under this agreement, both countries also agreed on founding a joint chamber of commerce called Pakistan-Afghanistan Joint Chamber of Commerce and Industry (PAJCCI). However, Pakistan continues to see stagnant transit trade flows with Afghanistan with the share of Iran and Central Asian economies gradually increasing.

The issues of smuggling and informal trade continue to sour the relations between border agencies, in turn, prompting Pakistan to start fencing the border. Where the APTTA allows transit trade route between Afghanistan and India, it also raises concerns for the local business community in Pakistan which says that Indian goods may enter Pakistan through Afghan border and distort the local market.[3] A key reason for smuggling has also been high tariffs. The federal tax ombudsman of Pakistan noted that a number of high tariffs prompt smuggling of vehicles, electronics, and cigarettes from Afghanistan.[4]

It was realised that some of the goods smuggled to Pakistan through Afghanistan first enter Afghanistan under the APTTA and are then diverted to Pakistan.[5] The purpose of taking this route is to avoid high custom duties. It was advised by local businesses to bring down tariff rates on both sides to avoid smuggling of goods across the borders. Both sides also raise the issue of smuggling and bribes at borders. With the help of vehicle tracking and integrated logistics system, the issue of smuggling is being sorted out. Other trade barriers include: hefty security deposits on trucks involved in transit trade, high insurance charges, and costly shipment tracker. These impediments in transit trade result in transaction costs for all involved in this chain.

According to Husain and Elahi, an improvement in bilateral political relations will certainly help improve prospects for economic cooperation:

> Relations between Pakistan and Afghanistan have historically been tense. Cross-border infiltration, refugees, drug trafficking, militant groups, and disputes over counterterrorism policy and dialogue with terrorist networks have contributed to an entrenched trust deficit and have eroded relations. These issues have impacts beyond the security sector, complicating efforts to build stronger trade and economic ties. Despite tensions, Pakistan is today Afghanistan's largest trading partner, and Afghanistan is Pakistan's second-largest trading partner.[6]

LEVERAGING CPEC FOR REGIONAL INTEGRATION

The trade volume of Pakistan with China was one-fifth of its total volume and highest among all its neighbours for the year 2019. Since the initiation of CPEC, the relations between the two countries touched new heights not only in terms of foreign policy but also in terms of economic integration. Although the trade volume from 2016–2021 increased by more than 43 per cent yet the trade balance has remained negative in all these years.[7] Pakistani exports are unable to penetrate the Chinese markets in big volumes. To some extent, the second phase of China Pakistan FTA, operationalised in January 2020, could turn things in favour of Pakistan's exporters. Pakistan's low competitiveness attributed to low productivity level, high energy cost, less-skilled labour force, limited infrastructure facilities, and less efficient technology also contributed to poor export prospects in the Chinese markets. The untapped export potential of Pakistani exports to China is $1.1 billion.[8] This available export potential for Pakistani goods is in various sectors, including leather, apparel, cotton (fabric), fish and shellfish, and fruits.

China has untapped export potential of around $7.6 billion and its leading potential exports include: machinery, electronic equipment, chemicals, fertilisers, synthetic textile fabric, plastics and rubber, metal products, ferrous metals, motor vehicle parts, and medical instruments.

CPEC could play a role in boosting bilateral trade as well as transit trade with India. Besides, the Chinese private sector could be attracted towards Pakistani SEZs being developed in collaboration with the Chinese. Husain notes:

> The scope of China-Pakistan economic relations should not remain limited to CPEC but also broadened to include Trade, bilateral investment, Financial services and Transfer of Technology. The Free Trade Agreement (FTA) with China should be renegotiated and the terms allowed to ASEAN countries made applicable to Pakistan also. Pakistani exports should be allowed less than equal reciprocity access. As the world's largest exporting nation, the penetration of Pakistani goods and products provides an attractive means for boosting employment and growth in Pakistan. In financial services, currency swaps between Yuan and Pak Rupee, expansion of Chinese bank branches in Pakistan and allowing Pakistani banks to open branches in China and availability of credit lines for cross border trade would reduce the transaction costs of doing business for both the countries. The second order effects of CPEC projects would be further spread as trade and financial cooperation are intensified. China has become a powerhouse in emerging technologies with applications to health, agriculture and industry that include clean energy, genetics, biotechnology and ICT. Pakistan should seek assistance of the Chinese scientists in training and collaborating in research with our scientists by establishing laboratories and regular exchange programs. This would solidify the Research and Development base of Pakistan and this trained manpower, in turn, would adapt and diffuse these technologies for increasing productivity in our various sectors.[9]

China's support in the development of Gwadar Port and city area also needs to be leveraged for optimal economic gains, locally and internationally. This port is still far from being in the condition to be compared to the regional trailblazers. Dr Husain had pointed towards having realistic assumptions about developments in Gwadar but continue to move forward and benchmark with the best in the region. He notes:

> There is no room for complacency about Gwadar's future as a deep-sea port and hub in view of intense competition from Salalah, Jebel Ali, Bandar Abbas and Charbahar. Commercial promotion and presentations about this new port's benefits to the businesses such as a vast hinterland should remain a continuous activity. To attract talent, the living conditions and habitat in Gwadar should be upgraded. Gwadar's development as an urban center, particularly in providing potable drinking water supply, electricity and roads should not lose sight of the requirements of the population of the district, and the adjoining areas in Makran division. Local population of the district and adjoining areas should be trained, employed and given all possible opportunities to fully participate in Gwadar's development. Potable drinking water remains a serious problem for the residents of Gwadar and expeditious arrangements should be made to meet this pressing need. Fisheries Industry in Gwadar which provides sustenance and livelihoods to a large section of population should be taken up for modernization.[10]

CONCLUSION

Trade with India is often referred to as the low-hanging fruit by Dr Husain. He recognises the welfare gains to various communities on both sides of the border involved with small- and medium-sized exporting firms who could benefit from land route trade between the two neighbours. Furthermore, he continues to explain that despite tensions between China and India both have maintained normal trade relations.[11]

Notes

1. Ishrat Husain, 'Pakistan's Economy and Regional Challenges,' *International Studies* 55, no. 3 (2018): 253–270.
2. Trade Map, 'Bilateral trade between Pakistan and Afghanistan Product: TOTAL All products.'
3. Ishrat Husain and Muhammad Ather Elahi, 'The Future of Afghanistan-Pakistan Trade Relations.' United States Institute of Peace, Peace brief no. 191 (2015).

4. Sayed Waqar Hussain, Asmat Ullah, and Bashir Ahmad Khilji, 'The Causes of Transit Related Pak-Afghan Cross Border Smuggling,' *The Dialogue* 9, no. 1 (2014).

5. Vaqar Ahmed and Saad Shabbir, 'Trade & Transit Cooperation with Afghanistan: Results from a Firm-level survey from Pakistan,' Sustainable Development Policy Institute, Working Paper #153 (2016).

6. Husain and Elahi, 'The Future of Afghanistan-Pakistan Trade Relations.'

7. 'External Trade Statistics of last 5 years,' Pakistan Bureau of Statistics.

8. Export Potential Map, 'Spot export opportunities for trade development.'

9. Ishrat Husain, 'CPEC and Pakistan's Economy: A Way Forward,' Centre for Excellence, CPEC (2018b).

10. Ibid., 17.

11. Ishrat Husain, 'Towards an Asian Century: Future of Economic Cooperation in SAARC Countries,' Concluding remarks, Islamabad Policy Research Institute (2014): 24–25.

List of Contributors

Abid Q. Suleri, Sustainable Development Policy Institute (SDPI)

Dr Abid Qaiyum Suleri is the head of Sustainable Development Policy Institute since 2007. He is a member of different policymaking forums and advisory boards, including the Prime Minister's Economic Advisory Council, Pakistan Climate Change Council, National Advisory Committee of the Planning Commission of Pakistan, Trade Policy Advisory Committee, Agricultural Universities Vice Chancellor's Search Committee, Government of Punjab, Board of Studies and Board of Faculty of various public sector universities and different committees/councils formed by the Higher Education Commission of Pakistan, Ministry of Planning, Development & Reforms, Ministry of Finance, and Ministry of Climate Change. He is also serving as member of different international policymaking forums, including advisory board of intergovernmental organization CAREC Think-Tanks Network, Member of the steering committee of World Commission on Forced Displacement (UK), and Co-Chair of the Board of Climate Action Network South Asia. He was a part of three judicial commissions on environmental issues. He is also editor-in-chief of SDPI's peer reviewed journal, *Journal of Development Policy, Research and Practice*. Dr Suleri has a PhD in food security from the University of Greenwich, UK.

Abdul Salam Lodhi, Balochistan University of Information Technology, Engineering and Management Sciences

Dr Abdul Salam Lodhi is Professor Economics at the Balochistan University of Information Technology, Engineering and Management Sciences (BUITEMS), Quetta. Presently, he is working as Director University College of Zhob, BUITEMS. Earlier, he also served as Dean Faculty of Management Sciences and Chairman Department of Economics, from September 2014 to May 2017, and January 2013 to September 2014 respectively. He joined BUITEMS in 2006 and before joining BUITEMS, he worked as Head of the Economics Department at the Balochistan Agriculture College, Quetta, and on various other positions in the Agriculture Department of the Government of Balochistan (1999–2006). He has a PhD in Economics from Bonn Graduate School of Development Economics, University of Bonn, Germany. His PhD thesis was on 'Education, Child Labor and Human Capital Formation in Selected Urban and Rural areas of Pakistan'. He is the author of several national and international research articles and presented his research on different international forums.

Ahmed Ali Siddiqui, Institute of Business Administration (IBA)

Ahmed Ali Siddiqui holds a bachelor's and master's degree in Business Administration from the Institute of Business Administration (IBA), Karachi, with six gold medals. His areas of specialisation include Islamic Finance and MIS. He has over 14 years of experience in Islamic banking and is involved in pioneering work in the field of Islamic finance in Pakistan. He also holds the post of Senior Executive Vice President & Head, Product Development & Shariah Compliance (PDSC) at the Meezan Bank Limited and is leading one of the largest research departments in the Islamic banking world with over 40 dedicated team members. He is also the Secretary for Shariah Supervisory Board at Meezan Bank. His previous assignment includes launching of Car Ijarah—Pakistan's first Islamic car financing scheme and Easy Home—Pakistan's first Islamic Housing Finance as Product Manager in Pakistan. Siddiqui is also part of the Joint Financial Advisors team to the government of Pakistan for issuance of local currency sovereign sukuk and Islamic financing transactions.

Ali Salman, Policy Research Institute of Market Economy (PRIME)

Ali Salman is founder and executive director of PRIME, an independent think tank in Islamabad. He is also co-founder and CEO of Islam and Liberty Network, a global platform for researchers and academics working on Islam and freedom. Salman's diverse career spans more than twenty years in the government, private sector, social enterprise, international development, think tanks, and universities. He is the recipient of the Fulbright Scholarship, Royal Netherlands Fellowship, and Charles Wallace Fellowship and holds master's degrees in economics, public policy, and business administration. He writes op-eds in the *Express Tribune*.

Beenish Javed, Policy Research Institute of Market Economy (PRIME)

Beenish Javed holds a degree in Master of Philosophy in Economics from the Pakistan Institute of Development Economics (PIDE), Islamabad. Currently, she is a Research Economist at the Policy Research Institute of Market Economy (PRIME)—a public policy think tank based in Islamabad. While at PRIME, she has worked on a wide array of issues, ranging from climate change, agriculture, and gender roles to trade liberalisation, contract enforcement, public debt, and private property rights. She was an active participant of the ATLAS Think Tank Essentials Training Program and has represented PRIME at the 2019 Asia Liberty Forum (ALF) held in Colombo, Sri Lanka. In addition, she participated in the International Academy for Leadership's 2019 training programme held in Gummersbach, Germany. Her areas of interest include International trade and development and environmental economics.

Bushra Yasmin, Fatima Jinnah Women University

Dr Yasmin is Associate Professor of Economics and Faculty Advisor of the Faculty of Arts and Social Sciences at the Fatima Jinnah Women University (FJWU), Rawalpindi. She has been serving at teaching and research institutes for the last twenty-two years and is the member of various statutory bodies. She did her PhD from Quaid-i-Azam University with a research fellowship from the University of Sussex, UK. She accomplished her post-doctorate in International economics from the Harvard University, USA, as a Fulbright Scholar. She has Star Award, Fulbright Award and Australian Award for Women in Executive Leadership to her credit. She is an active researcher and has been published widely in the journals of national and international repute. She has been awarded with International research grant by PSSP Competitive Grants Program, Planning Commission, USAID and IFPRI and National project by the Punjab Commission on the Status of Women (PCSW). She played a vital role in establishing the Department of Economics at FJWU and initiated a series of workshops on quantitative analysis. She organised an international conference and also launched the mentoring programme at her institute. She is an efficient and highly motivated administrator who is always ready to take up the challenges, especially for women empowerment.

Faheem Sardar, Prime Minister's Secretariat

Faheem Sardar is the MD of TANGENT* which is an independent economics think tank and corporate advisory whose ideology is to strengthen results and governance. TANGENT* provides its services to organisations, start-ups, and individuals at the strategic, operational, and tactical levels in policy, research, advisory, and outreach. He was the CEO of Askari Securities Ltd. for nine years and worked extensively in the capital market, ranging from regulating, to forensics, to business development. Earlier, he was the GM and Chief Operating Officer of the Lahore Stock Exchange. He has also worked with the Saudi Pak Investment Co Ltd., and Securities & Exchange Commission of Pakistan (SECP). He is also a trainer of corporate governance at the Pakistan Institute of Corporate Governance. He is also part of the SECP's investor education initiative. He is the author of *The New Finance Construct*, *Mind Conquest* and *CEO at 34* and has contributed various articles on the capital market, the economy, and societal aspects. His books are also part of the National Library Collection of Pakistan and the National Book Foundation. He has read from his books at the National Book Foundation Book Day in April 2016, 2017, and 2018. His books have been recommended for curricula in various universities. He has been engaged with universities in teaching advanced finance and managerial concepts through courses, discussions, seminars, and mentoring sessions.

Ghulam Nabi, Center for Environment Economics and Climate Change (CEECC)

Ghulam Nabi is a Research Associate at the Center for Environment Economics and Climate Change (CEECC). The CEECC is works under the Pakistan Institute of Development Economics (PIDE) with focus on complex connections and wide interactions between economics and the environment. Nabi has been involved in number of seminars as a participant and organiser. He is also the author of articles for national and international journals.

Ghulam Samad, Senior Research Officer, Central Asia Regional Economic Cooperation (CAREC) Institute

Dr Ghulam Samad is a Senior Research Officer at the Central Asia Regional Economic Cooperation (CAREC) Institute. Before joining the CAREC Institute, he was Senior Research Economist at the Pakistan Institute of Development Economics (PIDE). He also served as an Economist at the Planning Commission of Pakistan. He holds a PhD in Economics from the Colorado State University, USA. He brings together an experience spanning over fifteen years of high-level research and teaching, along with providing valuable contributions to peer-reviewed national and international journals, and several international books on key economic themes.

Hadia Majid, Assistant Professor, LUMS

A Fulbright Scholar, Dr Hadia Majid holds a PhD in Development Economics from The Ohio State University. Her research agenda considers the impact of monetary and public resource constraints on individuals in Pakistan. Her work includes cash transfer evaluations, public goods provisioning, human capital acquisition in the context of intra-household decision-making, and factors affecting women's access to earned income. Here, she documents and explores the barriers to women's labour supply and their access to decent, empowering work. She has published in international journals and is currently editing a book titled, *Gender at Work in Pakistan*. Her work has been funded by several agencies such as ESRC-DFID, IDRC, IGC, IFPRI among others and she has acted as a consultant for government and non-governmental agencies on gendered labour market outcomes. Her expertise lies in RCT, quasi-experimental, and quantitative driven fieldwork. She has also done qualitative work with low-literate, low-income informal and formal sector women workers.

Hamid Mahmood, Ministry of Planning and Development

Hamid Mahmood holds a Master's degree in Public Policy from Royal Holloway College, University of London, UK. He is currently serving as Director in the Islamabad Capital Administration since February 2021. He is looking at the portfolio of Agriculture and Fisheries Department, Chief Commissioner Office, ICT, Islamabad and also providing services as Deputy Project Direct for PSDP project titled, 'Rehabilitation and Improvement of Fish Seed Hatchery In Rawal Dam, ICT'. Previously, he served as Assistant Chief in the various sections of the Ministry of Planning, Development & Special Initiatives, Islamabad including Poverty Alleviation, Macroeconomics, CPEC, Trade, SDGs, etc. He has more than twelve years of experience in the development sector. His interest areas are development economics, public policy, and economic reforms. He has been involved in a number of projects and assignments at the Ministry of Planning and served as coordinator in Panel of Economists, Macroeconomic stabilisation, Institutions and Reforms group, etc. He has more than ten international peered review publication at his name.

Johannes F. Linn, Brookings Institute

Johannes F. Linn is a Non-resident Senior Fellow at the Brookings Institution, a Distinguished Resident Scholar at the Emerging Markets Forum in Washington, DC, and a Senior Fellow at the Results for Development Institute. He also is the co-founder and co-chair of the international Scaling Up Community of Practice, which currently has over 600 participants. In 2019, he served as Global Facilitator for the 1st Replenishment of the Green Climate Fund. In 2011, 2014, and 2017, he chaired three Replenishment Consultations of the International Fund for Agricultural Development. From 2005–2010, he was Director of the Wolfensohn Center for Development at Brookings. Before that, he worked for three decades at the World Bank, including as the Bank's Vice President for Financial Policy and Resource Mobilization and Vice President for Europe and Central Asia. He holds a bachelor's degree from the Oxford University and a doctorate in economics from the Cornell University.

Liaqat Ali Shah, China-Pakistan Economic Corridor (CoE-CPEC)

Dr Liaqat Ali Shah is Project Director in the Ministry of Planning, Development & Special Initiatives and Executive Director Centre of Excellence for CPEC in PIDE. Before joining the ministry of planning/PIDE, he was a faculty member at the Management Sciences Department of COMSATS University at Islamabad Campus. He has a major in mechanical engineering from the University of Engineering & Technology, Peshawar, Master's and PhD degree in industrial management from Arts et Métiers ParisTech, France. Moreover, he was a Post-doctoral Fellow at the University of Technology of Compiègen (UTC) at Picardie region of France and Post-Doctoral Fellow at Ecole des Mines de Nantes (EMN) Engineering School at Pays de Loire France. He has worked in National Engineering and Scientific Commission (NESCOM) as Assistant Manager (Technical) and has served as industrial systems analyst in Montupet automotive industry, France.

M. Aman Ullah, Government of Punjab

Dr Aman holds a PhD in Economics from the University of Auckland, New Zealand. He is the author of several publications and recipient of many scholarships and grants. Currently, Dr Aman is serving as Joint Chief Economist for the Planning and Development Board, Government of Punjab. Along with supervising the work of the Punjab Bureau of Statistics, he is also the Focal Person of the Government of the Punjab for Sustainable Development Goals, China-Pakistan Economic Corridor (CPEC), and the Punjab Growth Strategy. He has held various important positions in P&D Board: Chief Economist and Director of Punjab Economic Research Institute. Dr Aman has a diverse experience in the public sector. Before joining the Government of Punjab, he worked with the Planning Commission of Pakistan for many years.

Maaz Javed, Pakistan Institute of Development Economics (PIDE)

Maaz Javed is a researcher at the Sustainable Development Policy Institute (SDPI) and a PhD scholar from Pakistan Institute of Development Economics (PIDE). His dissertation work involves research on price formation mechanism for varying market micro-structures. His research interests lie in the area of trade and development economics, ranging from theory to design to implementation. At SDPI, he has been involved in many collaborative research projects. He worked in several areas, such as regional trade integration, Afghanistan Pakistan transit trade, poverty alleviation, quality of FDI, and most recently on digital trade integration. As a researcher, he has the exposure of working with international development partners, such as UN-ESCAP, National Endowment for Democracy (NED), and Center for International Private Enterprise (CIPE). His future research aims to dig more into regional trade aspects and its interconnection to achieving SDGs.

Muhammad Arif, International Islamic University Islamabad (IIUI)

Dr Muhammad Arif is an academician, trainer, researcher, and social entrepreneur. He completed his PhD in tourism marketing from Bodo Graduate School of Business, University of Nordland, Norway. He has been in academics for the last twenty years sharing with the students in the areas, including marketing and research. At present, he is serving in the faculty of management science, International Islamic University, Islamabad. He is an active trainer in the areas of leadership, critical thinking, and evidence-based decision-making. Dr Arif also did some research-based consultancies for organisations in public, private, and development sector. He preferred to research in solution-driven (or applied) research for the society. Recently, in collaboration with the Board of Investment, Pakistan he did SWOT Analysis of Pakistan's Business Environment. The study is based on in-depth interviews with the top twenty-two MNCs CEOs based in Pakistan.

He is an avid supporter of informed decision-making. In order to promote this social cause, since September 2017, he has been publishing a weekly e-newsletter and podcast titled, *Weekly Business Insights* comprising of extractive summaries of the articles from the top ten business magazines.

Naeem Zafar, Government of Sindh

Dr Zafar has around thirty years of diverse experience in public policy, development management, university teaching, economic research, power generation, and manufacturing. He is currently working with the Government of Sindh as a Chief Economist. Prior to this, he worked with United Nations as senior advisor, Planning Commission as member social sector and at IBA as assistant professor. He earned his PhD from the Northern Illinois University where he researched on foreign aid and economic growth. His areas of interest include: financial economics, labour economics and econometrics. In addition, he has worked on various projects, including consumer confidence survey, social protection policy among others.

Saranjam Baig, Government of Gilgit-Baltistan

Dr Saranjam Baig teaches economics and public policy at the Karakoram International University, Gilgit Pakistan and International Political Economy at Sultan Qaboos University, Muscat, Oman. He has also been working with Mahbubul Haq Human Development Centre (MHDC) and the University of La Verne, California. He received his education at the Claremont Graduate University, California, with a Master's in Economics and a Doctorate Degree in Economics and Political Science. He also holds an MS in Development Studies from the University of Glasgow, Scotland, UK. He is an avid researcher. His work has been published in many local and international journals.

Shakeel Ahmad, United Nations Development Programme (UNDP)

Shakeel Ahmad has around eighteen years of experience in the development sector— project development, public policy with substantive expertise on issues of poverty, microfinance, gender equality, and broader governance and institutional development. He is part of UNDP Pakistan senior management team and chief of Development Policy Unit. He has worked closely with high level government and political offices. He is a development economist by training. He has studied Development Management from the London School of Economics (LSE). He has a degree in Agricultural Economics (Gold Medallist) from the Agriculture University, Peshawar.

Tariq Banuri, Higher Education Commission (HEC)

Tariq Banuri is the Chairman, Higher Education Commission, Government of Pakistan. He holds a PhD in Economics from the Harvard University. He started his career as a member of the erstwhile Civil Service of Pakistan (CSP) and served in a number of positions, including as Professor of Economics, University of Utah (2012–2018), Director, UN Division for Sustainable Development, founder and first Executive Director of the

Sustainable Development Policy Institute (SDPI), Islamabad, Director, Asia Centre of the Stockholm Environment Institute (SEI), and Executive Director of the Global Change Impact Studies Centre (GCISC), a statutory corporation established under the GCISC Act 2013. He has served on national as well as international forums for policy and research, including as Coordinating Lead Author on the Nobel Prize-winning Inter-governmental Panel on Climate Change (IPCC), member of the UN Secretary General's Advisory Group on Energy and Climate Change (AGECC), member of the UN Committee on Development Policy (CDP), member of the Pakistan Environmental Protection Council, member of the Central Board of Governors of the State Bank of Pakistan (SBP), and member/secretary of the Presidential Committee on Higher Education. In 2002 he was awarded the Sitara-i-Imtiaz (SI) for his services in areas of research and education.

Vaqar Ahmed, Sustainable Development Policy Institute (SDPI)

Dr Vaqar Ahmed is currently Joint Executive Director, Sustainable Development Policy Institute (SDPI) and serves as a Board Member of the Fauji Foundation Welfare Advisory Board. He is also the honorary Research Fellow at Partnership for Economic Policy, Canada, and Technical Advisor to the Government of Punjab's Urban Unit. Earlier, he served the UNDP as Advisor and has undertaken assignments with the Asian Development Bank, World Bank, and Ministries of Finance, Planning and Commerce in Pakistan. He was also the former Head of Macroeconomics Section in the Ministry of Planning & Development in Pakistan. He remained the technical associate and member of the task forces constituted by the Government of Pakistan, including the Advisory Panel of Economists (2008), Task Force on Private Sector Development (2009), Working Group for Pakistan Vision 2025, and Working Group for Twelfth Five Year Plan (2019). He has published extensively on various aspects of international trade, public finance, and private sector competitiveness. His book, *Pakistan's Agenda for Economic Reforms*, was published by the Oxford University Press in 2018. He is a visiting faculty member and researcher in different international institutes, including the University of Laval in Canada, University of Le Havre in France, National University of Ireland, Quaid-e-Azam University, and the Pakistan Institute of Trade and Development. Apart from South Asian countries, he has worked in Africa, USA, the European Union and the Far East on assignments related to these regions. He was the recipient of 2015 Young Leaders Fellowship award by the French Ministry of Foreign Affairs.

Zafar Hayat, International Monetary Fund (IMF)

Dr Zafar Hayat served the SBP in its various departments including Research, Monetary Policy, and Banking Inspection. He has a PhD in economics from the Massey University, New Zealand with a specialisation in Pakistan's monetary policy. His primary area of interest is Pakistan's monetary policy and has published numerous relevant policy-oriented articles in reputable international and local journals.

Bibliography

A.T. Kearney, and Jazz. 'Digital Entrepreneurship Ecosystem in Pakistan 2017: How Pakistan can build a world-class digital ecosystem.' Islamabad: A. T. Kearney, 2017.

Abbas, Ghulam. 'CCP to prepare rules for online businesses.' *Pakistan Today*. April 22, 2020.

Abidi, Hina, Farhan Shafiq, Rimsha Arshad, Maria Pirwan, and Ahmed Hassan. 'Stories of Entrepreneurship.' *Market Forces* 10, no. 2 (December 2015).

Acemoglu, Daron, and James Robinson. *Why Nations Fail: The Origins of Power, Prosperity, and Poverty*. London: Profile Books, 2012.

_____. 'The Role of Institutions in Growth and Development.' Commission on Growth and Development. Working Paper No. 10. World Bank, 2008.

Ács, Zoltán J., László Szerb, Esteban Lafuente, and Ainsley Lloyd. 'The Global Entrepreneurship Index.' The Global Entrepreneurship and Development Institute, 2019.

Ahmad, Iftikhar, and Zhou Taidong. 'Special Economic Zones in Pakistan: Promises and Perils.' PIDE Research Report Series, 2020.

Ahmad, Manzoor. 'Improving Regional Trade to Support Pakistan's Economic Growth.' *The Lahore Journal of Economics* 19 (September 2014): 461–469.

Ahmed, Maryam Mohiuddin, Arslan Khalid, Alainna Lynch, and Emily Darko. 'The State of Social Enterprise in Bangladesh, Ghana, India and Pakistan: The State of Social Enterprise in Pakistan.' British Council, 2016.

Ahmed, Vaqar. 'Who is failing Pakistani startups?' *Arab News*. February 22, 2021.

_____, M. Javed, R. Tabassum, A. Javed, M. F. Ferracane, and W. Anukoonwattaka. 'National Study on Digital Trade Integration in Pakistan.' United Nations Economic and Social Commission for Asia and the Pacific. Bangkok, 2021. Unpublished.

_____. *Pakistan's Agenda for Economic Reforms.* Karachi: Oxford University Press, 2017.

_____, and Mustafa Talpur. 'Corporate Tax Reforms in Pakistan.' Sustainable Development Policy Institute, 2016a.

_____, and Saad Shabbir. 'Trade & Transit Cooperation with Afghanistan: Results from a Firm-level survey from Pakistan.' Working Paper #153. Sustainable Development Policy Institute, 2016b.

_____, and Mustafa Talpur. 'Towards a Fair and Just Fiscal Policy in Pakistan.' Policy Review. Sustainable Development Policy Institute, July 2015.

_____, Ahsan Abbas, and Saira Ahmed. 'Public Infrastructure and Economic Growth in Pakistan: A Dynamic CGE-Microsimulation Analysis.' In *Infrastructure and Economic Growth in Asia. Economic Studies in Inequality, Social Exclusion and Well-Being.* Edited by John Cockburn, Yazid Dissou, Jean- Yves Duclos, and Luca Tiberti. Springer, 2013.

_____, and Cathal O'Donoghue. 'External Shocks in a Small Open Economy: A CGE-Microsimulation Analysis.' *Lahore Journal of Economics* 15, no. 1 (2010a): 45–90.

_____, and Cathal O'Donoghue. 'Case Study: Global economic crisis and poverty in Pakistan.' *International Journal of Microsimulation, International Microsimulation Association* 3, no. 1 (2010b): 127–129.

_____, Guntur Sugiyarto, and Shikha Jha. 'Remittances and Household Welfare: A Case Study of Pakistan.' Asian Development Bank, Economics Working Paper Series, no. 194 (February 2010c).

Akın, Çiğdem. 'Multiple Determinants of Business Cycle Synchronization.' SSRN, 2012.

Alam, Shaista. 'The trade integration and Pakistan's export performance: Evidence from exporter dynamic database.' *International Journal of Development Issues* 17, no. 3 (2018): 326–345.

_____. 'Exchange rate volatility and Pakistan's Import demand: An Application of Autoregressive Distributed Lag model.' *International Research Journal of Finance and Economics* 16, no. 48 (2010): 7–23.

Ali, Bushra, and Emily Darko. 'Grants, incubators and innovation: a snapshot of social enterprise activities in Pakistan.' Pakistan: ODI (December 2015).

Ali, Liaqat, and Iqbal Ahmad Panhwar. 'Impact of Trade Liberalization on Economic Development in Pakistan: A Co-integration Analysis.' *Global Management Journal for Academic & Corporate Studies* 7, no. 1 (2017): 19.

Anwar, Z. 'Central Asia in World Attention.' *Central Asia* 41 (1997): 183.

APP. 'Pakistan's cash programme instrumental in mitigating COVID-19 impact: WB.' *Pakistan Today*. May 5, 2020.

Arestis, Philip, and Malcolm Sawyer. 'A critical reconsideration of the foundations of monetary policy in the new consensus macroeconomics framework.' *Cambridge Journal of Economics* 32, no. 5 (February 2008): 761–779.

Arif, Muhammad. 'Understanding a Big Elephant and its Small Chain: Pakistan's SWOT Analysis.' Unpublished report, 2019.

Artaza, Ignacio. 'Urbanisation in Pakistan Cumulatively, cities in Pakistan generate 55% of the GDP.' *The Express Tribune*. June 05, 2019.

Ashraf, Malik Muhammad. 'Welcome moratorium by FATF.' *The Nation*. April 10, 2020.

Asian Development Bank. 'Asian Development Outlook (ADO) 2020: What Drives Innovation in Asia?' April 2020.

————. 'ADB, Kashf Foundation Partner to Expand Women's Access to Credit in Pakistan.' 2019.

————. 'Report and Recommendation of the President to the Board of Directors.' Project Number: 37220 (November 2008).

Awan, Ahmad Bilal, and Zeeshan Ali Khan. 'Recent progress in renewable energy – Remedy of energy crisis in Pakistan.' *Renewable and Sustainable Energy Reviews* 33 (May 2014): 236–253.

Azhad, Qahafa. 'List of Startup Accelerators, Incubators, and Venture Capital Firms in Pakistan.' *Ideagist*. November 18, 2018.

Baig, Saranjam, M. Qasim, L. Xuemei, and Khalid Mehmood Alam. 'Is the China-Pakistan Economic Corridor an Opportunity or a Threat for Small and Micro-Entrepreneurs? Empirical Evidence from Northern Pakistan.' *Sustainability* 12, no. 5 (2020): 1727–1746.

————, Aftab Ahmed Khan, Amjad Ali Khan, and Salma Bano. 'Rural Tourism, Income, and Rapid Urbanization: Exploring the Nexus using a Multidisciplinary Approach.' *International Journal of Economic and Environmental Geology* 10, no. 4 (2019a): 01–06.

————. 'Policy Considerations for Designing Effective Anti-Corruption Strategies in Pakistan.' *Global Social Sciences Review* 4, no. 2 (2019b): 291–297.

————. 'Moral Suasion or Policy Reforms? How to Tackle Sectarian Violence in Pakistan: The Case Study of Gilgit-Baltistan.' *Global Social Sciences Review* 4, no. 1 (2019c): 271–280.

Ball, Laurence, and Niamh Sheridan. 'Does Inflation Targeting Matter?' National Bureau of Economic Research, Working Paper 9577 (March 2003).

Banuri, Tariq, and Edward Amadeo. 'Policy, Governance, and the Management of Conflict.' In *Economic Liberalization: No Panacea*. Edited by Tariq Banuri. Oxford: Oxford University Press, 1992.

Bernanke, Ben S., Mark Gertler, and Simon Gilchrist. 'Chapter 21: The financial accelerator in a quantitative business cycle framework.' *Handbook of Macroeconomics* Vol. 1, Part C (1999): 1341–1393.

Bokil, Madhavi, and Axel Schimmelpfennig. 'Three Attempts at Inflation Forecasting in Pakistan.' IMF Working Paper No. 05/105 (May 2005).

Brewer, Gene A., Sally Coleman Selden, and Rex L. Facer II. 'Individual Conceptions of Public Service Motivation.' *Public Administration Review* 60, no. 3 (2000): 254–264.

Brockhaus, Robert H. 'The Psychology of the Entrepreneur.' In *Encyclopedia of Entrepreneurship*. Edited by C. A. Kent, D. L. Sexton, and K. H. Vesper, 39–57. Englewood Cliffs, NJ: Prentice-Hall, 1982.

Buchanan, Leigh. 'The Most Important Entrepreneurs of the Past Decade.' *INC*. December 24, 2019.

Burdekin, Richard C. K., and Pierre L. Siklos. 'Exchange Rate Regimes and Shifts in Inflation Persistence: Does Nothing Else Matter?' *Journal of Money, Credit and Banking* 31, no. 2 (May 1999): 235–247.

Business Recorder Research. 'Corona and Pakistan's on-demand economy.' March 19, 2020.

———. 'Oil: To hedge or not?' March 11, 2020.

Buurman, Margaretha, Robert Dur, and Seth Van den Bossche. 'Public Sector Employees: Rise Averse and Altruistic.' IZA Discussion Papers No. 4401. Bonn: Institute for the Study of Labour, 2009.

Cecchetti, Stephen G., and Michael Ehrmann. 'Does Inflation Targeting Increase Output Volatility? An International Comparison of Policymakers' Preferences and Outcomes.' NBER Working Paper No. 7426 (December 1999).

Chaudhary, M. Aslam, and Naved Ahmad. 'Sources and impacts of Inflation in Pakistan.' *Pakistan Economic and Social Review* 34, no. 1 (Summer 1996): 21–39.

Chaudhury, Dipanjan Roy. 'PM Modi proposes emergency covid-19 fund for SAARC nations.' *The Economic Times*. March 16, 2020.

Chibba, Michael. 'Financial Inclusion, Poverty Reduction and the Millennium Development Goals.' *European Journal of Development Research* 21, no. 2 (April 2009): 213–230.

Chief Justice Balochistan High Court. 'Zhob Taraki krnay k bajae zawalpazeer mard doctors se Gyne ka operation karana baes e sharam hy.' *Jang*. December 8, 2019.

Christensen, Clayton M., Efosa Ojomo, and Karen Dillon. 'Cracking Frontier Markets.' *Harvard Business Review* (January–February 2019).

Corbo, Vittorio, Oscar Landerretche, and Klaus Schmidt-Hebbel. 'Assessing inflation targeting after a decade of world experience.' *International Journal of Finance & Economics* 6, no. 4, Special Issue: Exchange Rates and Monetary Policy Issues (October 2001): 343–368.

Coulibaly, Dramane, and Hubert Kempf. 'Does Inflation Targeting decrease Exchange Rate Pass-through in Emerging Countries?' Banque de France Working Paper No. 303 (November 2010).

Coy, Peter. 'Free Trade Is Dead. Long Live Managed Trade.' *Bloomberg Businessweek*. January 23, 2020.

Cridge, Stella. 'The role of founder experience in industrial development: firm entry, growth and diversification in Pakistan's textile industry during trade liberalization.' PhD Thesis. London School of Economics, 2009.

Demirgüç-Kunt, Asli, Leora Klapper, and Dorothe Singer. 'Financial Inclusion and Inclusive Growth: A Review of Recent Empirical Evidence.' Policy Research Working Paper: No. 8040. World Bank, 2017.

———, Saniya Ansar, and Jake Hess. 'The Global Findex Database 2017: Measuring Financial Inclusion and the Fintech Revolution.' World Bank, 2018.

Deutsche Gesellschaft für. Internationale Zusammenarbeit (GIZ) GmbH. 'Study on Producing Skilled Workforce for Potential Economic Sectors in Gilgit Baltistan.' TVET Report, 2017.

Doss, Cheryl. 'Intrahousehold Bargaining and Resource Allocation in Developing Countries.' *World Bank Research Observer* 28, no. 1 (2013): 52–78.

Durrani, Fakhar. 'Will coronavirus affect CPEC and Pak economy?' *The News*. February 7, 2020.

Easterby-Smith, Mark, Richard Thorpe, and Paul Jackson. *Management Research*. Los Angeles; London: SAGE Publications, 2008.

Easterly, William R. *The Elusive Quest for Growth: Economists' Adventures and Misadventures in the Tropics Development Research Institute*. MIT Press, 2001.

Edwards, Sebastian. 'Openness, Trade Liberalization, and Growth in Developing Countries.' *Journal of Economic Literature* 31, no. 3 (1993): 1358–1393.

Eisenmann, Thomas R. 'Entrepreneurship: A Working Definition.' *Harvard Business Review*. January 10, 2013.

Ellis, Peter, and Mark Roberts. 'Leveraging Urbanization in South Asia: Managing Spatial Transformation for Prosperity and Livability.' World Bank, 2016.

Faundez, Julio. 'Douglas North's Theory of Institutions: Lessons for Law and development.' *Hague J Rule Law* (2016): 373–419.

Financial Inclusion Insights. 'Pakistan Wave 5 report fifth annual FII tracker.' Technical Report, 2018.

Foord, Jo. 'Strategies for creative industries: an international review.' *Creative Industries Journal* 1, no. 2 (2008): 91–113.

Gartner, William B. 'A Conceptual Framework for Describing the Phenomenon of New Venture Creation.' *The Academy of Management Review* 10, no. 4 (October 1985): 696–706.

Gavin William T. 'Inflation Targeting: Why it Works and How to Make it Work Better.' Federal Reserve Bank of St. Louis Working Paper (2003).

Georgellis, Yannis, Elisabetta Iossa, and Vurain Tabvuma. 'Crowding out intrinsic motivation in the public sector.' *Journal of Public Administration Research and Theory* 21, no. 3 (2011): 473–493.

Goncalves, Carlos, and Joao M. Salles. 'Inflation targeting in emerging economies: What do the data say?' *Journal of Development Economics* 85, no. 1–2 (2008): 312–318.

Gounder, Rukmani, and Zhongwei Xing. 'Impact of education and health on poverty reduction: Monetary and non-monetary evidence from Fiji.' *Economic Modelling* 29, no. 3 (2012): 787–794.

Gruber, Jonathan. *Public Finance and Public Policy*. 3rd ed. New York: Worth Publishers, 2011.

Haider, Mehtab. 'Creditors pledge Rs708b for Pakistan to fight Covid-19.' *The News*. April 28, 2020.

———. 'Brain drain.' *The News*, April 2019.

Haldane, A. G. *Targeting Inflation*. London: Bank of England, 1995.

Hamid, Naved, and Faizan Khalid. 'Entrepreneurship and Innovation in the Digital Economy.' *The Lahore Journal of Economics* 21 (2016): 273–312.

Hanif, Usman. 'In Pakistan, economists press for policy easing amid COVID-19 crisis.' *The Express Tribune*. April 3, 2020.

Harijan, Khanji, Muhammad Aslam Uqaili, and Mujeebuddin Memon. 'Renewable Energy for Managing Energy Crisis in Pakistan.' In *Wireless Networks, Information Processing and Systems. IMTIC 2008. Communications in Computer and Information Science*, Volume 2. Edited by D. M. A. Hussain, A. Q. K. Rajput, B. S. Chowdhry, and Q. Gee, 449–455. Springer, 2008.

Hayat, Zafar, Jameel Ahmed, and Faruk Balli. 'What monetary discretion can and cannot do under boom and bust cycles? Evidence from an emerging economy.' *Journal of Economic Studies* 46, no. 6 (October 2019): 1224–1240.

———, and Muhammad Rehman 'Does Inflation Bias Stabilize Real Growth? Evidence from Pakistan.' *Journal of Policy Modeling* 40, no. 6 (November–December 2018): 1083–1103.

———. 'Pakistan's Monetary Policy: Some Fundamental Issues.' *The Pakistan Development Review* 56, no. 1 (Spring 2017): 31–58.

———, James Obben, and Shamim Shakur. 'An empirical assessment of monetary discretion: The case of Pakistan.' *Journal of Policy Modeling*, Elsevier 38, no. 5 (2016): 954–970.

Hedrick-Fong, Yuwa. 'Exporting services promises to be the new frontier of global trade.' *Forbes*. January 3, 2020.

Hu, Yifan. 'Empirical Investigations of Inflation Targeting.' IIE Working Papers Series WP No. 03-6 (2003).

Husain, Ishrat. 'CPEC & Pakistan Economy: An Appraisal.' Centre of Excellence for CPEC, Pakistan Institute of Development Economics, 2020.

———. *Governing the Ungovernable: Institutional Reforms for Democratic Governance*. Karachi: Oxford University Press, 2018a.

———. 'Pakistan's Economy and Regional Challenges.' *International Studies* 55, no. 3 (2018b): 253–270.

———. 'Capacity to reform.' *Dawn*. August 13, 2018c.

———. 'CPEC and Pakistan's Economy: A Way Forward.' Centre of Excellence, China-Pakistan Economic Corridor (2018d).

———. 'Economic policymaking.' *Dawn*. July 30, 2018e.

———. 'Why Institutional Capacity Matters and Where Reforms Should Start.' The Wilson Center, 2018f.

———. 'Analysis of Pakistan's Debt Situation: 2000-2017.' Fourth National Debt Conference. Islamabad: PRIME Institute, 2017a.

———. 'Policy imperatives for CPEC.' *Dawn*. April 10, 2017b.

———, and Muhammad Ather Elahi. 'The Future of Afghanistan-Pakistan Trade Relations.' Peace brief no. 191. United States Institute of Peace, 2015a.

———. 'A Roadmap for Governance Reforms Tuesday.' *Blue Chip Magazine*. April 14, 2015b.

———. 'Bureaucracy needs reforms.' *Dawn*. January 25, 2014a.

———. 'Towards an Asian Century: Future of Economic Cooperation in SAARC Countries.' Concluding remarks. Islamabad Policy Research Institute (2014b): 24–25.

_____. 'Economic Governance and Institutional Reforms.' *Pakistan: Moving the Economy Forward*. Lahore: Lahore School of Economics, 2013.

_____. 'Economic Reforms in Pakistan: One Step Forward, Two Steps Backwards.' *The Pakistan Development Review* 51, no. 4 (2012): 7–22.

_____. 'A confused federalism.' *Dawn*. June 21, 2009.

_____. 'Financing Human Development in Pakistan.' Speech at the Pakistan Development Forum held at the Convention Center. Islamabad, 2005a.

_____. 'Pakistan's economic turnaround - an untold story.' Pakistan Supplement Global Agenda. Davos: World Economic Forum Annual Meeting, 2005b.

_____. 'Key Issues in Managing Pakistan's Economy Inaugural Address.' The Lahore Journal of Economics (2004a).

_____. 'Unleashing entrepreneurship.' UN Secretary General's Report on Unleashing entrepreneurship. Karachi, 2004b.

_____. *Pakistan: The Economy of An Elitist State*. Karachi: Oxford University Press, 1999.

Hussain, Altaf. 'Gilgit-Baltistan Reforms 2009.' Forum of Federations (2009).

Hussain, Sayed Waqar, Asmat Ullah, and Bashir Ahmad Khilji. 'The Causes of Transit Related Pak-Afghan Cross Border Smuggling.' *The Dialogue* 9, no. 1 (2014).

I-genius. 'Opportunity Pakistan Report: Commission on Social Entrepreneurship &Innovation.' 2014.

International Monetary Fund. 'Review of the Debt Sustainability Framework for Market Access Countries.' IMF Policy Paper. January, 2021.

_____. 'World Economic Outlook: 'The Great Lockdown.' April 2020.

_____. 'Pakistan: First Review Under the Extended Arrangement Under the Extended Fund Facility and Request for Modification of Performance Criteria.' December 23, 2019.

Institute of Policy Studies. 'Northern Areas of Pakistan-Facts, Problems and Recommendations.' RSP Report (2011).

International Union for Conservation of Nature. 'Northern Areas Strategy for Sustainable Development.' NASSD Background paper, 2003.

Isenberg, Daniel. 'What an Entrepreneurship Ecosystem Actually Is.' *Harvard Business Review*. May 12, 2014.

Ismail, Muhammad, and Fazal Husain. 'Fiscal Discretion and its Impact on Pakistan Economy.' *The Pakistan Development Review* 51, no. 4 Part II (2003).

Jalil, Aiman. '12 million women without CNIC.' *The Express Tribune*. November 30, 2017.

Johnson, David R. 'The effect of inflation targeting on the behavior of expected inflation: evidence from an 11 country panel.' *Journal of Monetary Economics* 49, no. 8 (2002): 1521–1538.

Jones, Jonathan D., and Nasir M. Khilji. 'Money Growth, Inflation, and Causality (Empirical Evidence for Pakistan, 1973—1985).' *The Pakistan Development Review* 27, no. 1 (Spring 1988): 45–58.

Kabeer, Naila. 'Women's economic empowerment and inclusive growth: labour markets and enterprise development.' Discussion Paper No. 29. Centre for Development Policy & Research, School of Oriental & African Studies. University of London, 2012.

Kahn, George, and Klara Parrish. 'Conducting monetary policy with inflation targets.' *Economic Review* 83, no. Q III (1998): 5–32.

Karimi, Farzad, and Akbar Tavakoli. 'The Analysis of Trade Integration and Business Cycles Synchronization with Emphasis on Regional Arrangements among OIC Nations.' Global Trade Analysis Project (2010).

Katz, Jerome A. 'The chronology and intellectual trajectory of American entrepreneurship education, 1876–1999.' *Journal of Business Venturing* 18 (2003): 283–300.

Kemal, A. R. 'Key Issues in Industrial Growth in Pakistan.' The Lahore Journal of Economics (September 2006).

Kemal, M. Ali. 'Is Inflation in Pakistan a Monetary Phenomenon?' *The Pakistan Development Review* 45, no. 2 (Summer 2006): 213–220.

Kemp, Tom. *Industrialization in the Non-Western World*. London: Longman, 1989.

Khan, A. M. M. *Product Report Sports Goods*. Karachi: Trade Development Authority Pakistan, 2019.

Khan, Abdus Sami. 'Policy Analysis of Education in Balochistan.' UNESCO, 2001.

Khan, Ashfaque H., and Yun-Hwan Kim. 'Foreign Direct Investment in Pakistan: Policy Issues and Operational Implications.' EDRC Report Series No. 66 (July 1999).

Khan, Ashraf. 'Monetary and Capital Markets Department Central Bank Legal Frameworks in the Aftermath of the Global Financial Crisis.' IMF Working Paper WP/17/101 (May 2017).

Khan, Ehsan Mehmood. 'Constitutional Status of Gilgit Baltistan: An Issue of Human Security.' Margalla Papers (2017).

Khan, Mohsin S., and Axel Schimmelpfennig. 'Inflation in Pakistan: Money or Wheat?' IMF Working Paper No. 06/60 (April 2006).

Khan, Mubarak Zeb. 'Large-scale manufacturing shrinks for eighth month in row.' *Dawn*. September 21, 2019.

Khan, Saleem, Sher Ali, and Saima Urooge. 'The Analysis Of Regional Bilateral Trade Between Pakistan and Central Asian Republics.' *Pakistan Journal of Applied Economics* 29, no. 1 (2019): 93–106.

Khan, Shaukat Hameed. 'Productivity and Entrepreneurship in Pakistan: The Role of Public Policy.' *The Lahore Journal of Economics* 21 (2016): 427–446.

Khan, Tajwer. 'Foreign Direct Investment in Pakistan: Fiscal Year 2020.' *Daily Times.* May 12, 2020.

Kiani, Khaleeq. 'Autonomy with accountability.' *Dawn.* December 17, 2018.

King, Mervyn. 'The Inflation Target Ten Years on.' *Bank of England Quarterly Bulletin* (Winter 2002).

Klasra, Kaswar. 'Microfinance is a growing business in Pakistan.' *ACCA.* March 1, 2018.

Kreutzmann, Hermann. 'Boundaries and space in Gilgit-Baltistan.' *Contemporary South Asia* 23, no. 3 (2015): 276–291.

Krueger, Anne. 'Why Trade Liberalisation is Good for Growth.' *The Economic Journal* 108, no. 450 (September 1998): 1513–1522.

Kugelman, Michael, and Ishrat Husain. 'Pakistan's Institutions: We Know They Matter, But How Can They Work Better?' The Wilson Center, 2018.

Kundi, Imran Ali. 'IMF allows exclusion of corona prevention expenses' from fiscal deficit.' *The Nation*, March 7, 2020.

Kuratko, Donald F., Michael H. Morris, and Minet Schindehutte. 'Understanding the dynamics of entrepreneurship through framework approaches.' *Small Business Economics* 45, no. 1 (2015): 1–13.

Kuttner, Kenneth N., and Adam S. Posen. 'Does Talk Matter After All? Inflation Targeting and Central Bank Behavior.' Federal Reserve Bank of New York Staff Report No. 88 (1999).

Lagarde, Christine. 'Pakistan and Emerging Markets in the World Economy.' International Monetary Fund. October 24, 2016.

Lanvin, Bruno, and Paul Evans. 'Global Talent Competitiveness Index 2018.' INSTEAD, The Adecco Group and TATA Communications (2018).

Levin, A., F. Natalucci, and J. Piger. 'The macroeconomic effects of inflation targeting.' *Federal Reserve Bank of St. Louis* 86, no. 4 (2004): 51–80.

Li, Xuemei, Khalid Mehmood Alam, and Shitong Wang. 'Trend Analysis of Pakistan Railways Based on Industry Life Cycle Theory.' Journal of Advanced Transportation (January 2018).

Lin, Shu. 'On the International Effects of Inflation Targeting.' *The Review of Economics and Statistics* 92, no. 1 (February 2010): 195–199.

_____, and Haichun Ye. 'Does inflation targeting make a difference in developing countries?' *Journal of Development Economics* 89, no. 1 (2009): 118–123.

Lodhi, Abdul Salam. *Education, Child Labor and Human Capital Formation in Selected Urban and Rural Settings of Pakistan*. Bern: Peter Lang Publishing, 2013.

Lund, Susan, James Manyika, Jonathan Woetzel, Jacques Bughin, Mekala Krishnan, Jeongmin Seong, and Mac Muir. 'Globalization in transition: The future of trade and value chains.' *McKinsey Quarterly* (2019).

Majid, Hadia, and A. Malik. 'Who listens to the underprivileged? Vulnerabilities of women workers in an urban informal economy.' Mimeo. Lahore University of Management Sciences, 2019a.

_____. 'Women's Work and Household Income: Examining 25 Years of Data.' Gender Identities at Work in Pakistan Workshop. January 3, 2019b.

_____. 'Female Labor Supply in Pakistan: Mapping the Last Three Decades.' Forman Christian College Pakistan: The Long View, 2047 Workshop. December 2, 2016.

Manyika, James, Sree Ramaswamy, Jacques Bughin, Jonathan Woetzel, Michael Birshan, and Zubin Nagpal. '"Superstars": The dynamics of firms, sectors, and cities leading the global economy.' McKinsey Global Institute (October 2018).

Manzoor, Rabia, Shehryar Khan Toru, and Vaqar Ahmed. 'Health Services Trade between India and Pakistan.' The Pakistan Journal of Social Issues, Volume VIII, 2017.

Maroof, Zaib, Shahzad Hussain, Muhammad Jawad, and Munazza Naz. 'Determinants of industrial development: a panel analysis of South Asian economies.' *Quality & Quantity: International Journal of Methodology* 53, no. 3 (May 2019): 1391–1419.

Mina, An Xiao, and Jan Chipchase. 'Inside Shenzhen's race to outdo Silicon Valley.' Technology Review. December 18, 2018.

Mir, M. A. 'Emphatic "No" by AJK for G-B's provincial status.' *The Express Tribune*. January 14, 2016.

Mishkin, Frederic S., and Klaus Schmidt-Hebbel. 'Does Inflation Targeting Make a Difference?' NBER Working Paper No. 12876 (January 2007).

_____, and Adam S. Posen. 'Inflation Targeting: Lessons from Four Countries.' Economic Policy Review, Federal Reserve Bank of New York, Vol. 3 (August 1997): 9–110.

Mollick, André Varella, René Cabral, and Francisco G. Carneiro. 'Does Inflation Targeting Matter for Output Growth? Evidence from Industrial and Emerging Economies.' *Journal of Policy Modeling* 33, no. 4 (July 2011): 537–51.

Moyo, Dambisa. 'Are Businesses Ready for Deglobalization?' *Mirror Mirror.* December 16, 2019.

Nasir, S. M., S. M. Raza, and S. B. H. Abidi. 'Wind Energy in Balochistan (Pakistan).' *Renewable Energy* 1, no. 3–4 (1991): 523–526.

Nazir, Ahad, Asad Afridi, Vaqar Ahmed, Dan Gregory, Muhammad Arif, and Syed Murtaza Kazmi. 'Developing Inclusive and Creative Economies: Creative and Social Enterprise in Pakistan.' Sustainable Development Policy Institute, 2021.

Neumann, Manfred J. M., and Juergen von Hagen. 'Does Inflation Targeting Matter?' *Federal Reserve Bank of St. Louis Review* 84 (July 2002):127–148.

North, Douglass C. 'Institutions.' *The Journal of Economic Perspectives* 5, no. 1 (Winter 1991): 97–112.

Olson, William C., and Nicholas Onuf. *The Growth of a Discipline: Reviewed.* In *International Relations: British and American Perspectives.* Edited by Steve Smith, 1–28. Oxford: Basil Blackwell, 1985.

Pasha, Hafiz A. 'Inflow of External Financing.' *Business Recorder.* February 18, 2020a.

———, and Shahid Kardar. 'Revisiting economic impact of coronavirus.' *Business Recorder.* April 14, 2020b.

———. 'Growth and Inequality in Pakistan: Agenda for Reforms.' Friedrich Ebert Stiftung, 2018.

———. 'Growth of the Provincial Economies.' Institute for Policy Reforms, IPR Brief (December 2015).

———, and Zafar H. Ismail. 'Determinants of Industrial Estates in Pakistan.' *Pakistan Economic and Social Review* 26, no. 1 (Summer 1988): 1–19.

Perry, James L. 'Measuring Public Service Motivation: An Assessment of Construct Reliability and Validity.' *Journal of Public Administration Research and Theory: J-PART* 6, no. 1 (January 1996): 5–22.

———, and Lois R. Wise. 'The Motivational Bases of Public Service.' *Public Administration Review* 50, no. 3 (May/June 1990): 367–373.

Pervaiz, Abeer, and Mohammad Saud Khan. 'Entrepreneurial Relations of Pakistani Entrepreneurs: A Macroeconomic and Cultural Perspective.' *SAGE Open* (October 2015): 1–13.

Petursson, Thorarinn G. 'Inflation Targeting and its Effects on Macroeconomic Performance.' SUERF Conference Proceedings and Studies, no. 5 (2005).

Pinsker, Joe. 'One City in Pakistan Makes Nearly Half of the World's Soccer Balls.' *The Atlantic*. July 2, 2014.

Prashantham, Shameen. 'Partner with entrepreneurs inside and out.' MIT Sloan Management Review (2019).

Puri, Luv. 'Pakistan's Northern Areas: Time for a Reality Check.' *Economic and Political Weekly* 44, no. 39 (2009): 13–15.

Qayyum, Abdul. 'Money, Inflation, and Growth in Pakistan.' *The Pakistan Development Review* 45, no. 2 (Summer 2006): 203–212.

Rana, Shahbaz. 'SBP poured $24b into inter-bank market between two IMF programmes.' *The Express Tribune*. January 20, 2020.

Rizvi, Azhar. 'Entrepreneuring Pakistan: 27 stories of struggle, failure and success.' South Carolina: CreateSpace Independent Publishing Platform, 2018.

Roger, Scott. 'Inflation Targeting Turns 20.' *Finance and Development* 47, no. 1 (March 2010).

Sabir, Sameer, Tania Aidrus, and Sarah Bird. 'Pakistan: A Story of Technology, Entrepreneurs and Global Networks - A Case Study.' MIT Sloan Management Review (2010).

Sachs, Jeffry. *The End of Poverty: Economic Possibilities for Our Time*. New York: The Penguin Press, 2005.

Samad, Ghulam, Vaqar Ahmed, and Rauf Khalid. 'Economic Contribution of Copyright-based Industries in Pakistan.' *The Pakistan Development Review* 57, no. 1 (2018): 99–114.

Sarfraz, Sohail. 'Ishrat for effective use of CNIC to detect tax evasion.' *Business Recorder*. December 3, 2019.

Schumpeter, Joseph A. *Capitalism, Socialism and Democracy*. New York: Harper & Brothers, 1950.

Schwab, Klaus. 'The Global Competitiveness Report 2019.' World Economic Forum (2019).

Sellon, Gordon H., and Stuart E. Weiner. 'Monetary policy without reserve requirements: analytical issues.' *Econometric Reviews* 81 (1996): 5–24.

Sharif, Muhammad, Umar Farooq, and Arshed Bashir. 'Illegal Trade of Pakistan with Afghanistan and Iran through Balochistan: Size, Balance and loss to the Public Exchequer.' *International Journal of Agriculture and Biology* 2, no. 3 (2000): 199–203.

Siddik, Md. Nur Alam. 'Does Financial Inclusion Promote Women Empowerment? Evidence from Bangladesh.' *Applied Economics and Finance* 4, no. 4 (2017): 169–177.

Siddique, Salman. 'Foreign investors return to Pakistan's debt market amid global health crisis.' *The Express Tribune*, April 22, 2020.

Siegmann, Karin Astrid, and Hadia Majid. 'Empowering growth in Pakistan?' No 595, ISS Working Papers - General Series from International Institute of Social Studies of Erasmus University Rotterdam (ISS). The Hague, 2014.

Siregar, Reza, and Siwei Goo. 'Effectiveness and commitment to inflation targeting policy: Evidence from Indonesia and Thailand.' *Journal of Asian Economics* 21, no. 2 (2010): 113–128.

SMEDA. 'Survey on Impact of Covid-19 (Coronavirus) on SMEs.' April, 2020.

Son, Hyun, and Nanak Kakwani. 'Economic growth and poverty reduction: Initial conditions matter.' United Nations Development Programme, International Poverty Centre, Working Paper 2 (August 2004).

Soumitra Dutta, Bruno Lanvin, and Sacha Wunsch-Vincent. 'Global Innovation Index.' Cornell University, INSEAD, World Intellectual Property Organization (2019).

Stone, Andrew, Brian Levy, and Ricardo Paredes. 'Public Institutions and Private Transactions. The Legal, and Regulatory Environment for Business Transactions in Brazil and Chile.' No. 891, Policy Research Working Paper Series. The World Bank, 1992.

Syed, Abdur-Rahim, and Asim Bokhari. 'Starting up: Unlocking entrepreneurship in Pakistan.' McKinsey & Company (2019).

Tahir, Saniya. 'Degradation of rangeland resources in Balochistan.' *Envirocivil*. April 26, 2014.

Taylor, John. 'Low inflation, pass-through, and the pricing power of firms.' *European Economic Review* 44, no. 7 (2000): 1389–1408.

The Economist. 'It has become harder for the Asian tigers to prosper through exports.' December 5, 2019a.

_____. 'Pakistan's army is to blame for the poverty of the country's 208 citizens.' 2019b.

The News. 'IMF representative terms performance of Pakistan's economy satisfactory.' April 21, 2020.

_____. 'Pak external debt may rise to $90 bn in next four years.' December 13, 2015.

Trainer, David. 'The Unicorn Bubble Is Bursting.' *Forbes*. October 7, 2019.

Truman, Edwin M. *Inflation Targeting in the World Economy*. New York: Columbia University Press, 2003.

Wallis, J. J., and Douglass C. North. 'Defining the State.' *Working Paper*. Mercatus Centre, George Mason University, 2010.

World Bank, and IMF. 'Joint World Bank-IMF Debt Sustainability Framework for Low-Income Countries.' March 6, 2020.

World Economic Forum. 'The Global Gender Gap Report 2020.' Technical Report, 2020.

Yasmin, Bushra. 'The Foreign Capital Inflows and Growth in Pakistan: A Simultaneous Equation Model.' *South Asia Economic Journal* 6, no. 2 (2005): 207–219.

———, Aamrah Hussain, and Muhammad Ali Choudhry. 'Analysis of factors affecting Foreign Direct Investment in Developing Countries. '*Pakistan Economic and Social Review* XLI, no. 1 and 2 (2003): 59–76.

Zada, Naseeb, and Khalid Khan. 'General Equilibrium Analysis of Pakistan's Free Trade Agreements: "A Global CGE Approach".' (2017).

Zain, Omar Farooq. 'A Socio-Political Study of Gilgit Baltistan Province.' *Pakistan Journal of Social Sciences (PJSS)* 30, no. 1 (September 2010): 181–190.

Zeger, Van der Wal, and Assel Mussagulova. 'Motivation of Public Servants in Pakistan.' United Nations Development Programme. Global Centre for Public Service Excellence, 2017.

Index